Nonprofit Kit For Dummies
2nd Edition

W9-AVJ-263

Cheat Sheet

Securing Your Nonprofit Status in Ten (Fairly) Easy Steps

- Choose a name for your nonprofit. While you're at it, select and reserve a Web domain name.
- Form your incorporating board of directors.
- Obtain a Federal Employer Identification Number by submitting IRS Form SS-4. You can find a copy of the form on the IRS Web site (`www.irs.gov`).
- Write Articles of Incorporation and submit them to the appropriate office in your state government with the required fee. Check out CD0402 for the Web sites of state offices.
- Develop organizational bylaws — the rules by which you will operate.
- Hold your first board meeting.
- Review IRS Publication 557, instructions for filing for tax exemption. Visit the IRS Web site at `www.irs.gov` to download this publication.
- File IRS Form 1023 if you're applying to become a 501(c)(3) tax exempt organization, preferably within 15 months of the date of incorporation. The latest version of Form 1023 can be found on `www.irs.gov`.
- Sit back and relax. Celebrate when your letter of determination arrives!
- Register as a charity in your state.

Note: You don't have to follow these steps exactly as we've ordered them here. See Chapter 4 for all the details.

Raising Money — Another Kind of 12-Step Program

- Set clear, reasonable, yet ambitious fundraising goals based on a clear assessment of your organization's likeliest supporters. See Chapter 13.
- Don't depend on one grant, one event, one donor, or one approach: Balance your resources among multiple sources.
- Make a fundraising budget. See Chapter 13.
- Remember that individual donors represent the largest total source for private contributions. See Chapter 14.
- Write a strong case statement for your organization, telling its story in terms of how it benefits people (or trees or salamanders or whatever constituents your mission serves). See Chapter 14.
- Ask. If you don't ask for a contribution, you won't get one. See Chapter 14.
- Make it easy for donors to respond to your request.
- Begin by asking for support among those people closest to your nonprofit — the board, volunteers, constituents, and staff. See Chapter 14.
- Include some fun in your fundraising. Special events can win friends and inspire new supporters. See Chapter 15.
- Examine each potential grantmaker's interests, focus, limitations, and policies. See Chapter 16.
- Demonstrate the needs of the constituents your nonprofit wants to serve and present a clear plan for addressing those needs. See Chapter 17.
- Acknowledge your donors' support and work to deepen their involvement in your organization. See Chapter 14.

For Dummies: Bestselling Book Series for Beginners

Nonprofit Kit For Dummies,® 2nd Edition

Cheat Sheet

Eleven Annual Tasks for Every Nonprofit Manager

- **Prepare your budget.** Project income and expenses for the coming year and compare to actual numbers for the current year. Ask the board of directors to approve the projected budget. See Chapter 10.

- **Evaluate performance.** Review your programs and your employees once a year. Set goals and objectives for both people and activities. See Chapters 8 and 9.

- **File your forms.** File your 990 Form with the IRS when it's due (four and a half months after the close of your fiscal year), and prepare any required reports for state and local authorities. See Chapter 5.

- **Have a party.** Recognize and acknowledge your volunteers, board members, and employees with at least one celebration every year. See Chapter 7.

- **Review your insurance.** See that you pay your premiums in full and that your organization is covered for all risks. See Chapter 12.

- **Prepare a fundraising plan.** Make realistic estimates and prepare an action plan showing how each fundraising activity will be carried out. See Chapter 13.

- **Back up your computers.** In fact, you should do this task weekly, but it's often forgotten. Don't lose your donor list or your financial records due to a computer crash.

- **Review terms of board members.** Make a chart to keep track of when officer and board member terms expire, reminding you to recruit new members and fill officer slots. See Chapter 6.

- **Read your mission statement.** Better still, frame it and hang it over your desk so you're always reminded of why you're doing what you're doing. See Chapter 3.

- **Review your organizational plan.** Plans are made to be followed and, as necessary, revised. If you haven't looked at your org plan in awhile, do so now. See Chapter 9.

- **Take a vacation.** You'll come back to work with new ideas and renewed energy.

Four Reasons Why Planning Is Important

- Guides the activities of your organization

- Helps you figure out how to best allocate your resources

- Creates a framework to evaluate your work

- Makes sure everyone understands your organization's goals and objectives

Three Primary Responsibilities of a Board of Directors

- To pay close attention to what's going on and make decisions based on good information

- To put the welfare of the organization above other interests when making decisions

- To act in accordance with the mission and goals of the nonprofit organization

Wiley, the Wiley Publishing logo, For Dummies, the Dummies Man logo, For Dummies, the For Dummies Bestselling Book Series logo and all related trade dress are trademarks or registered trademarks of John Wiley & Sons, Inc. and/or its affiliates. All other trademarks are property of their respective owners.

For Dummies: Bestselling Book Series for Beginners

Nonprofit Kit

FOR

DUMMIES®

2ND EDITION

Nonprofit Kit

FOR

DUMMIES®

2ND EDITION

by Stan Hutton and Frances Phillips

Wiley Publishing, Inc.

Nonprofit Kit For Dummies® 2nd Edition

Published by
Wiley Publishing, Inc.
111 River St.
Hoboken, NJ 07030-5774
www.wiley.com

For general information on our other products and services, please contact our Customer Care Department within the U.S. at 800-762-2974, outside the U.S. at 317-572-3993, or fax 317-572-4002.

For technical support, please visit www.wiley.com/techsupport.

Wiley also publishes its books in a variety of electronic formats. Some content that appears in print may not be available in electronic books.

Library of Congress Control Number: 2005933553

ISBN-13: 978-0-7645-9909-5

ISBN-10: 0-7645-9909-7

Manufactured in the United States of America

10 9 8 7 6 5 4 3 2

2B/RU/RR/QV/IN

WILEY

About the Authors

Stan Hutton became involved in the nonprofit world after co-founding a non-profit organization in San Francisco. Since that time, he has worked as non-profit manager, fundraiser, consultant, and writer. He served as executive director of the Easter Seal Society of San Francisco and a fundraiser for Cogswell College. For five years, he wrote for and managed a Web site about nonprofits for About.com. He has worked at the San Francisco Study Center and the Executive Service Corps of San Francisco. He currently is a program officer at the Clarence E. Heller Charitable Foundation.

Frances Phillips is a senior program officer at the Walter and Elise Haas Fund, where she also directs The Creative Work Fund. She also teaches grant writing and creative writing at San Francisco State University. Previously, Frances worked as executive director of Intersection for the Arts and of the Poetry Center and American Poetry Archives at San Francisco State University; and as a partner in the public relations and fundraising firm Horne, McClatchy and Associates. Frances serves on the boards of the California Alliance for Art Education and Grantmakers in the Arts; and she is co-editor of the Grantmakers in the Arts *Reader*.

Dedication

We dedicate this book to the devoted nonprofit managers, staff members, volunteers, and board members who are working long hours to improve living conditions, advance the arts and learning, and protect the environment.

And to our daughter, Alice, who is also a writer and who probably will have the good sense not to bore her own children at the dinner table with details of her latest book.

Authors' Acknowledgments

This book started with our agent Maureen Watts, who had the idea and approached us to write it. Many thanks to her, and to project editor Chrissy Guthrie, copy editor Sarah Faulkner, acquisitions editor Stacy Kennedy, and technical editor Mickie Rops, who guided us through shaping and revising our manuscript for this edition. We also thank our colleagues who gave us permission to include examples of their work on the CD that accompanies this book.

We owe much of our knowledge of the nonprofit sector to a remarkable array of professionals with whom we have worked. It is impossible to list everyone who has helped and inspired us but we would be remiss if we did not name a few. Lori Horne, Jean McClatchy, and Ginny Rubin showed Frances the satisfaction of raising money for good causes. She is grateful to the boards of the Poetry Center at San Francisco State and Intersection for the Arts for giving her a chance to be a nonprofit executive director; and to her current and past colleagues at the Walter and Elise Haas Fund — particularly Bruce Sievers and Pamela David. Stan wants to add his thanks to Arthur Compton, Louise Brown, Neil Housewright, John Darby, Jan Masaoka, and Bruce Hirsch, all of whom have given him opportunities to work in the nonprofit sector and provided guidance along the way.

Publisher's Acknowledgments

We're proud of this book; please send us your comments through our Dummies online registration form located at www.dummies.com/register/.

Some of the people who helped bring this book to market include the following:

Acquisitions, Editorial, and Media Development

Project Editor: Christina Guthrie

Acquisitions Editor: Stacy Kennedy

Copy Editors: Michelle Dzurny, Sarah Faulkner

Editorial Program Assistant: Courtney Allen

Technical Editor: Mickie S. Rops

Media Development Specialist: Angela Denny

Editorial Manager: Christine Meloy Beck

Media Development Manager:
Laura VanWinkle

Editorial Assistants: Hanna K. Scott,
Nadine Bell, David Lutton

Cover Photos: © Wiley Publishing, Inc.

Cartoons: Rich Tennant
(www.the5thwave.com)

Composition Services

Project Coordinator: Jennifer Theriot

Layout and Graphics: Carl Byers, Andrea Dahl, Lauren Goddard, Stephanie D. Jumper, Barbara Moore, Barry Offringa

Proofreaders: Jessica Kramer, Dwight Ramsey, TECHBOOKS Production Services

Indexer: TECHBOOKS Production Services

Special Help
Carmen Krikorian

Publishing and Editorial for Consumer Dummies

Diane Graves Steele, Vice President and Publisher, Consumer Dummies

Joyce Pepple, Acquisitions Director, Consumer Dummies

Kristin A. Cocks, Product Development Director, Consumer Dummies

Michael Spring, Vice President and Publisher, Travel

Kelly Regan, Editorial Director, Travel

Publishing for Technology Dummies

Andy Cummings, Vice President and Publisher, Dummies Technology/General User

Composition Services

Gerry Fahey, Vice President of Production Services

Debbie Stailey, Director of Composition Services

Contents at a Glance

Table of Contents

Introduction

*I*t may sound corny, but we <u>feel a certain sense of mission</u> when it comes to nonprofits. We've started them, directed them, raised funds for them, consulted for them, volunteered for them, given money to them, and written about them. We've been associated with nonprofits in one way or another for more years than we care to remember.

Why have we continued to work for nonprofit organizations? Yes, we care about others and want to see the world a better place — our values are important to us. But, to be honest, that's not the reason we've worked for nonprofit organizations for so many years. We believe the reason is that we <u>can't think of anything more interesting or more challenging to do.</u>

Starting a new program is exciting. Getting your first grant is thrilling. Working with the multifaceted personalities that come together on a board of directors is fascinating. Learning a new skill because no one else is there to do it is fun. Seeing the faces of satisfied clients, walking along a restored lakeshore, hearing the applause of audiences — all are gratifying.

That's why we do it.

About This Book

We try to cover the gamut in this book — everything you need to know to start and manage a charitable organization, from applying for your tax exemption to raising money to pay for your programs. On the CD, you'll find supplemental information, including forms to help you create a budget, examples of grant proposals, and links to Web sites where you can find more help. We also attempt to give a bird's-eye view of the economy's nonprofit sector. When you look at financial resources, for example, nonprofits are much like the rest of the world: Most of the wealth is held by relatively few nonprofit organizations; a respectable number of them are in the middle; and many more struggle to make ends meet.

We try to be honest about the difficulties you'll sometimes face. You probably won't be able to achieve everything you set out to accomplish, and you'll always wish you had more resources to do more things.

Still, we can't imagine doing anything else. Maybe you'll feel the same way after you jump into the nonprofit world.

Conventions Used in This Book

When writing this book, we used a few conventions that you should be aware of:

- Anytime we introduce a new nonprofit-related term, we *italicize* it.
- Web sites and e-mail addresses appear in monofont to help them stand out.
- When we refer to nonprofit organizations, unless we say otherwise, we're talking about organizations that have been recognized as 501(c)(3) nonprofits and that also are considered public charities by the IRS.
- All corresponding CD elements are labeled with the chapter number and the order in which the element appears in the chapter. For instance, the first CD element in Chapter 2 is labeled CD0201.

What You're Not to Read

We'd love for you to read the entire book, because we worked so hard on it, but if you're pressed for time or just want to cut to the chase, you can skip the following:

- **Sidebars:** These gray-shaded boxes contain interesting info that's related to the topic at hand but isn't essential.
- **Paragraphs marked with the "Technical Stuff" icon:** The info contained here is completely skippable, but you'll enhance your knowledge and understanding if you take the time to read these tidbits.

Foolish Assumptions

When writing this book, we made some assumptions about who may be interested in reading it:

- Maybe you have an idea that will help solve a problem in your community, and you believe that starting a nonprofit organization is the best way to put your idea into action.
- Maybe you serve on a board of directors and wonder what you're supposed to be doing.
- Maybe you work for a nonprofit and need some ideas about fundraising, managing your organization, or working with your board of directors.
- Or maybe you're simply curious about the nonprofit sector and want to find out more about it.

If you're one of these people, we're confident this book will answer your questions and give you the info you're seeking.

How This Book Is Organized

This book is organized into six parts. You don't have to read it from cover to cover; you can dip in for reference at any point — jumping from Part IV to Part II to Part V if you like. We won't tell anyone.

Part I: Getting Started with Nonprofits

Read Part I if you want an introduction to nonprofits and information about establishing a nonprofit organization. You can also find a chapter to help you answer the question "Do I want to start a nonprofit organization or not?" If you decide that the answer is yes, we provide guidance for setting up a legal structure and winding your way through the IRS requirements.

Part II: Managing a Nonprofit Organization

This part covers the nuts and bolts of managing an organization — finding and hiring employees, setting up procedures (and responsibilities) for your board of directors, getting publicity for your programs, and recruiting and retaining volunteers. Planning and budgeting are two important aspects of keeping a nonprofit on track and in the black. And if you're managing a building or thinking of buying one for your organization, you can find some tips here.

Part III: Successful Fundraising

Part III focuses on the fundamental reality of nonprofit organizations — fundraising is essential. Start by creating your fundraising plan and then implement it by raising funds from individuals, writing grant proposals, running annual campaigns, and, if you're really ambitious, launching a capital campaign.

Part IV: The Part of Tens

This is the famous Part of Tens, containing a little whimsy on philanthropic organizations, suggestions on where to find answers to questions you may have, and some quick, practical advice on a topic that's dear to everyone's heart: raising money.

Part V: Appendixes

In this part, you can find a glossary of commonly used terms in the nonprofit sector, along with a bibliography of organizations, and a list of reference books and Web sites that can help you continue learning about all aspects of working and volunteering in nonprofits. You can also find information about using the CD that comes with this book.

And don't forget the accompanying CD! We collected examples of just about everything we could think of — letters, grants, budgets, contracts, and more — and put them on the CD in the back of this book to help guide you in your work. You can also find a list of offices to contact to find out about nonprofits in your state and links to dozens of other useful Web sites.

Icons Used in This Book

We use the following icons throughout the book to flag particularly important or helpful information.

This icon means that you can find more helpful information and management tools on the CD that accompanies this book.

The remember icon stands watch at information that you should keep ready for application.

You may not need this technical stuff today, but — who knows? — it may be invaluable tomorrow.

This icon is posted next to little hints and suggestions gleaned from our experience over the years.

Warnings are just what you think they might be. We alert you to information that you shouldn't forget.

Where to Go from Here

If you're new to the nonprofit world, we suggest beginning with Chapter 1, where you find fundamental information to get you started in the right direction. If you're familiar with nonprofits already but want to better understand your responsibilities as a board member, you find the answers in Chapter 6. If you're a new board member and want to understand the organization's finances when spreadsheets are passed out at board meetings, we provide guidance about both making a budget and understanding financial statements in Chapter 10.

If you're like every other nonprofit worker or volunteer, you want to know how to get money for your organization. Chapters 13 through 18 cover this topic. Chapter 13, Crafting a Fundraising Plan, is a good place to begin.

Part I

Getting Started with Nonprofits

The 5th Wave — By Rich Tennant

CHILDRENS DEVELOPMENT FOUNDATION

MISSION STATEMENT
1. TUTOR THE CHILDREN
2. MENTOR THE CHILDREN
3. COOK AND EAT THE CHILD[...]

"I'm not sure I can reconcile point 3 with the other two points."

In this part . . .

*I*n this part, we introduce the nonprofit sector and the key role that it plays in our society and economy. We define different types of nonprofit organizations, focusing on the kind that can receive tax-deductible contributions.

We walk you through the steps for starting a nonprofit organization: the questions you should ask, the planning you should do, the mission you should define, and the documents you need to master. We invite you to use all your skills, from dreaming to networking to filling in the blanks for the Internal Revenue Service.

After your organization receives nonprofit status from the IRS, you need to attend to various reports every year. Sound scary? Fear not — we show you the way.

Chapter 1

Tuning In to the World of Nonprofit Organizations

*I*t's morning in America. The radio alarm clicks on in your rural hometown. After tuning in to the weather, news, and livestock reports, you finish the kitchen chores while listening to an interview with a poet teaching at the small college in town. You hurry your two young kids away from *Sesame Street* and into the minivan for the regular a.m. run to the co-op preschool next to the volunteer fire station. Seeing the station reminds you to unload the bag of canned goods you bought for the county food drive. You drop the bag at the firehouse door and go take on the day.

It's morning in America. The radio alarm clicks on in your big-city apartment. After tuning in to the weather and stock market reports, you finish the kitchen chores while listening to a symphony recorded at the nearby concert hall. You drag your teenagers out of bed before leaving for work, reminding them that you'll pick them up tonight at the youth center. You hurry down the street to the subway, grab a newspaper, and notice that the city's largest hospital has a headline — a staff physician is getting results with a startling new treatment. You read about it on the train as you head to the office.

Both mornings are filled with nonprofit organizations. The rural town offers public radio and television, *Sesame Street,* a private college, a volunteer-run preschool, and a community food bank. The city scene includes public radio, a symphony orchestra, a youth club, and a hospital. Behind those layers of nonprofit organizations is another layer: the small press publisher and distributor of the poet's latest book, the medical school where the physician was educated, the economic think tank that analyzes stocks and commodities, and the agency providing emergency preparedness training to volunteer firefighters.

The nonprofit sector isn't a distinct place, not some plaza or district that you come upon suddenly as you weave your way through your day. It's more like a thread of a common color that's laced throughout the economy and our lives. You can find it and its influence no matter where you are — from the wilderness to the metropolis.

So, What's a Nonprofit Organization?

People hear the term *nonprofit organization* and picture Mother Hubbard's cupboard, as in awfully bare or zero bank balance. In fact, some nonprofit organizations turn very tidy profits on their operations, and that's good, because cash flow keeps an enterprise humming, whether it's a for-profit business or not.

The main difference between a for-profit and a nonprofit enterprise is what happens to the profit. In a for-profit company like Ford, Microsoft, Disney, or your favorite fast-food establishment, profits are distributed to the owners, including shareholders. But a *non*profit can't do that. Any profit remaining after the bills are paid has to be plowed back into the organization's service program or kept in reserve. So profit can't be distributed to individuals, such as the organization's board of directors.

What about shareholders — do nonprofits have any shareholders to pay off? Not in terms of a monetary payoff, like a stock dividend. But in a broad, service sense, nonprofits do have "shareholders." They're the people who benefit from the nonprofit's activities, like the people who tune in to public radio and TV or receive free food through the county food program.

Introducing the one and only 501(c)(3)

When we use the term *nonprofit organization* in this book, for the most part, we're talking about an organization that has been incorporated (or recognized in some way) under the laws of its state and that the Internal Revenue Service has classified as a 501(c)(3). If that term is new to you, add it to your vocabulary with pride. In no time, "five-oh-one-see-three" will roll off your tongue as if you're a nonprofit expert. Other kinds of nonprofit organizations *do* exist; they're formed to benefit their members, to influence legislation, or to fulfill other purposes. They receive exemption from federal income taxes and sometimes relief from property taxes at the local level. (Chapter 2 discusses these organizations in greater detail.)

Nonprofit organizations classified as 501(c)(3) receive extra privileges under the law. They are, with minor exceptions, the only group of tax-exempt organizations that can receive contributions from individuals and organizations that are tax deductible for the donor.

Being a nonprofit organization doesn't mean that an entity is exempt from paying all taxes. Nonprofit organizations pay employment taxes just like for-profit businesses do. In some states, but not all, nonprofits are exempt from paying sales tax, so be sure that you're familiar with your local laws.

Activities of the nonprofit sector

The Internal Revenue Service tax code describes allowable purposes of 501(c)(3) nonprofit organizations as serving religious, educational, charitable, scientific, and literary purposes.

Here's a quick summary of the activities undertaken by nonprofit charitable organizations:

- ✔ **Arts, culture, and humanities** — This category includes art museums and concert halls.

- ✔ **Education** — You'll find schools in this category, of course, along with libraries and education support organizations, such as organizations providing student scholarships.

- ✔ **Environmental** — These organizations work toward preserving and conserving natural resources and protecting the environment against damage and overuse.

- ✔ **Animal related organizations** — Here you'll find zoos, aquariums, and humane societies.

- ✔ **Health** — This big area encompasses hospitals, clinics, medical research organizations, and many more.

- ✔ **Human services** — Everything from youth development organizations to services for homeless individuals comes under this category.

- ✔ **International and foreign relations** — Groups that work with foreign policy, refugees, and international economic development programs are covered here.

- ✔ **Public and societal benefit** — This category includes civil rights organizations and groups promoting citizen participation.

- ✔ **Religion related** — Although churches aren't required to obtain tax-exempt status, many congregations create charitable programs and seek 501(c)(3) status for their programs.

Check out CD0101 for a more detailed list of the activities that nonprofits take on.

A sector by any other name

Not everyone thinks that *nonprofit sector* is the best term. That's because of the array of organizations with different kinds of nonprofit status. Some of these organizations are formed to benefit their members — like fraternities and labor unions — and don't share a broad public-serving intent. Another reason nonprofit sector may not be the best choice of terms is its negative connotation. After all, what's worse than not making a profit? But, as we point out earlier, and we remind you again in later chapters, not making a profit isn't the determining factor. Alternative terms that you may hear include the following:

✔ **Voluntary sector:** This term emphasizes the presence of volunteer board members and the significance of voluntary contributions and services to the work of 501(c)(3) organizations. In this definition, the organizations alone don't represent the meaning of *nonprofit;* the definition includes the vast web of their supporters who participate as volunteers and donors.

✔ **Independent sector:** This term emphasizes the public-serving mission of these organizations and their volunteers and their independence from government. (Independent Sector is also the name of a nonprofit organization that sponsors research, publications, and public programs about the sector.)

✔ **Charitable sector:** This term emphasizes the donations these organizations receive from individuals and institutions.

✔ **Third sector:** This term emphasizes the organization's important role alongside government and the for-profit business economy.

We're going to use the term *nonprofit sector* throughout this book, but we want you to understand its limitations and be familiar with other commonly used terms.

Bigger than a breadbox

The nonprofit sector is larger than many people realize. Here are some figures from the National Center for Charitable Statistics, based on IRS data, about the number of 501(c)(3) public charities in 2005 in the U.S.

✔ More than <u>800,000 organizations</u> are registered as public charities with the IRS.

✔ Assets held by these groups total $1.5 trillion.

✔ One-half of all the assets are owned by fewer than 2,000 charities.

✔ Over three-quarters of nonprofit charities have an annual gross revenue under $100,000.

Finding Your Mission and Entering the Nonprofit World

People form nonprofit organizations in order to work toward changing conditions in the world, either for a specific group of people or society in general. The overall goal or purpose of a nonprofit is known as its mission. Taking the time needed to clearly outline a nonprofit's mission is time well spent because the mission guides the activities of the organization, helps the nonprofit's directors allocate resources wisely, and serves as a measure for evaluating the accomplishments of the group. We think developing a mission statement is so important that we devote an entire chapter (Chapter 3) to guiding you through this process.

Examining your personal mission before embarking on the path of launching a nonprofit is important. You're creating a legal entity that has responsibilities for reporting to both the state and federal governments. If the organization grows to the point where you must hire employees, you're responsible for paying regular salaries and providing adequate benefits. And although you can be compensated for your work as a nonprofit staff member, you aren't able to develop equity in the organization or take away any profits at the end of the year. Look at Chapter 2 for more information to help you make this important decision.

Setting up a nonprofit

Nearly all nonprofit organizations are established as corporations under the laws of a particular state. If you're located in Iowa and you plan to do most of your work in that state, you follow the laws in Iowa to set up the basic legal structure of a nonprofit corporation. Although you'll find some differences from state to state, in general, the process requires writing and submitting articles of incorporation to the state and developing *bylaws*, the rules under which the corporation will operate.

After your nonprofit is established under your state laws, the next step is applying for 501(c)(3) status from the Internal Revenue Service. This step entails completing and submitting IRS Form 1023. You need to specify in some detail the proposed activities of the new organization, and you're asked for projected revenue and expenses for the year in which you apply and three years into the future. To be honest, you can't complete this form in one afternoon. It requires substantial time and thought to develop the material that you must include. We discuss the incorporation and IRS application process in Chapter 4.

Planning and flexibility are paramount

If you start and run a nonprofit organization, you'll discover that planning is your best friend. Every task from budgeting to grant writing requires that you make plans for the future. And you need to do a substantial amount of planning before you're ready to send in your exemption for nonprofit status.

Don't be frightened by this recommendation to plan. The act of planning comes down fundamentally to thinking through what you're going to do as well as how and when you're going to do it. Your plan becomes the road map that guides you toward achieving your goals and your nonprofit mission. Planning is something that you should pay attention to every day.

You should always begin with a plan, but that doesn't mean that plans shouldn't be altered when the situation calls for it. Circumstances change; flexibility and adaptability are good traits to nurture if you're running a nonprofit organization. Chapters 9 and 10 cover planning and budgeting. Chapters 11 and 13 discuss planning for marketing and fundraising.

Getting Inspired and Inspiring Volunteers

The nonprofit sector is exciting. It encourages individuals with ideas about solving social problems or enhancing arts, culture, the environment, or education to act on those ideas. It creates a viable place within our society and economy for worthy activities that have little chance of commercial success. We think that it combines the best of the business world with the best of government, bringing together creativity, zeal, and problem solving from the business side with a call to public service from the government side.

We also find volunteerism inspiring. Everyone has heard stories of tightly knit communities where neighbors gather to rebuild a barn. That spirit of pitching in to help is the best part of living in a community in which people share values and ideas.

Many people live in places that contain people from a wide variety of backgrounds. The nonprofit sector provides an array of institutions in which all people can come together, with both those who resemble them and others who are unlike them, to work toward the common good. Volunteerism enables everyone to pitch in to rebuild "the barn" in a wide variety of contexts.

Applying the term *voluntary sector* to nonprofit organizations came about for a good reason. In the United States, according to the Bureau of Labor Statistics, 64.5 million people volunteered at least once between September 2003 and September 2004.

When you're working in a nonprofit, you'll likely be supervising volunteers — and they'll likely supervise you. What we mean is that (with very few exceptions) nonprofit boards of directors serve as unpaid volunteers. And if you're the executive director, your supervisors are the trustees or board members of the organization. At the same time, you likely depend on volunteers to carry out some or all of the activities of the organization. You may even be a volunteer yourself.

The word supervision sounds harsh, and we don't mean to suggest that nonprofits are or should be run with an iron hand. The board of directors does have ultimate responsibility, however, for the finances and actions of a nonprofit organization, and, therefore, people serving in that capacity have a real duty to make sure that the organization has sufficient resources to carry out its activities and that it's doing what it's supposed to be doing.

We prefer to think of nonprofits as being an organized group activity. You need to depend on others to reach goals, and they need to depend on you. We talk about boards of directors in Chapter 6 and working with volunteers in Chapter 7. If your nonprofit employs paid staff or hopes to someday, Chapter 8 provides some guidance in hiring and managing employees.

Finding the Resources to Do Your Job

One distinctive feature of the nonprofit sector is its dependency on contributions. We devote many pages of this book — most of Part III — to advice about getting contributions.

Gifts from individuals of money, goods, services, and property make up the largest portion of that voluntary support. This part is also the oldest of the voluntary tradition in the United States and goes back to colonial times. Since the late 19th century, private philanthropic foundations have emerged as another major source of support, and in the 20th century — particularly after World War II — the federal government and corporations became important income sources. Many nonprofits also sell some kind of service, and a trend in the sector shows earned income becoming a larger portion of total revenues.

Among private, nongovernmental sources of support, gifts from living individuals — as opposed to bequests from people who have died — have always represented the largest portion of total giving, but philanthropic giving by foundations and corporations has been growing. Table 1-1 outlines sources of private contributions in 2004. The best fundraising approach for most organizations is to take a balanced approach that includes individual giving as well as grants and corporate contributions.

Table 1-1	Sources of Private Contributions: 2004	
Source of Income	*Amount of Total Giving*	*Percentage of Total Giving*
Individuals	$187.92 billion	75.6%
Foundations	$28.80 billion	11.6%
Bequests	$19.80 billion	8.0%
Corporations	$12.00 billion	4.8%
Total	$248.52 billion	100%

Source: Giving USA Foundation(tm) — AAFRC Trust for Philanthropy/Giving USA 2005

Comparing income

Table 1-2 gives a quick overview from *Giving USA 2005* showing how the various kinds of nonprofit organizations compare in securing revenues.

Table 1-2	2004 Contributions by Type of Recipient Organization	
Organization Type	*Contributions in Billions*	*Percentage*
Religion	$88.30	35.5%
Education	$33.84	13.6%
Foundations	$24.00	9.7%
Health	$21.95	8.8%
Unallocated/Other	$21.36	8.6%
Human services	$19.17	7.7%
Arts, culture	$13.99	5.6%
Public/society benefit	$12.96	5.2%
Environment/Animals	$7.61	3.1%
International	$5.34	2.1%
Total	$248.52	99.9%

Source: Giving USA Foundation(tm) — AAFRC Trust for Philanthropy/Giving USA 2005

Fundraising for fun and profit

Every nonprofit organization depends on generous donors for the cash it needs to pay its bills. Even if you have income from ticket sales, admission charges, or contracted services, you'll find that raising additional money is necessary to keep your organization alive and thriving.

You can see from Table 1-1 that individual giving is the largest single source of contributed income to nonprofit organizations. But you can't just sit waiting by the mailbox for the donations to begin arriving. Two basic rules of fundraising are that people need to be asked for donations and thanked after giving one. Chapter 14 focuses on raising money from individuals, Chapter 15 covers raising money with special events, and Chapter 18 discusses campaign fundraising, which is used when you need to raise extra money for your building or your endowment.

Grants from foundations and corporations make up a smaller percentage of giving to nonprofits, but their support can be invaluable for start-up project costs, equipment, technical support, and, sometimes, general operating costs. Keep in mind that the figures given in Table 1-1 don't apply equally to every nonprofit. Some organizations get most of their income from foundation grants; others get very little. Chapter 16 introduces you to resources to help you find potential grant sources. Chapter 17 takes you through the process of crafting a grant proposal.

Fundraising works better if people know you exist. That knowledge also helps get people to your theater or to sign up for your programs. Here's where marketing and public relations enter the picture. Chapter 11 helps you figure out what your media message should be and how to circulate it to the world.

Make no mistake about it, fundraising is hard work, but if you approach the task with a positive attitude and make your case well, you can find the resources you need.

Chapter 2

Deciding to Start a Nonprofit

Maybe you've been thinking about starting a nonprofit organization for years, or maybe an idea to solve a social problem or provide a needed service just popped into your head. It doesn't matter how or when you got the idea. It could be time to make it a reality.

But before you file your incorporation papers, understand the positive and not-so-positive factors that can make or break your new organization. Like starting any business, starting and managing a nonprofit organization isn't a simple matter, so be prepared for lots of hard work. You must be equipped to manage money and raise funds — which isn't always an easy task — and you must be able to work closely with and inspire others, whether they are board members, staff, or volunteers. After reviewing the pros and cons of starting your nonprofit organization, you may even decide that now isn't the right time to take this important step.

In this chapter, we pose some questions that you should think about (and answer) before you begin the process of incorporation and applying for tax exemption. If some of your answers point to the conclusion that your idea is worth pursuing, but now isn't the right time and place to start a brand-new nonprofit organization, we give you an alternative to consider.

When we use the term *nonprofit* in this book, we're referring to organizations that have been recognized by the IRS as public charities under section 501(c)(3) of the tax code. Later in this chapter, we describe some of the other kinds of nonprofits to point out the distinct attributes of these 501(c)(3) public charities.

Weighing the Pros and Cons

Before you jump headfirst into making your nonprofit dream a reality, you should understand some basic facts about nonprofit organizations. We begin with some of the pros:

- Exemption from taxes on most income to the nonprofit

- For some types of nonprofits, the ability to receive contributions that are deductible for the donor

- The possibility of receiving grant funds from foundations and corporations

- The feeling that you're contributing to the solution of a problem or the improvement of society

Just about everyone would consider these facts as positive, but they aren't the whole story. If you're thinking of starting a nonprofit to get rich or to avoid paying taxes, consider the following list of cons:

- Nonprofit employees' salaries are subject to income tax like all compensation.

- If your organization has more than $25,000 in revenue a year, you have to file an annual report with the IRS and make these reports available to the public.

- You can't start a nonprofit organization to benefit a particular individual or family member.

- Competition for grants from foundations, corporations, and government agencies is tough, and so is getting donations from individuals. You'll be up against more established nonprofits with successful track records.

- Well over half of the nonprofit organizations in the United States either choose to operate without paid staff or do so because of a lack of funds.

- If you decide to move on to other pursuits, you can't take with you any assets accumulated by the organization you've built.

Bottom line: Think carefully about your motivation for launching a nonprofit organization. Remember that nonprofit organizations are permitted special privileges because they are formed to benefit the public, not individuals.

Doing Your Basic Homework

Beyond thinking about the fundamental burdens you'll face in starting and running a nonprofit organization, it's a good idea to apply some common sense, too. Nonprofits don't operate in a vacuum and neither should you.

Personal commitment and inspiration can take your organization far, but you also need to find out how your community may receive your particular idea. Before going full steam ahead with your organization, you need to investigate your competition, get community support, decide how to fund your organization, recruit the right managers for your organization, and develop a game plan. Read on to find out how to get your nonprofit off to the right start.

Checking out the competition

If you wanted to open a grocery store, you wouldn't choose a location next to a successful supermarket because the market can bear only so much trade. This principle holds true for nonprofits, too. You may have the best idea in the world, but if someone else in your community is already doing it well, don't try to duplicate it. Just as if you were starting a business, you must examine your competition.

If your area doesn't have a similar program, ask yourself why. Maybe your community doesn't have enough potential clients or audience members to support the project. Or maybe funders don't perceive the same needs in the community as you do.

Assessing the needs of your area is a good way to evaluate the potential market for your nonprofit's services. You may want to use some or all of the following methods to determine your community's needs:

✔ Telephone surveys or written questionnaires to a random sample of residents in your community

✔ Interviews with local foundation and civic officials

✔ Focus groups with people who are likely to benefit from the organization

For more details on assessing your community's needs, see Chapter 9.

Finding people to help you

Your chances of success increase if you begin with support from others, and the more help you have, the better. Sure, you can probably find examples of a single-minded visionary who battles through all sorts of adversity to establish a thriving nonprofit, but starting and running a nonprofit organization is essentially a group activity.

When starting a nonprofit, you need to find people to serve on the board of directors and to support your efforts with donations of money and volunteer time. The first people you usually identify as supporters are family and friends. How can they turn you down? But, in the long run, you need that support from others who believe in the organization's mission, too.

Some people hesitate to share their idea with others because they believe that someone might steal it. We think this fear is largely unfounded. You'll be better off if you invite others to join you in the undertaking, whatever it is.

To find people to help you and support your organization, take every opportunity to speak about your idea before civic groups, religious groups, and service clubs. You can pass out fliers or set up a booth at a volunteer fair. Talk to your friends and coworkers. Put on your salesperson's cap and convince the community that it needs your program.

If you're having a hard time drumming up support, it may be a sign that you need to refine your idea or that others view it as impractical. It may be time to go back to the drawing board.

Figuring out how you'll pay the bills

Funding your nonprofit organization is a big issue. Even if you begin as a volunteer-run organization and work from a home office, you still need funds for letterhead, supplies, equipment, postage, and insurance. You'll also have filing fees of at least several hundred dollars for your incorporation and tax-exemption applications. Many nonprofit start-ups are funded by the founder in the beginning. Are you able to pay all the start-up expenses before revenues start flowing to your new nonprofit?

Putting together a budget will help you decide whether the start-up expenses are manageable for you. You'll be creating lots of budgets sooner or later, so you may as well get an early start.

If you're not able to fund the operation by yourself in the early months, you need to make a compelling case that your new organization will provide an important service to the community and convince donors that you have the knowledge and experience to provide it. You can solicit contributions from individuals before the IRS grants the organization tax-exempt status, as long as you reveal that your exemption is pending. (These contributions become deductible to the donor when and if you receive the tax exemption.) Start-up grants from foundations or corporations are rare and next to impossible to obtain before the IRS recognizes your organization's tax-exempt status, so don't plan on receiving any grants from outside organizations.

New organizations can avoid the awkward period between start-up and receiving tax-exempt status by beginning as a sponsored program of an existing nonprofit organization. This arrangement is known as *fiscal sponsorship*. We discuss fiscal sponsorship in more detail later in this chapter.

Taking a long, hard look in the mirror

Ask yourself whether you're the right person to start a nonprofit organization, and answer honestly. If your organization offers a service, especially in the health and social services fields, do you have the qualifications or license necessary to provide those services? In addition to being professionally qualified, you also need to consider whether you feel confident about your management, fundraising, and communication skills.

When starting and working in a new nonprofit organization, you also need to be able to stretch yourself across many different skill areas. You may be dressed to the nines one day to pitch your project to the mayor or to a corporate executive, and the next day, you may be sweeping the floor of your office or unplugging a clogged toilet. In other words, you need to be versatile and willing to take on just about any task that needs to be done.

When potential donors are evaluating grant proposals, they certainly look to see whether the organization's leadership has the background, experience, and knowledge necessary to carry out the proposed program. This doesn't necessarily mean that you need to be an experienced nonprofit manager, but try to assess your background to see how you can apply your experience to the nonprofit you hope to start.

Planning — and then planning some more

If there ever was a time to plan, this is it. Planning is what turns your initial idea into a doable project.

Planning is also a good way to find potential holes in your thinking. For example, you may believe that your community doesn't have adequate animal rescue services. You may be right, but when you begin to break down the idea of starting an animal shelter, you may find that this project costs more money or requires more staff or facilities than you first thought it would. Armed with that knowledge, you can adjust your plan as necessary or scrap the idea altogether.

To begin planning, write a one- or two-page synopsis of your nonprofit idea. In your synopsis, include what you're trying to do and how you plan to do it. Then make a list of the resources you need to accomplish your mission. Resources may include money, volunteers, and an appropriate space to carry out your activities. After you've prepared your synopsis and list of resources, talk to as many people as you can about your idea, asking for help and honest feedback about your project. The purpose of this planning process is to think your nonprofit idea through step by step. If you need help in the planning process, take a look at the information on planning in Chapter 9.

Understanding Nonprofit Ownership

We once received a telephone call from a man who was shopping for a nonprofit. "Do you know if there are any nonprofits for sale in New Hampshire?" he asked. Although this question doesn't come to us often, it illustrates a misconception about the status of nonprofit organizations. No one person or group of people can *own* a nonprofit organization. You don't see nonprofit shares traded on stock exchanges, and any equity in a nonprofit organization belongs to the organization itself, not to the board of directors or the staff. Nonprofit assets can be sold, but the proceeds of the sale must benefit the organization, not private parties.

If you start a nonprofit and decide at some point in the future that you don't want to do it anymore, you have to walk away from it and leave the running of the organization to someone else. Or, if the time has come to close the doors for good, any assets the organization owns must be distributed to other nonprofits fulfilling a similar mission.

 When nonprofit managers and consultants talk about "ownership" of a nonprofit organization, they're using the word metaphorically to make the point that board members, staff, clients, and the community have a stake in the organization's future success and its ability to provide needed programs.

Benefiting the public

People form nonprofit organizations to create a public benefit. In fact, nonprofit corporations are referred to sometimes as *public benefit corporations*. A nonprofit organization can't be created to help a particular individual or family, for example. If that was possible, we'd all have our separate nonprofit organizations.

You can start a nonprofit to aid a specific group or class of individuals — everyone suffering from heart disease, for example, or people living below the poverty level — but you can't create a nonprofit for individual benefit or gain. But just because you're working for the public's benefit doesn't mean that you can't receive a reasonable salary for your work. And, despite the name "nonprofit," such an organization can have surplus funds — essentially, a profit — at the end of year. In a for-profit business, the surplus money would be distributed to employees, shareholders, and the board of directors; however, in a nonprofit organization, the surplus funds are held in reserve by the organization and aren't distributed.

Accounting to the public

People are paying more attention to nonprofit organizations these days. A few examples of excessive salaries reported in the media and concern about how some nonprofits have spent donated funds have prompted donors, legislators, and the general public to ask more questions regarding nonprofit finances and management.

Although nonprofit organizations aren't public entities like governmental agencies and departments, their tax-exempt status and the fact that contributions are tax-deductible require them to be more accountable to the public than a privately owned business.

We discuss nonprofit disclosure requirements in more detail in Chapter 5, but at a minimum, federal law requires that nonprofits with annual revenues totaling more than $25,000 must file a report (Form 990) every year with the IRS, summarizing income and expenses and revealing staff and consultant salaries that are more than $50,000. States also have their own reporting requirements, and both state and federal legislatures are considering more extensive nonprofit accountability laws.

Even if your nonprofit has revenues of less than $25,000, you should still consider filing a 990 report so you can share information with potential donors. In addition, filling out a 990 report lets the IRS know that your nonprofit is still alive and kicking.

A word about excessive compensation

Although nonprofit employees have no absolute limit on the amount of compensation they can earn, the IRS does have the authority to penalize individuals (and organizations) who receive (or pay) excessive compensation. Whether the IRS considers benefits "excessive" depends on the situation. For instance, a staff member earning $100,000 annually from an organization with a budget of $125,000 probably needs to worry, but someone earning $100,000 from a nonprofit with a $5 million budget probably doesn't.

An employee found to receive excessive compensation may be required to pay an excise tax, and in dire cases, the nonprofit organization may lose its tax-exempt status. Chapter 5 offers more information on excessive compensation.

So, when setting your nonprofit's executive director's salary, take care that the amount of compensation is justified by salary surveys of similar organizations. Also factor in the local cost of living, the size of the nonprofit's budget, and the type of services being provided.

Federal law also requires nonprofits to make copies of their three most recent 990 reports, as well as their application for tax exemption, which is available for public inspection. State and local laws in your area may require additional disclosures. Posting your 990 reports and other required documents on the Web is an acceptable way to meet disclosure requirements.

Download a copy of the 990 report from the IRS Web site at www.irs.gov. You can also view completed 990 forms from other nonprofit organizations at GuideStar (www.guidestar.org).

Nonprofits Aren't One-Size-Fits-All

The words "nonprofit" and "charity" go together in most people's minds, but not all nonprofits are charitable organizations. The most common examples are business and trade associations, political advocacy groups, fraternal societies, and clubs. Although these nonprofits enjoy exemption from corporate income taxes, people who donate to them may not claim a tax deduction for their contributions.

Most nonprofits, charitable or not, are incorporated organizations that are formed under the laws of the state in which they are created. Some nonprofits have other legal structures, such as associations or trusts, but these are in the minority. The IRS grants tax-exempt status to a nonprofit after reviewing its stated purpose. (See Chapter 4 for information about incorporation and applying for a tax exemption.) Nonprofit types are identified by the section of the IRS code under which they qualify for exempt status.

In this section, we provide an overview of types of nonprofit organizations and some of the rules and regulations that you'll be subject to if you decide to incorporate and seek tax-exempt status from the IRS. You may discover, for example, that your idea will have a better chance for success if you create a social welfare organization — a 501(c)(4) — or even if you start a for-profit business.

Knowing them by their numbers

To get the full flavor of the various categories of nonprofit organizations, see the information at the IRS Web site (www.irs.gov) or review IRS publication 557. The following list summarizes various classes of nonprofit organizations:

- **501(c)(3):** These organizations are formed for educational, scientific, literary, charitable, or religious pursuits; and to test for public safety and prevent cruelty to children and animals. Nonprofits in this category are classified either as public charities or private foundations. Foundations are subject to additional reporting requirements. This book focuses on the special attributes of and restrictions on 501(c)(3) organizations, which include limits on the amount of legislative lobbying they may do. We discuss these lobbying restrictions below.

✔ **501(c)(4):** These organizations are known as *social welfare organizations* and are formed for the improvement of general welfare and the common good of the people. Advocacy groups tend to fall into this category because organizations with this classification are allowed more leeway to lobby legislatures as a part of their mission to improve the general welfare. Certain employee organizations also come under this classification. Contributions to these organizations aren't deductible for the donor.

✔ **501(c)(5):** Labor unions and other groups formed to work for better conditions for workers are in this category. These groups also may lobby for legislation.

✔ **501(c)(6):** Business and trade associations that provide services to their members and work toward the betterment of business conditions are placed in this classification. This category includes chambers of commerce and real estate boards, for example. Again, lobbying for legislation is allowed.

✔ **501(c)(7):** This section covers social clubs formed for recreation and pleasure. Country clubs and organizations formed around a hobby come under this classification. These organizations must be funded primarily by memberships and dues.

✔ **501(c)(9):** A voluntary employees' beneficiary association organized to pay insurance benefits to members and their dependents.

✔ **501(c)(19)/501(c)(23):** These categories cover veterans' organizations for people who have served in the U.S. military. 501(c)(23)s are veterans' organizations formed before 1880.

Several other 501(c)-type organizations are so specialized in nature that we won't go into them here. One of our favorites is the 501(c)(13), which covers cemetery companies.

Political committees and parties have their own special classification, too. They're recognized under IRS code section 527 and are organized for the purpose of electing persons to office. They have special reporting requirements and aren't required to be incorporated.

Odd little rules and regulations to add to your file

Entire volumes have been written about IRS regulations and laws pertaining to nonprofits. Don't worry — we just want to give you an overview of some facts that may help you decide whether starting a 501(c)(3) nonprofit organization is your best choice.

Nonprofits and political activities

Nonprofits can't campaign to support or oppose the candidacy of anyone running for an elected office. If you want your organization to do so, you must form a political committee under IRS section 527. However, the stipulations on nonprofits lobbying for specific legislation are less clear. In the following list, we try to break down the stipulations for you a bit:

- ✔ Social welfare organizations and labor unions have more leeway when it comes to legislative lobbying than the 501(c)(3) organizations. In fact, lobbying can be the primary activity of these organizations. Groups that lobby must inform their members what percentage of dues they use for lobbying activities, and they can't work toward a candidate's election.

- ✔ Charitable organizations, or nonprofits that the IRS considers public charities under section 501(c)(3), may participate in some legislative lobbying if it's an "unsubstantial" part of their activities. The IRS doesn't define "unsubstantial" but determines this question on a case-by-case basis.

- ✔ Public charities can spend a higher portion of their budget on lobbying activities if the organization chooses to elect the *h designation,* which refers to section 501(h) of the IRS code. Electing the h designation requires more financial reporting to the IRS, but it allows the nonprofit to spend a greater percentage of its income on lobbying activities. The IRS allows more expenditures for direct lobbying (when members of the nonprofit talk with a legislator about an issue at hand) than for grassroots lobbying.

- ✔ Private foundations, although they, too, are recognized under section 501(c)(3), may not participate in any legislative lobbying. The only exception to this rule is when pending legislation may have a regulatory impact on the foundation.

Going deeper into the details of these laws and reporting requirements is really beyond the scope of this book. However, if you're contemplating involving your nonprofit in serious legislative activity, consult an attorney or tax specialist for advice. Information also is available at the Charity Lobbying in the Public Interest Web site (`www.clpi.org`). Penalties for engaging in too much political activity can include loss of your organization's tax exemption.

The situation with churches

Churches are in a category all by themselves. The IRS doesn't require them to file for a tax exemption, nor does it require them to file annual reports to the IRS. Some churches, however, do want the IRS to acknowledge their tax-exempt status as a 501(c)(3) organization.

Some churches file annual reports because their social service programs may include anything from preschools to soup kitchens. These programs can apply for foundation funding and government grants or contracts to help pay the costs of providing the services. But it's highly unlikely that grants or contracts will be given to church programs that haven't been recognized officially as tax-exempt.

Taxes, taxes, taxes

Nonprofit organizations may be subject to unrelated business income tax, known as UBIT. When a nonprofit earns more than $1,000 a year from a trade or business that's unrelated to its exempt purpose, this income is taxable. Also, some corporate sponsorship funds may be subject to UBIT if they are perceived by the IRS as advertising dollars. IRS Publication 598 (www.irs.gov) tells you all you need to know about this subject.

Some states exempt *some* nonprofits from paying state sales and use taxes. Check the laws in your state to see whether your organization is exempt from paying these taxes. The same is true of property taxes — it depends on your local jurisdiction. Your nearest tax assessor can tell you whether you have to pay property taxes.

Nonprofit employees, of course, must pay income tax on their salaries and other taxable compensation.

Nonprofits owning for-profits

Nonprofits can own for-profit businesses. We don't recommend it, because you're going to have enough on your plate, especially when you're starting out, but it is possible. The business is subject to all regular taxes, just like all other for-profit businesses. Profits from the business become assets of the nonprofit and must be used to further the organization's goals and programs.

Very small organizations

If your nonprofit has less than $5,000 in annual revenues, it doesn't need to apply for a tax exemption. You can even go a bit over $5,000 in a year if your average annual income over a three-year period is less than $5,000.

When your income averages more than that amount, however, you have 90 days following the close of your most recent tax year to file for a tax exemption.

Nonprofit compensation

Nonprofit organizations have one common feature, regardless of their type: No board member, staff member, or other interested party can benefit from the earnings of a nonprofit. Instead, assets are forever dedicated to the purpose of the organization. If the organization dissolves, the nonprofit must transfer the assets to another organization that performs a similar function.

This doesn't mean that people are required to work for nonprofit organizations for free. Nonprofits can and should pay reasonable salaries to their staff members, if they have any. But keep in mind the difference between paying a salary and splitting the profits at the end of year.

Comparing Nonprofits and For-Profits

Believing that nonprofit organizations have special advantages isn't uncommon. And to some extent, it's true. How many for-profit businesses, for example, get help from volunteers and generous donors? On the other hand, the advantages to owning your business exist, too. In this section, we discuss the similarities and differences between nonprofits and for-profits to help you decide which direction you'd like to go.

How they're alike

We want to start with the similarities between the nonprofits and for-profits because, believe it or not, there are several. For instance:

- ✔ Good business practices are important to both.
- ✔ Good planning based on good information is also a critical factor in the success of both nonprofits and for-profits.
- ✔ Management skills, the ability to communicate clearly, and attention to detail make a difference whether you're working in a nonprofit or somewhere else.
- ✔ A little bit of luck doesn't hurt, either.

The term *entrepreneur* usually is used to describe someone who starts a new business. But any person or group that sets out to establish a nonprofit organization is entrepreneurial. After all, you're starting out on a path that may lead to great success, and you'll assume some risks along the way. We hope that you won't risk your house or your savings account to get a nonprofit going, but you may have uncertain income for a while. In addition, you always risk the chance of damaging your professional reputation if things don't go as well as you hoped.

How they differ

Although for-profits and nonprofits require similar professionalism and dedication from their leaders, they differ when it comes time to interpret their "bottom line" and successes.

The biggest difference between nonprofits and for-profits is the motivation for doing what you do — the "mission" of the organization. For-profit businesses exist to make money — a profit. Nonprofits exist to provide a public benefit.

Evaluating the success of a for-profit endeavor is easy: Did you make money, and, if so, how much did you make?

We're not saying this to cast stones at the capitalist system or to in any way disparage the millions of folks who work for profit-making endeavors. After all, the nonprofit sector depends on profits and wealth for its support. And, of course, nonprofits have to balance the books, too. Even nonprofits prefer to end the year with more money than they had when they started. They just don't call it profit; they call it a surplus.

For a nonprofit to be successful, it needs to change some aspect of the human condition; it needs to solve a problem, provide education, or build a monument. And because the goals of nonprofits are so lofty and progress toward achieving them is often slow, evaluating nonprofit success is sometimes difficult. That's why nonprofits are often said to have a *double bottom line* — that is, the financial results and the social change they create.

Using a Fiscal Sponsor: An Alternative Approach

If you're simply interested in providing a service, maybe you don't want to waste your time with the bureaucratic and legal matters that can complicate a new nonprofit start-up. Or maybe you have a project that will end after a year or two, or you simply want to test the viability of an idea. Why bother to establish a new organization if it's going to close when you finish your project?

You may not need to start a nonprofit to carry out the program you're thinking of starting. *Fiscal sponsorship* may be the best route to take. In this approach, your new project becomes a sponsored program of an existing 501(c)(3) nonprofit organization. Contributions earmarked for your project are tax deductible because they're made to the sponsoring agency.

Here's a hypothetical example. Joanna Jones, a paralegal for a Chicago law firm, has an interest in immigration law and wants to provide part-time assistance to recent immigrants from South Asia who are having visa problems. She has created an annual budget and spoken to several funders who have expressed a desire to make three-year grants to the project. However, in order to accept funding, Jones must either create a 501(c)(3) organization or find an alternative. Someone suggested that she seek a fiscal sponsor as that alternative.

After doing some research, she contacted the Angeline Community Center, a nonprofit organization that provides health and other services to low-income groups, including the immigrant population she hopes to help. The community center agreed to become the fiscal sponsor. The foundation funders made their grants to Angeline Community Center, earmarked for the immigration counseling program.

Jones now provides immigration counseling services under the auspices of the Angeline Community Center. Under this arrangement, the community center provides basic accounting services for the project and is ultimately responsible to the funders to ensure that their grants are used as they were intended.

Important points to ponder

A fiscal sponsor sometimes is called a "fiscal agent," but this term doesn't accurately describe the relationship between a fiscal sponsor and the sponsored project. The term *agent* implies that the sponsoring organization is acting on behalf on the project, when really the project is acting on behalf of the organization. The project is simply a program of the sponsoring nonprofit.

This distinction may seem nitpicky, but it's an important one to keep in mind in order to satisfy IRS requirements for this type of relationship. The 501(c)(3) sponsoring organization is responsible to both the funders and the IRS to see that the money is spent as intended and that charitable goals are met.

Here are important points to keep in mind if you decide to go the fiscal sponsor route:

- ✔ The mission of the fiscal sponsor must be in alignment with the project. In other words, if you have a project to provide free food to the homeless, don't approach your local philharmonic orchestra as a potential sponsor. Find a nonprofit that has similar goals in its mission statement.

- ✔ The board of directors of the sponsoring organization must approve the sponsorship arrangements. They are, after all, ultimately responsible.

- ✔ Both parties should outline a contract or memorandum of understanding detailing the responsibilities of each.

    See CD0201 for a sample fiscal sponsorship agreement.

- ✔ The fiscal sponsor customarily charges a fee for sponsoring a project, usually between 5 and 15 percent of the project's annual revenues, depending on what services it's providing to the project. Some fiscal sponsors can provide payroll services, office space, and even management support, if needed.

✔ Contributions to the sponsored project should be written to the sponsor, with a note that instructs that they be used for the project.

Some foundations are reluctant to award grants to fiscally sponsored projects, even announcing in their guidelines that they won't do it. One reason for this reluctance is their concern that boards of the sponsoring organizations exercise less oversight toward fiscal sponsorships than they do toward their agency's other programs. Those foundations also may be concerned that the sponsoring nonprofits are providing convenient access to 501(c)(3) status to entities that don't qualify for that tax status from the IRS. Not all foundations share these prohibitions. Some, in fact, are proponents of fiscal sponsorship as a way of supporting new ideas and timely programs. You can read much more about foundations and grant proposals in Chapters 16 and 17.

Fiscal sponsorship as a first step

Using fiscal sponsorship as a temporary solution while establishing a new nonprofit corporation and acquiring a tax exemption can be an effective approach for the following reasons:

✔ You avoid the period when you have a nonprofit corporation but no tax-exempt status.

✔ You have an opportunity to test the viability of raising funds for your idea.

✔ You have time to establish an organizational infrastructure and to create a board of directors in a more leisurely manner.

✔ You can pay more attention to building your program services in the crucial beginning stages of your project.

Finding a fiscal sponsor

If you're not sure who to ask about fiscal sponsorship, a good place to begin is at your local community foundation. Community foundations often have programs that provide fiscal sponsorship programs, and their mission statements are typically broad enough to cover any program that benefits the areas they serve.

If your area doesn't have a community foundation nearby, contact the nearest United Way office or another nonprofit that provides referrals and ask for help in finding the right agency to sponsor your project.

Chapter 3

Writing Your Mission Statement

· ·

In This Chapter

▶ Understanding the role of a mission statement

▶ Creating a mission statement

▶ Generating support for your mission statement

· ·

The purpose of your organization is stated in its mission; in fact, it's the reason the organization exists. The process of developing your mission statement is also important because it can help you test and refine your ideas. And after you've decided on your organization's mission statement, you can use it as a touchstone to return to when making decisions about your nonprofit.

Mission statements can be one-liners or go on for two or three pages. We suggest aiming for something in between these two extremes. A mission statement contained in one line resembles an advertising slogan, and a long, rambling statement is rarely read, even by the board of directors and staff members.

You need to spend some time thinking about what you want to include in your mission statement because it defines what your organization hopes to accomplish. You must craft the language you use to describe your purpose so that it's clear and to the point.

In this chapter, we give you some guidance about how you can create a simple yet compelling mission statement.

Mission Statement Basics

The mission statement is an organization's center. We were tempted to use the word *heart* rather than *center,* but we think that's stretching the metaphor a little. Or we could have said that mission statements are living, breathing organisms from which all organizational life flows, but that would truly be going too far. People are really at the heart of and bring the life to an organization. Mission statements just help give this human energy direction and form.

Can organizations operate without good mission statements? Yes, and some do. We're sure that some organizations out there haven't looked at their mission statements since the Carter administration but are still doing good things. Your chances of success are better, however, if you and the people associated with your organization know exactly what they're trying to do and how they're going to do it.

A mission statement should state the organization's purpose, how the purpose will be achieved, and who will benefit from the organization's activities. Organizational values and vision also may be included.

The mission should also be

- ✔ **Memorable:** You want to carry it around with you at all times.

- ✔ **Focused:** Your mission statement should be narrow enough to focus the activities of your organization but broad enough to allow growth and expansion.

- ✔ **Easy to read:** Write the statement in plain language so that it doesn't need a set of footnotes for folks to decipher it.

Working with a purpose

When thinking of your purpose, think of the end result you want. What would you like to see happen? What would the world (or your community) be like if your organization succeeded?

To say that you have to have a purpose seems almost too basic. Maybe you're thinking to yourself, "Of course I have a purpose. Why do you think I bought this book? I want to start a nonprofit to [fill in the blank]." But we bring this point up because the purpose is basic to a mission statement. Knowing and understanding your organization's purpose is essential to making the organizational decisions you need to make. Your purpose drives your fundraising efforts and your program planning.

Without a *clearly stated* purpose, you may have a difficult time explaining why your organization exists, which is a fundamental requirement when asking for money, recruiting board members, hiring and motivating staff, and publicizing your activities.

Describing how you work

Now that you know your purpose, the next step is deciding how you're going to make it happen. Mission statements usually include a phrase describing the methods your organization will use to accomplish its purpose. Think about the activities and programs your organization will provide to achieve its goal.

Don't confuse ends with methods. Providing a program is a method, not an end. The end (or desired result) you seek may be to ensure that all high school students have an equal opportunity to attend college. Your methods may include providing tutoring, offering scholarships, and promoting the value of a college education, to name a few.

When describing your methods, you don't want to be so specific that you have to rewrite your mission statement every time you add a new program, but you do want to state how your organization plans to fulfill its purpose. For example, will you focus on providing services to your clients, or will you be involved primarily with public education? If you plan to do both, say so.

Putting the beneficiaries on a pedestal

If you've determined your purpose, you probably know the primary beneficiaries of your activities. The mission statement should include this information. If you aim your programs at families, for example, make that clear in your statement.

Some organizations have a more general audience than others. If your purpose is preserving historic buildings, what group is the beneficiary of this activity? It may be current and future residents of a city, a county, or even a state. Again, thinking of who will benefit helps to focus organizational activities.

Adding your organizational values

People who work together in a nonprofit organization tend to share the same core values and beliefs. Nonprofits may be organized around religious principles, a certain philosophy of treatment, a belief in the extraterrestrial, or the benefits of eating four meals a day.

Whatever you believe, it's an important part of the passion that fuels your nonprofit. Include a phrase in your mission statement about your organizational values. Doing so helps remind you (and lets others know) why you're doing what you're doing.

Envisioning your future

Simply put, a *vision statement* is your dream of what your organization can become. Although vision statements can describe a future desired condition as a result of the organization's activities, they are more typically applied to the organization itself. Usually, the statement includes phrases like "the best," "recognized as a leader," or "become financially stable."

Here's an example of a vision statement from a fictitious agricultural policy think tank.

> *The ABC Agricultural Economics Institute will continue to encourage excellence in its staff by providing opportunities for communication, collaboration, and professional development. The institute's research projects and position statements on agricultural matters will be widely reported in the media and referred to in the setting of state and national agriculture policy.*

Some nonprofits include their vision statements in their mission statements, and others don't. We believe that holding a dream is a good thing, and we see some truth to the statement, "If you can't conceive of doing something, you can't do it." Still, we encourage you not to spend an excessive amount of time shaping your vision statement. Focusing on concrete ends and means is more important.

Keeping your focus narrow at first

Narrow mission statements are best for organizations that work within a limited geographical area and have a single, specific purpose. But what if your vision is broader than your county? What if you hope to expand your services to a regional, state, national, or even global level?

We recommend starting in the most focused way possible and growing the organization. So, for example, if you hope to establish counseling services across the nation for parents of children who have learning disabilities, beginning close to home is the best approach. Get your program going in your hometown before branching out to other areas.

The narrower your mission statement, the easier it is to convey your organization's purpose and activities. If you start out with a mission to provide counseling services to every parent in the United States who has a child with a learning disability, you're likely to run into trouble. You're trying to run before you can walk.

Mission statements can always be changed. As your organization achieves success locally and you determine that it's time to expand, you may want to review your mission anyway as a part of your organizational planning process. That's the time to consider setting a broader mission.

Check out two examples of a mission statement from the same organization — seven years apart. CD0301 was adopted in 1995; CD0302 is a revised mission statement adopted in 2002.

Keeping your statement short and sweet

In keeping with our notion that a good mission statement is easily expressed, we tend to favor short, pithy statements over long, rambling ones.

We understand, however, that some organizations want to describe their aims and activities more fully than what can be captured in a single short paragraph. For those organizations, we suggest that you begin your mission statement with a one-paragraph summary that states simply what your non-profit hopes to accomplish, how it plans to do it, and for whom. You may want to prepare your longer statement first and then go back and distill the essence of your mission into a short, succinct paragraph.

Beginning your mission statement with a summary paragraph and then expanding your vision with a longer statement is a little like having your cake and eating it, too. Treat your pithy first paragraph like an executive summary of a longer report. That way, you still have a short, clear statement to use when you need it.

Speaking of your mission . . .

An effective mission statement doesn't have to be fancy, just clear and complete. Here are a few good examples:

From a health clinic: "Our organizational mission is to establish and maintain a family health clinic to ensure access to affordable health care for the residents of Lincoln County. The clinic will achieve its mission by providing primary health care on a sliding fee basis, practicing preventive medicine, and promoting healthy lifestyles through a county-wide public education campaign."

From an organization promoting political awareness: "In order to ensure full participation in our country's political process, we inform citizens about the benefits and responsibilities of exercising their rights in a democratic society. We fulfill our mission by disseminating examples of citizen participation in grass-roots projects that improve local communities and by promoting town hall meetings that encourage individuals of diverse interests to join together in collaborative action."

From a private elementary school: "Our mission is to help our students to be well prepared for the high school curriculum and to instill the desire to be lifelong learners by providing our students with teachers who are skilled in classroom instruction and who themselves demonstrate the benefits of continuous learning far beyond their formal education."

Writing the Mission Statement

Before writing the final draft, get input from everyone involved. You want to hear as many ideas as possible, and you want everyone to agree on the essence of the organization's mission.

When it comes to putting words on paper, however, choose your best writer and turn her loose. We're not fans of committee-written prose. We've sat in meetings where committees discussed verb choice and the placement of commas without apparent end. The result of such efforts is usually murky prose that requires several readings to interpret the meaning.

Your mission statement is something that you carry around with you, in your head and in brochures. You want to be able to explain quickly and succinctly what your organization does. If you have to pull out a book to explain it, your audience is going to lose interest fast.

Getting input from your group

If you're starting a nonprofit with a group of people, everyone needs to agree on the mission statement. In this case, we recommend a meeting to solicit input from everyone. The biggest advantage to this kind of group activity is achieving full buy-in from everyone involved. After all, you want people to believe and accept the organization's mission statement. If they don't, they probably won't stay around to help.

You probably already have a good idea of your purpose. The task before you is to refine that idea so it's simply stated in a few words.

Bring a few prewritten suggestions to the group meeting. Present them as drafts to the group and ask for feedback. If your group is larger than five or six people, consider bringing in an experienced group facilitator to guide the discussion so that everyone's ideas are heard and the discussion remains on track.

Drafting the statement

When drafting your statement, the best advice we can offer is to stay away from jargon and flowery rhetoric. Avoid the buzzwords that are currently popular in your field. In fact, this is good advice in any kind of writing — grant proposals, memos, letters, and so on. You don't want your audience scratching their heads and wondering, "What does that mean?"

Here's an example of a vague, unclear mission statement:

> *The Good Food Society works to maximize the utilization of nutritious food groups to beneficially help all persons in their existence and health by proclaiming the good benefits of balanced nutrition.*

You probably get the idea that this organization wants people to have better eating habits so they can enjoy better health. But try reciting this statement to someone whom you're trying to convince to contribute to your organization. Can you say tongue-tied?

Long, multisyllabic words don't make a mission statement more impressive. If anything, they have the opposite effect. Instead of the preceding statement, try something like this:

> *Believing in the value of good nutrition, the Good Food Society aims to improve public health by providing information about the benefits of a balanced diet to parents of school-age children through its public education programs.*

This mission statement may not be perfect, but it states the organization's values, its long-term goal, the targeted group, and a general method for accomplishing the goal.

The statement also suggests that the Good Food Society has given some thought to how to best accomplish its mission — that is, to aim its information campaigns at parents, who presumably have some control over the food their children eat. The implied strategy is that if good eating habits are established in childhood, they will carry over into the child's adult life.

Giving your statement the elevator test

Mission statements should be used, not written and then stuck in a drawer somewhere and pulled out only when you're writing a grant proposal.

Imagine that you're riding in an elevator with someone who knows nothing about your nonprofit. You have 15 seconds to describe your organization's purpose and activities. Doing so is easy if you have a clear, short mission statement. Even if you have a longer mission statement, develop a 50- to 75-word spiel that you can recite from memory.

Getting Buy-In for Your Mission Statement

We talk a bit about buy-in in the section "Getting input from your group," earlier in this chapter, and we discuss it at even more length in Chapter 9. The important thing to keep in mind is that the more involved people are in creating a mission statement, the more likely they are to invest and believe in it.

When you're the sole founder

If you're setting out to start a nonprofit on your own, you'll soon discover that you need to gather more people around you. You need a board of directors and volunteers to help you move forward. We suggest that you begin by finding people who share your values and, if not your passion, at least your desire to accomplish your aims.

Bring these people together to discuss your mission. Even an hour or two spent talking about what your organization can do helps you and your supporters come together around a common theme.

When you have a group of founders

If you've already assembled a group and everyone has agreed that it's time to incorporate and seek tax-exempt status (see Chapter 4 for more on these topics), creating the mission statement should be one of the first things you do.

Having a group of like-minded people together gives you an advantage because you probably have identified your board of directors and key volunteers. But starting a nonprofit with a preformed group also carries some potential pitfalls. What happens, for example, if members of the group have different priorities?

Different factions almost always need to compromise in order to agree on a mission that enables the organization to use its limited resources in the most effective way. As the organization grows and more resources become available, more programs that address the concerns of the individual founders can be implemented. (See the sidebar, "A healthy compromise," for a real-life example of how a group overcame their differences.)

A healthy compromise

We know of a community-based group that wanted to start a neighborhood health center focusing on environmental health risks in the community. The group hoped to provide health screening services and public education about local environmental risks and to encourage local government to clean up toxic areas in the community.

The challenge this group faced was the different perspectives held by its different members. School-based participants wanted to focus on children and respiratory problems caused by the environment. Another faction became involved because its interest was in early detection of breast cancer. And a third faction believed that prostate cancer screening was of paramount importance.

What was the solution? This group decided to first establish a neighborhood meeting place where information about environmental factors in the community and all associated health risks could be presented. The group also scheduled a series of town hall meetings to give neighborhood residents an opportunity to express concerns about environmental health risks and get answers to their questions.

The school-based faction had to pull back on its initial plan to provide one-to-one counseling to children and their parents about respiratory ailments in the schools. At the same time, the breast and prostate cancer prevention advocates agreed to assign a lower priority to the door-to-door campaigns that they had originally insisted be implemented as soon as possible.

Remember that mission statements aren't carved in stone. They can be changed. We don't recommend wholesale changes in your basic purpose, but you can alter the mission statement to either narrow or broaden your organization's focus, depending on your progress toward achieving the mission and the needs you see in your community.

For groups that are working together to establish a nonprofit organization, we recommend that you find an outside facilitator to guide the group through the inevitable discussions about priorities and the direction of the new organization. Finding a neutral person who can bring an outsider's perspective to the group's deliberations is almost essential. A facilitator also takes responsibility for managing the group so you and your colleagues can be full participants in the meeting. You *can* do it yourself, but you may be happier (and spend less time in meetings) if you get someone to help you. See Chapter 21 for suggestions on finding help. If you aren't near a *nonprofit support organization* (a nonprofit that helps other nonprofits with technical assistance), ask other nonprofits near you for suggestions.

Chapter 4

Incorporating and Applying for Tax Exemption

In This Chapter

▶ Forming a nonprofit corporation

▶ Writing your organization's articles of incorporation

▶ Applying for an Employer Identification Number

▶ Creating bylaws — the rules of your nonprofit

▶ Scheduling board meetings

▶ Going for IRS tax exemption

---

*I*f you want to provide programs and services as a nonprofit organization, you need to set up the legal structure for your organization and apply for its tax exemption. Before you begin fulfilling your mission, you must take care of those jobs, which require attention to detail and ample planning.

This two-step process usually consists of forming a nonprofit corporation under the laws of your state and then submitting an application form to the Internal Revenue Service (IRS) requesting that your organization be recognized as tax exempt.

In this chapter, we provide a guide to the incorporation and exemption process and give you suggestions about where you can go for help. Keep in mind, though, that we're not attorneys, and the information in this chapter isn't meant to be legal advice. Although many nonprofits are formed without the aid of legal counsel, we think that consulting an attorney is a good idea, even if it's only to review your work. After all, you're taking on legal responsibilities. Why not use professional help?

For quick reference, we've put together a checklist for forming a nonprofit organization (CD0401).

Creating a New Entity — the Corporation

The first legal step in creating a nonprofit organization almost always is forming a *corporation*. We say "almost always" because exceptions exist. In the United States, for example, associations, trusts, and sometimes limited liability companies can operate as tax-exempt nonprofit organizations. And charitable groups with under $5,000 in annual revenues, as well as churches, aren't required to apply for tax exemption. We say more about associations and trusts later in this chapter, but for now, we want to focus on the most common legal structure for nonprofit organizations: the corporation.

A corporation is an entity or an organization that has legal standing. It's established by a group of individuals — the incorporators — under the laws of the state in which it's formed.

One advantage of creating a corporation is that the individuals who govern and work for it are separate from the abstract thing they create. Although board members can be liable for the corporation's actions if they don't exercise their duties and responsibilities carefully, in most cases corporations protect individuals from personal liability. So it's helpful to think of a corporation as separate from the people who start it because, well, it is.

When you start a corporation, you're creating an entity that's expected to continue in perpetuity. In other words, the corporation you create goes on living after you decide to do something else or after your death. Corporations can be closed or dissolved, but you must take legal steps to do so. You can't just take down your shingle and walk away.

Looking to your state law

In the United States, corporations are created and regulated under the laws of the state in which they're formed. Although the way a corporation is formed from state to state has more similarities than differences, you do need to create your nonprofit so that it conforms to the peculiarities of your state. Some states, for example, require a minimum of three directors; others require only one.

Check out CD0402 for a list of information about where to go to get specifics about incorporating in your state. Usually, the secretary of state's office handles incorporations. Some states have an incorporation package that includes the forms you need to file. You also can find state contact information on the IRS Web site at www.irs.gov.

Considering your corporation's governing documents

Think of a corporation as a tiny government with a constitution and laws. To set down the rules under which the organization will operate, you need to prepare the following important documents:

✔ The *articles of incorporation* make up the document that creates the organization. It names the organization and describes its reason for existence. In the case of a nonprofit corporation, it specifies that the corporation won't be used to create profit for its directors. The articles are signed by the corporation's incorporators, usually three people, who may or may not end up being directors of the organization.

✔ *Bylaws* specify how directors are elected, the length of their terms, the officers and their duties, the number of meetings to be held, who is and isn't a member of the corporation, how many members or directors are required to be in attendance for a quorum to be present, the rules for director attendance at board meetings, and how the bylaws may be amended. They also may list the standing committees of the board and grant or limit particular powers of the trustees.

As you draft these documents (see the "Writing the Articles of Incorporation" section later in this chapter for more specific information on writing them), remember that you're creating the legal rules under which your nonprofit will operate. Both articles of incorporation and bylaws may be changed by following the laws of your state (in the case of articles of incorporation) or the bylaws.

Deciding whether to have members in your corporation

Corporations may have members. They may even have different classes of members — voting and nonvoting, for example. Depending on state law, you usually have the option to create membership conditions in either the articles or the bylaws. If you have a choice and if you're going to have members, we recommend adding these conditions in the bylaws, which are easier to amend than the articles of incorporation.

Don't add members unless you have a very good reason to do so. In general, having members in your corporation adds additional responsibilities to the governance of the organization. If you have members, for instance, you need to have membership meetings, probably at least one per year, and the members will be involved in choosing directors for the organization.

However, you may have good reasons for getting as many people involved in your organization as possible, and having members is one way to achieve this goal. If your nonprofit is a neighborhood improvement group, for example, including as many people as possible in the governance of the organization may be important.

Many nonprofit organizations have "members," with membership cards and special rates on admissions to performances or exhibits. Don't confuse this kind of membership, which is a marketing and fundraising strategy, with legal membership in the corporation. You're free to start a membership program of this type without amending your bylaws or your articles of incorporation.

Choosing your corporation's name

Choosing a name for your new corporation may be one of the most important things you do as you set it up. A nonprofit's name is a little like a mission statement (see Chapter 3 for more on mission statements). You want it to suggest the types of programs and services you offer and the people you serve.

If your programs provide home health services to people over 65, don't name your nonprofit something generic like "Services for the People." Stay away from names that are so abstract that they have no meaning at all. A name like the Reenergizing Society prompts more questions than it answers. What or who is being reenergized? How are clients being reenergized? And why are they being reenergized? Use concrete, descriptive terms.

To avoid possible embarrassment, check the acronym that results from your organizational name. The Associated Workers For Union Labor, for example, isn't a title you want to abbreviate on your letterhead.

Also be careful that you don't select a name that's easily confused with that of another organization. Before you decide on a name, do an Internet search to see whether any other companies or organizations already have that name. The state agency that accepts your application for incorporation has procedures for ensuring that two corporations in your state don't end up with exactly the same name. However, these procedures can't help you uncover organizations with the same name in other states or with names that are similar and could be confused with your name. To help ensure that you have a distinctive name, you may want to include the name of the city or region where your organization is located — Tap Dancers of Happy Valley, for example.

You also can search the Federal Trademark Register (www.uspto.gov) to determine if the name you have chosen is trademarked by another organization. If you wish, you can register your own trademark with the federal government and with the state in which you incorporate.

If you incorporate your organization under one name but then decide that you're not totally pleased with it, you can register another name as a DBA, which stands for "doing business as." The original corporate name continues to be your organization's legal name, but you can use the DBA name on letterhead, annual reports, and press releases — everywhere except legal documents. A county office usually handles this type of transaction. Check your local laws.

Writing the Articles of Incorporation

We assume that you have the papers you need from the appropriate state office. (If not, use the state-by-state list on the CD [CD0402] for contact information.) That office may even have sent sample articles of incorporation and instructions about how to prepare your own. Pay close attention to the instructions. Follow them step by step. It may be as simple as filling in the blanks.

In this section, we give you some general guidance on drafting your articles. The articles need to be signed by the incorporators of the corporation. In some states, three incorporators are needed; in others, you need only one. If the articles need to be notarized, the signatures must be added in the presence of a notary public. Most states charge a fee for filing for incorporation. If your state requires one, include a check or money order with the articles.

Creating a heading

Put a heading on your articles so that they can be identified. The heading should be something like this one:

Articles of Incorporation of the XYZ Theater Company, Inc.

Sometimes you're required to add a short paragraph after the heading stating that the incorporators adopt the following articles under the [cite the state code number under which you're filing] of [give the state name].

Article 1

You insert the name you worked so hard to choose here. It's as simple as writing the sentence, "The name of the corporation is the XYZ Theater Company, Inc."

Could it be any easier?

Article II

Some states require that you state that the corporation is perpetual. If yours does, put it here and say something like this:

This corporation shall exist in perpetuity unless dissolved.

Chances are that the state will give you the language to use if it's needed.

Article III

This article is a good place to state the organization's purpose. This article is probably the most important because state authorities and the IRS review it to help them determine whether your organization qualifies as a charitable entity.

IRS Publication 557 contains information about the language needed in the articles of incorporation and sample articles. You can download this publication from the IRS Web site (www.irs.gov).

Remember that 501(c)(3) organizations must be organized for a charitable, religious, educational, literary, or scientific purpose. See Chapter 2 for more on various classes of nonprofits, such as the 501(c)(3). You've already done your mission statement, right? If not, see Chapter 3. If so, stating your purpose shouldn't be too hard. Using the XYZ Theater Company as an example, you might say this:

This corporation is established to provide theatrical productions of new and classic plays. It also will work to strengthen the theater arts, support emerging playwrights, and encourage persons to enter the acting profession by providing scholarships and grants to theater arts students and by promoting the benefits of dramatic entertainment to the general public.

This article must also include a statement of exempt purpose under the IRS code:

This corporation is organized exclusively for charitable, literary, and educational purposes, including for such purposes, the making of distributions to organizations that qualify under section 501(c)(3) of the Internal Revenue Code, or any corresponding section of any future federal tax code.

You must state that no proceeds of the corporation will enrich any individual, except that reasonable compensation may be paid for services to the corporation. Also add that if the corporation is dissolved, any assets remaining will be distributed to another corporation serving a similar purpose and qualifying as a tax-exempt, charitable organization under the provisions of 501(c)(3) of the Internal Revenue Code. You don't need to identify a particular non-profit corporation, just that assets will be distributed to one serving a purpose similar to yours.

Article III may be the most critical for getting your nonprofit corporation established and, ultimately, approved for tax exemption by the IRS. If your state doesn't provide good examples of the language required in this article, ask a lawyer about the requirements in your state.

Article IV

All articles of incorporation identify the name and address of an *agent of the corporation,* someone to whom mail can be addressed. This address is considered the address of the corporation until changed. Include the person's name and street address. Post office boxes usually aren't allowed to be used as addresses.

This person, by the way, doesn't need to be a director or incorporator of the corporation. The agent of the corporation can even be your attorney.

Article V

Put the initial directors' names and addresses in this article. Most nonprofits start with three initial directors. If you're incorporating in a state that requires only one director, we still recommend having three.

Article VI

List the incorporators' names and addresses in this article. *Incorporator* simply refers to the person or people who are creating the corporation. Often, the incorporators and the initial directors are one and the same. And again, whether you need one or more depends on your state requirements.

Article VII

If you want your corporation to have members, here's where you define the qualifications for membership. You can define classes of membership — voting and nonvoting, for instance. If you don't want members, all you have to say is, "This corporation has no members." Better yet, refer the question to your bylaws, which are easier to amend if you change your mind. If that's what you decide to do, you can say, "Membership provisions of this corporation are defined in the bylaws."

Corporate members aren't the same as the subscribers to a PBS station or the members of a museum or zoo, for example. Members of a corporation have the right to participate in governing the organization.

Article VIII

You may not need an Article VIII. Some forms have a blank space here to add additional provisions. We don't recommend doing so unless you're sure you know what you're doing. Maybe your group is adamant that all future directors must be elected by 85 percent of the membership. Such a provision probably would ensure that you'd never elect new directors, but who knows? Use this blank space cautiously.

Signed, sealed, and delivered

The articles must be signed by the incorporator(s) and mailed to the appropriate state office with the required fee, if any, enclosed. Some states offer an opportunity to expedite processing for a surcharge. Usually you only mail the original articles to the state office, but sometimes a state office requires one or more additional copies.

Your next step is to wait. It's hard to say how long the response will take — it depends on the efficiency of the state office and the volume of incorporation papers it receives.

Creating a nonprofit corporation alone doesn't make your organization tax exempt. You also need recognition from the IRS (see the section "Applying for Tax Exemption," later in this chapter) before your nonprofit is a "real" nonprofit.

If the articles are in order and your corporate name passes muster (meaning that no other organization in the state has the same name), you receive a certified copy of the articles, stamped with an official seal. Guard this piece of paper as if it was gold. Make copies and put the original away for safekeeping in a fireproof box. You've taken the first step toward starting your nonprofit.

Getting Your EIN

The first thing to do after you complete your incorporation is to apply to the IRS for an *Employer Identification Number,* or EIN. Even if you don't plan on hiring employees anytime soon, you need this number for your application for tax exemption and for all your state and federal reports. The EIN is a little like a Social Security number for organizations. It will be attached to your nonprofit forever. You don't have to pay a fee to get your EIN.

Getting an EIN is easy. Submit IRS Form SS-4, which you can download from `www.irs.gov` or complete online. It's even possible to apply by telephone. As IRS forms go, this one is simple and straightforward and only one page long.

The name of the applicant isn't your name; it's the name of your new organization. As with the incorporation papers, you need to identify an individual as the principal officer and include his Social Security number on the form. If your organization is a church or church-controlled organization, check that box in section 8a. If it's not, check the Other Nonprofit Organization box. Specify what sort of nonprofit organization you are. In most cases, "charitable" is sufficient.

You're asked in what state your organization is incorporated and when you started the business. Use the date on your incorporation papers as the start date. You're also asked how many employees you expect to hire in the next 12 months. If you don't expect to hire anyone, put in a zero. Your principal activity (line 15) is charitable. Also state the general field in which you're working, such as social services, education, or the arts.

The IRS estimates that you'll receive your EIN in four to five weeks if you apply by mail. If you want a faster turnaround, you can apply by telephone by calling the IRS Business and Specialty Tax Line. The person named as the principal officer on the form must make the call. Be sure that you have completed the SS-4 Form before you call. An IRS worker takes your information over the phone and assigns an EIN to your organization. You must fax or mail the form to the appropriate IRS office within 24 hours of making the call.

Even if your organization is an unincorporated association or a trust, you still need an EIN number if you plan to apply for a charitable tax exemption.

Developing Your Organizational Bylaws

Bylaws are the rules by which your organization operates. As with articles of incorporation, different states have different requirements about what needs to be included in the bylaws, so it's important to contact the appropriate agency in your state to get the specific information you need. Use the state contact information on CD0402 to find the office in your state.

In general, bylaws guide the activities of your organization and the procedures of your board of directors — how many directors, the length of their terms, how they're elected, what constitutes a quorum, and so on.

Bylaws are divided into articles just like the articles of incorporation are. Because more detail is included, however, the articles themselves are divided into sections (and subsections, if needed) to address various aspects of the articles.

Bylaws can always be changed. Almost always, however, amending the bylaws requires more than a simple majority; usually two-thirds of the directors must agree to a bylaw change.

If you review the bylaws of ten different organizations, you'll find variation in the order in which articles are presented. You may find the board of directors specified in Article III or Article V. Bylaws also vary in how specifically they spell out what's required. Some bylaws specify the number and type of standing committees; others give the board president the responsibility of making those specifications.

If you don't address a particular question in your bylaws — setting a quorum, for example — most states have a default position in their code that applies to the governing of nonprofit corporations.

Check out CD0403 for a general guide to creating bylaws for your new nonprofit.

Holding Your First Board Meeting

Your organization's first board meeting is more or less a formality, but documenting it is important because it officially kicks off your new nonprofit corporation. If you've named directors in your articles of incorporation, they should be present at the meeting. The first order of business is to elect the officers of the organization. For your second order of business, pass a resolution authorizing the board or its designate to open the necessary bank accounts, because you need a copy of this resolution to open an account.

Prepare minutes of the meeting, and keep them with your articles of incorporation. We say more about keeping records in Chapter 5, but now is a good time to start a *board book* — a loose-leaf notebook containing a copy of your articles of incorporation, bylaws, and the minutes of your first board meeting and every board meeting to follow.

Applying for Tax Exemption

The final step in becoming a tax-exempt charitable organization is to apply for tax exemption from the Internal Revenue Service. ***Note:*** "Tax exempt" doesn't mean that you're exempt from all taxes. You don't have to pay taxes on the organization's income, and donors who contribute to your organization can claim a tax deduction. But if your nonprofit employs staff, it's required to pay payroll taxes like any employer. And your liability for sales and property taxes depends on your state and local laws. Also, if your nonprofit has income that's unrelated to its charitable purpose, you're required to pay taxes on that revenue.

Who doesn't need to apply

If your organization is a church, a church auxiliary, or an association of churches, you don't need to apply for tax-exempt status. Also, if your nonprofit had an income of less than $5,000 in any previous year in which you operated, and if you don't expect your revenue to grow beyond this limit, you're not required to submit this application.

Keep in mind that you still may apply for tax exemption even though you're not required to

do so. Having a determination letter from the IRS acknowledging your tax-exempt status has some advantages. For example, you need to show proof of your exemption to get a bulk mail permit from the U.S. Postal Service. It's also a public acknowledgment that contributions to your organization are deductible to the donor. If you hope to receive foundation grants, your organization should be recognized as tax exempt by the IRS.

To apply for tax exemption, you request what's known as a *determination letter* or *ruling* — a letter from the IRS stating that it has determined that your organization qualifies as a tax-exempt organization under the applicable sections of the IRS code. You'll send copies of this letter to foundations, government agencies, and state tax authorities — in short, to anyone to whom you need to prove that yours is a tax-exempt nonprofit organization.

Be sure to check with your state about what you need to do to register your nonprofit as a tax-exempt organization. Registration and reporting requirements vary from state to state. Chances are you received this information when you contacted your state office to begin your incorporation process, but if you didn't, you should contact the appropriate state government office. You can find contact information for all states on CD0402.

You request tax-exempt status by submitting to the IRS the Application for Recognition of Exemption or IRS Form 1023. You can download the form from the IRS Web site at www.irs.gov. Be sure to download the form's instructions at the same time and read the next section, "Tackling Form 1023."

Tackling Form 1023

Yes, Form 1023 is long, and yes, it's a little scary. If you can get help from your accountant or attorney, we recommend that you do so. Don't discount getting help from your friends and associates, either. Two heads are usually better than one.

Read the instructions carefully. The application package includes line-by-line explanations as well as the various schedules that you may need to submit if you're applying as a church or school, for example. If a schedule isn't required for your type of nonprofit, don't submit a blank one. Toss it into the round file.

Understanding the difference between public charities and private foundations

Public charities and private foundations are both 501(c)(3) organizations (see Chapter 2 for more on 501(c)(3) organizations), but you should understand the important differences between them before you begin completing the application for tax exemption. Private foundations have different reporting requirements than public charities and may be required to pay taxes on their income. Contributions to private foundations are deductible, but not to the same extent as contributions to public charities.

So one important determination that the IRS makes based on your application for tax-exempt status is whether your organization is classified as a public charity or a private foundation. Part X of Form 1023 addresses this question. We assume you're striving for public charity status. If so, check the "No" box in line 1a and skip to line 5 about which we have more to say later in this chapter.

Establishing public charity status

The IRS applies several measures to determine whether an organization is a public charity. Generally, for a nonprofit to be considered a public charity, it must receive one-third of its revenues from public sources. It's complicated, and we can't cover all the nuances and technicalities. But, fundamentally, it comes down to how much of your organizational income you get from the public.

Imagine two nonprofits. The first is a small, storefront historical museum that intends to get most of its revenue from grants and contributions from the public. The second is a chamber orchestra that also receives grants and contributions but gets half its income from ticket sales and performance fees. Both organizations probably can qualify for public charity status, but under two different IRS code sections. The museum must apply for public charity status under IRS code section 509(a)(1). The orchestra must apply under section 509(a)(2).

Both of these organizations will undergo what's referred to as the public support test. To pass this test, the museum needs to demonstrate, over a four-year average, that one-third of its revenue comes from contributions from the general public, support from government agencies, or grants from organizations that get their support from the public, such as United Way. So if your museum's average revenue is $60,000 per year and at least $20,000 a year comes from donations, state grants, and support from United Way, you're home free.

But what if your organization doesn't get a third of its revenue from the public? Fortunately, the organization may be able to qualify under another test that gives more leeway on the percentage of public support. Under this test, only 10 percent of total revenue needs to come from those public categories. But the organization also must demonstrate that it has an ongoing fundraising program that's reaching to the public for more donations. Other factors also are considered. If the museum's contributions come in many small gifts rather than a few large ones, it's more likely to be given public charity status. It's even better if the museum's board of directors is broadly representative of the community. And if the organization makes its facility available to the general public, as we're sure this museum would, that's another feather in its cap.

The chamber orchestra is expecting contributions, too, but more of its income comes from selling tickets to its concert series and from fees it receives from performing at schools and retirement homes. For nonprofits that expect to generate significant income from fees for services related to their exempt purpose, the IRS allows those fees to be calculated as public support. In other words, contributions from the public *and* their earned income must make up one-third of their revenues. The orchestra needs to be sure that it gets less than one-third of its total income from business unrelated to its charitable purpose and investments. As long as it maintains this distribution of income, it keeps its public charity status.

When you get to Part X of Form 1023, you need to check a box indicating which public charity classification you seek. In line 5, if you think that your nonprofit is more like the museum, a (509)(a)(1), you probably want to select the "h" box; if you're closer to the chamber orchestra, a (509)(a)(2), the "g" box is yours. If you're not sure — and, frankly, who would be? — you can let the IRS decide which category you fit by selecting the "i" box.

Take schools as an example. To apply as a school, you have to submit Schedule B. Your school must provide regular instruction and have a student body and a faculty. In other words, you can't just start an organization and call it a school.

Every IRS rule has an exception or two, and qualifying as a public charity is, well, no exception. Churches, schools, hospitals, public safety testing organizations, and a few others are automatically considered public charities. If you have an intense interest in this rule, read Chapter 3 of IRS Publication 557 available from the IRS Web site at www.irs.gov. If you think that your organization falls into one of these categories, check the appropriate box in Part X, line 5 (a through f) and answer the questions on the appropriate schedule included with Form 1023. But we don't recommend doing so unless you're absolutely certain that you know what you're doing. If you need further advice regarding these categories, we suggest you consult an attorney.

Describing your activities

You need to attach a narrative description of your charitable activities and how you plan to carry them out in Part IV of the application. You must provide more detail here than you have in your articles of incorporation or in your mission statement. The IRS wants you to list what you're going to do in order of importance, approximately how much time you'll devote to each activity, and how each activity fulfills your charitable purpose.

When you fill out this form, chances are you haven't started operating yet, so you're simply listing *proposed* activities. If you've done a business plan (which we recommend), refer to the plan to make sure that you cover all your activities. (See Chapter 9 for help with planning.) If you've been operating your organization, explain what you've been doing and how it relates to your charitable purpose.

A nonprofit that provides family counseling and public education about strengthening families might say something like this:

> *The charitable purpose of the Claremont Family Counseling Center is to promote the benefits of positive family interaction in the following ways:*
>
> *The primary activity will be to provide professional family counselor services, on a sliding scale fee basis, to families in Claremont County and surrounding counties. No family will be refused service due to the inability to pay for services, and services will be available to all members of the general public. (75%)*
>
> *The center will maintain a Web site that provides referral information, suggestions for strengthening family interactions, reference materials concerning families, and e-mail and bulletin board posting capabilities. (10%)*
>
> *Staff members will present information about families to local schools, service clubs, and churches through multimedia presentations. (10%)*
>
> *Brochures will be prepared and distributed on request. (5%)*

You're asked more questions about your specific activities in Part VIII of Form 1023, including, for example, how and where you intend to raise funds, whether or not you operate a bingo game or other gaming activities, and your involvement with foreign countries and organizations. Answering yes to these and other questions means that you must attach explanations.

You're also asked if your organization will attempt to influence legislation. If you answer yes, you're given an opportunity to elect section 501(h) of the IRS code. If you do so, your organization's expenses for allowable lobbying activities are measured by a percentage of your revenue. Chapter 5 has more information about this subject.

Reporting salaries and conflicts of interest

The IRS revised Form 1023 in 2004 to include more information about staff salary levels, board member compensation, and business and family relationships of board members and staff. If you pay or plan to pay any staff member or consultant over $50,000 per year, you need to report this fact. If you compensate or plan to compensate members of your board, this information must be shared on Form 1023. You're also asked if the organization has a conflict of interest policy and if compensation has or will be set by comparing salaries of your staff to salaries of similar organizations. Although the IRS says these practices aren't required to get a tax exemption, they are recommended. The instructions for Form 1023 contain a sample conflict of interest policy statement.

Part V of the application stretches over two pages and clearly is a reaction to increased public and legislative concern about financial abuse and self-dealing in both the nonprofit and business sectors. We say more about the increased scrutiny aimed at the nonprofit sector in Chapter 5. It's important to keep in mind that nonprofits are, in a sense, "quasi-public" organizations because the government is granting them special status as tax-exempt organizations.

Dealing with financial information

The IRS wants to see financial information. (Surprise, surprise.) New organizations have to estimate their income and expenses for three years — the current year and two years following. Making financial projections sends shivers down the backs of many folks, but it's really not that difficult. Ideally, you've made plans for your nonprofit already, and you can take the figures from your business plan. If you haven't written a business plan, now's a good time to do so. See Chapter 9 for planning information and Chapter 10 for help in creating a budget.

When you estimate your income, keep in mind the requirements for qualifying as a public charity. Diverse sources of income are important, both for qualifying as a 509(a)(1) or (2) organization and for the stability of your nonprofit.

You also need to choose your annual accounting period. This period is usually referred to as your fiscal year. It can be any 12-month period you desire. Most organizations choose as their fiscal year either the calendar year (January 1 through December 31) or the period from July 1 to June 30. Most government agencies operate on a July 1 through June 30 fiscal year, and nonprofits that get support from government grants and contracts often prefer to operate on the same basis. Some organizations offering services to schools set the fiscal year to correspond with the academic year. But the choice is yours. You can set your fiscal year from November 1 to October 31 if you like.

Your first accounting period doesn't need to be a full 12 months; in fact, it probably won't be. If you form your organization in September and select a calendar year as your fiscal year, your first accounting period covers only four months, September through December.

If you have an accountant, seek advice about the best accounting period for your organization. Remember that your fiscal year determines when future reports are due to the IRS and also when you prepare year-end financial reports for your board of directors. The annual 990 report is due, for example, four and a half months after the close of your fiscal year. So if your fiscal year is the same as the calendar year, the report is due on May 15. If you always spend early May traveling to the Caribbean, you may want to pick another accounting period.

Advance versus definitive rulings

If your nonprofit is new, the IRS has little evidence to determine whether your organization qualifies as a public charity. Therefore, it's not uncommon for newly-formed organizations to receive what's known as an advance ruling. If your nonprofit has been operating for less than eight months, an advance ruling is your only option.

An *advance ruling* means that your organization is treated as a public charity for five years. At the end of that period, you must submit IRS Form 8734, and the IRS reviews your status. If the sources of your revenue qualify you as a public charity, you'll receive a new determination letter recognizing your public charity status as definitive. Getting a definitive ruling doesn't mean that you can go off and do anything you want with your nonprofit, of course. You still need to continue to show the appropriate sources of income, over any four-year period, to maintain public charity status.

Advance rulings may seem tenuous, but they offer nonprofits an opportunity to develop the appropriate revenue streams and to become well-established organizations. Don't be put off by an advance ruling. The IRS isn't picking on you; it's standard operating procedure.

If you've been operating for more than eight months, you have the choice of asking for an advance or definitive ruling. If you're in this situation, we suggest that you seek professional advice before making the selection.

Collecting the other materials

In addition to the completed application, you need to submit conformed (exact) copies of your articles of incorporation and the certificate of incorporation if your state provides one. If bylaws have been written for your organization, submit them, too, but bylaws alone don't qualify as organizing documents.

Present this material as attachments to your application. Put your organization's name, address, and EIN (Employer Identification Number) on each attachment and specify the section of the application that each attachment refers to. The application package you receive from the IRS has a checklist of the materials that must be included.

Every nonprofit applying for tax exemption must have an organizing document. Usually, this document is the articles of incorporation, because most nonprofit organizations are incorporated. However, in the United States, associations, trusts, and, in some states, limited liability companies also may apply for tax-exempt status. An organizing document for an association may be the articles of association or a constitution; a trust is usually organized by a trust indenture or deed.

Paying the fee

The fee for filing IRS Form 1023 is $500 for organizations that have had or anticipate having revenue of over $10,000 per year. If your organization has been operating without a tax exemption and has income of less than $10,000 per year, or if you anticipate having revenues of less than $10,000 per year in the future, the fee is set at $150.

We don't recommend trying to save $350 on the application fee unless you're very certain that revenues to your organization will remain under $10,000. We understand that the $350 difference in the fees can loom very large for a start-up nonprofit, but why play with fire? Although the penalties for misstating your income aren't clear, we wouldn't want you to find out the hard way.

Send the form with all the appropriate attachments and schedules. Don't forget the application fee. Keep a copy of everything for your records. Then take a break! You deserve it.

Getting along until the exemption comes

After you file your application, your organization is in never-never land for a while. You don't have your exemption yet. Although making an accurate prediction is difficult, the IRS can take between two and six months to act on your application. The process may take longer if the application is returned for corrections.

During this period, your organization can operate and even solicit contributions. You must tell donors that you've applied for a tax exemption and are waiting to hear from the IRS. Assuming that your application is approved, if your organization was incorporated within 15 months (27 months with a more-or-less automatic extension) of submitting Form 1023, your tax-exempt status is retroactive to the date of incorporation. If your organization had been operating for a longer period before you submitted Form 1023, the exemption may be retroactive only to the date on which you submitted the application.

Another option is using a fiscal sponsor during this period. See Chapter 2 for information about using and finding fiscal sponsors.

Don't put off filing for your exemption. Filing sooner rather than later makes life simpler.

Chapter 5

Safeguarding Your Nonprofit Status

Keeping your nonprofit status isn't hard if you follow the rules. Nonprofit organizations are private organizations, but because they're granted special tax status and presumably are acting on behalf of the public, they're required to disclose more information than privately held for-profit companies are. Nonprofit status is a privilege.

A good way to think about it is to compare nonprofits to companies that sell shares of stock to the public. These companies must follow the rules and regulations set forth by the Securities and Exchange Commission about disclosing financial information. Nonprofits in the United States must follow the rules of the Internal Revenue Service to make financial information available for public scrutiny. In some cases, state and local governments also have disclosure rules.

Your nonprofit organization can get into trouble with authorities in a few ways. This chapter lays out the reporting requirements that you need to follow and some pitfalls to avoid in order to maintain your 501(c)(3) status. See Chapter 2 for more on 501(c)(3) organizations.

We don't aim to scare you! Just keep good financial records and stick to your mission, and you'll be fine.

Disclosing What You Need to Disclose

Disclose is a funny word, isn't it? It seems to imply that you're hiding something that must be pried from your clutches. Don't think of it that way. The IRS regulations that lay out the rules for disclosure refer to "the public inspection of information." That's much more genteel.

In this section, we briefly cover what you're expected to disclose as well as what you're not expected to disclose to the public.

What you do need to show

What information must be disclosed to the public? (Sorry, we can't help ourselves. We like the word.) It's simple, really. It's your three most recent filings of IRS Form 990 and your application for exemption — if you filed for your exemption after July 15, 1987.

If you have a question that this chapter doesn't cover, refer to IRS Publication 557 (www.gov.org).

Form 990 is the annual report that you must file with the IRS. We talk more about filing the 990 later in this chapter, but in a nutshell, it's a report of your annual finances and activities as a nonprofit organization. Don't panic! We've filled them out many times and survived.

Current IRS regulations state that the three most recent 990 reports and attachments to the report must be available for public inspection at the organization's primary place of business during regular business hours. A staff member may be present during the inspection, and copies may be made for the person requesting them. If you make copies on your own copier, you can charge the same as the IRS charges: $1 for the first page and 15 cents for each additional page.

The information provided in this chapter is about 501(c)(3) organizations that are considered public charities. If your organization is a private foundation, special disclosure rules apply especially to you. Check with the Council on Foundations (www.cof.org) about disclosure requirements.

If you work out of your home or you really have no primary place of business, you can arrange to meet at a convenient place or mail copies to the person who requested them. You have two weeks to do so. The information also can be requested in writing, and if it is, you have 30 days to respond.

If you applied for your exemption after July 15, 1987, you must include your application for exemption and all the supporting materials submitted with it in the information you make available for inspection. Although the IRS doesn't say so, we assume that you include your articles of incorporation and your bylaws, if you attached them to your application.

You need to know the rules and regulations about public inspection of non-profit materials, but frankly, in the many years we've been working for non-profits, no one has ever asked to see our 990 forms. This doesn't mean that you won't be asked, however. Follow the Boy Scout motto and be prepared.

On your 990, you will need to disclose compensation paid to board members. This information will be available for public inspection, as will employee salaries and contractor payments over $50,000 per year.

What you don't need to show

You don't need to reveal your donor list. Donors who contribute over $1,000 must be named on a schedule attached to your 990 report, but you can black out names and addresses of these donors before you make the form available for public inspection.

Other items that may remain private include the following:

- ✔ Trade secrets and patents
- ✔ National defense material
- ✔ Communications from the IRS about previous unfavorable rulings or technical advice related to rulings
- ✔ Board minutes and contracts

IRS regulations go into more detail, but we think these four items sum up the major points. If you have a question about an item, consult your attorney or tax adviser.

The public disclosure rules offer a nice tool for anyone who gets a bee in his bonnet and wants to harass your organization. So if you start getting request after request after request, check with the nearest IRS office. IRS officials have the authority to relieve you of the disclosure responsibilities if they agree that harassment is occurring.

Check your state and local government requirements about whether your nonprofit must make other information available under local laws.

Using the Web to satisfy disclosure requirements

You can avoid the hassle of photocopying Form 990 by placing the required information on the Web. If you do so, be sure that you post an exact copy of the materials, not a summary or a retyped copy. You can scan material with a scanner and put it on your Web site as a graphic, but the best way to do it is to put the materials in PDF format by using Adobe Acrobat, available from Adobe (www.adobe.com).

GuideStar (www.guidestar.org) keeps a database of basic information about U.S. nonprofit organizations as well as PDF files of 990 returns. You can add information about your nonprofit to the GuideStar database. Some states also maintain Web databases of 990s of nonprofits incorporated in their jurisdictions. Remember that you need to make available your three most recent 990 returns and your application for exemption.

If someone arrives at your office and asks to inspect your 990s, you still need to allow them the privilege. Web access to the materials only relieves the responsibility of mailing out copies.

Avoiding Excessive Payments and Politicking

Paying excessive compensation and engaging in campaign politics can get a charitable nonprofit organization in trouble. It doesn't happen often, but you need to be aware of the rules.

Determining a reasonable amount of pay and benefits

In past years, if the IRS discovered wrongdoing in a nonprofit, it had little recourse but to take away the organization's exempt status. However, since revised tax laws were passed in 1996, the IRS has the authority to apply "intermediate sanctions" in cases of excess benefits for nonprofit staff or disqualified persons associated with the nonprofit. Board members and their family members — really anyone who can influence the organization's activities — are disqualified persons.

Excess benefits can include excessive salaries for staff members or a business deal arranged to benefit a disqualified person in which the nonprofit overpaid for a service. So if you sit on a board of directors that decides to rent office space from your uncle at two or three times the going rate, you and your uncle may be in trouble. If you do decide to rent from your uncle, be sure that you can document that you're paying a market rate rent. Also, you shouldn't participate in the board vote about renting the space.

An excessive benefit for a nonprofit staff member is any sum that's above a "reasonable amount." You're probably thinking, "What's a reasonable amount?" and you're right to ask the question. In the case of executive compensation, it's up to the board of directors to find out what a fair salary is for nonprofit managers in your area and for an organization of your size and scope.

If the IRS finds that someone in your nonprofit has received an excessive benefit, the financial penalties are severe. A 25 percent excise tax is levied on the "excess amount," and the full excess amount must be paid back to the organization in less than a year. If payment isn't received in that time, the tax can go up to a healthy 200 percent.

Here are three tips on avoiding excess benefits problems:

- ✔ No board member should participate in a board decision that benefits herself or her family. Certainly, no executive director should participate in setting her own compensation.
- ✔ Rely on credible independent information about reasonable costs in business deals and compensation matters.
- ✔ Document the reasons why you make the decisions you make.

We don't want to frighten you with visions of huge tax bills. We're not saying that you can't pay nonprofit staff well or that you have to undertake a scientific study to determine fair compensation. Use your head, be reasonable, and exercise caution.

Document board decisions by keeping minutes of board meetings. You don't need to keep a verbatim record of board deliberations, but you want your minutes to reflect the discussions that take place and the decisions that are made. Maintain what's known as a *board book* — a loose-leaf notebook that contains copies of your articles of incorporation, bylaws, amendments to bylaws, notices sent to announce board and membership meetings, and a chronological record of your board meeting minutes.

Using caution when getting involved in politics

We aren't saying that you shouldn't get involved in politics, because it's your right to do so if you wish. If you want to give your personal support and endorsement to a candidate, by all means do it. But be sure to separate yourself from your nonprofit organization when you do. Nonprofits in the 501(c)(3) category can't support or endorse candidates for political office.

If you want to talk to your legislator about the passage of a bill that benefits your clients, go ahead and make an appointment. But if you find yourself traveling to your state capital or to Washington, D.C., on a regular basis, step back and consider how much organizational time and money you're spending on the activity. Charitable nonprofits can spend an "insubstantial" amount on direct lobbying activities. If it's 5 percent or less of your organizational budget, you're probably within the limits allowed, according to the people who pay attention to these things.

Be more cautious with what's known as *grass-roots lobbying,* or attempting to influence the general public to vote in a particular way. If lobbying is important to your overall mission as a 501(c)(3) public benefit nonprofit, you can elect the "h" designation, which requires more financial reporting to the IRS but allows you to spend more money on these activities. To do so, file IRS Form 5768 after you have a look at the regulations in IRS Publication 577.

Why all the fuss?

Nonprofit organizations face increasing regulation and public scrutiny in the years to come. Why? Three reasons come to mind:

- ✔ Concern about how nonprofit organizations used contributions that were made for disaster relief efforts, including the tragedy of September 11, 2001

- ✔ A series of widely reported cases in which some nonprofits, both public charities and private foundations, have paid very high salaries to executives and trustees and otherwise pushed the limits of ethical behavior

- ✔ The number and degree of corporate accounting and insider trading scandals that have been revealed over the past few years in the for-profit sector

These factors have focused more public and legislative attention on how nonprofit organizations (and for-profit corporations) operate and how their affairs are regulated.

The U.S. Congress and many state legislatures have passed, or are considering, stricter reporting requirements for the nonprofit sector. Greater accountability is being asked of nonprofit leaders, both managers and board members, in how money is raised, how conflicts of interest are avoided, and how funds are spent, especially for salaries and expenses. The Michigan Nonprofit Association (www.mnaonline.org) has developed *Principles and Practices for Nonprofit Excellence in Michigan* that provides good overall guidance in this area.

If you're involved with a start-up nonprofit that's operating on a shoestring, you may be asking yourself why you need to worry about getting paid too much. And you're right, you probably don't need to worry. But you should stay informed of changes in reporting requirements and the need to have good, ethical operating policies in place, keeping good financial records, and documenting your organizational decisions with board and committee meeting minutes.

If you're already involved with a medium or large nonprofit, you should be aware of the need for independent financial audits and board policies that guard against excessive compensation, self-dealing, and conflicts of interest.

Because the regulatory situation is changing, and because it varies from state to state, we suggest visiting the Web sites of Independent Sector (www.independentsector.org) and BoardSource (www.boardsource.org) to keep abreast of the latest developments. The National Council of Nonprofit Associations (www.ncna.org) maintains a chart of pending legislation in U.S. states.

Sending in Form 990

The formal name for this report is *Return of Organization Exempt From Income Tax,* but everyone refers to it as "the 990." It *is* IRS Form 990, after all. With some exceptions, this basic report must go to the IRS each year to report on your nonprofit organization's finances and activities.

The report must be postmarked no later than the 15th day of the fifth month after the end of your annual accounting period; in other words, after the close of your fiscal year. When you filed your application for exemption, you selected your accounting period. Many nonprofits use the calendar year as their fiscal year. If that's your case, your 990 has to be out the door on May 15.

At first glance, the 990 is an imposing form with many spaces to fill in and instructions presented in small type. Take your time, seek help when you need it, and prepare a rough draft before you fill in the final copy.

Who doesn't need to file a 990?

How do you know whether you need to fill out a 990? We'll start with the easiest case first. If your organization is a church or a church-related organization, you don't need to file. You can if you want to, but doing so isn't required.

Also (and this case applies to many nonprofits in the United States), if your organization normally has revenues of no more than $25,000 per year, you are excused. Skip directly to the fundraising chapter in this book. Just kidding.

Even if your income is below $25,000, some states still require that you file a 990. Check your state laws.

Other nonprofits are excused as well, but they typically aren't 501(c)(3) organizations. If you're interested in finding out what they are, take another look at IRS Publication 557 if you aren't bored with it by now.

How to use the 990-EZ return

If your nonprofit had less than $100,000 of gross receipts (all income before you subtract expenses) in your last fiscal year, and if it has total assets of less than $250,000, you can use the 990-EZ form. It's a shortened version of the 990, only two pages long, although if you have one or more large contributions, you may have to file Schedule B. More about that later in this section.

Fill in the identifying information at the top of the form. If you've filed in past years, you'll receive a package of forms in the mail with a peel-off label that you can use for your name and address. Be sure to add your *Employer Identification Number* (EIN). See Chapter 4 for more on EINs. Also check the correct box to indicate whether you're using a cash or accrual accounting method. If you need help with that question, see Chapter 10.

All 501(c)(3) organizations that file either the 990 or the 990-EZ must attach Schedule A, which reports employees and contractors who earn more than $50,000 per year. If it doesn't apply to your organization, just fill in the identifying information and write "Not Applicable" where appropriate.

If your 501(c)(3) organization received in the past year a contribution of cash, a grant, or property from a single individual that was valued at over $5,000, *or* if a gift totaled more than 2 percent of your total grants and contributions, you must file Schedule B with your 990 or 990-EZ. If a person gives you two gifts of $2,500 within the year, you must file the schedule. If you don't have grants or gifts in this range, be sure to check the appropriate box on your 990 or 990-EZ forms to let the IRS know you aren't required to file Schedule B.

Parts 1 and 11

In Part I, you report your financial activities over the past year. Chances are that the two lines that have the highest amount of revenue are line 1 (contributions, gifts, and grants) and line 2 (program service revenue, including government fees and contracts). You may have some income from membership fees for line 3 and income from investments or interest on a savings account for line 4.

Lines 5 through 8 deal with income from sales of materials or assets and income from special events. You're asked to report the costs and expenses associated with the materials sold and any direct expenses associated with special events. In other words, the IRS wants to see a net amount for sales and special events. The total you end up with on line 9 is your total revenue for the year.

Don't confuse your total revenue with your gross receipts. Gross receipts include all the income you received from sales and special events before you subtract expenses. You may have total revenue of less than $100,000 but gross receipts over that amount. If you do, you can't use Form 990-EZ. You need to file the long form. Sorry.

Report your expenses on lines 10 through 16 in their appropriate categories and total the amount on line 17. Subtract line 9 from line 17, and you have your surplus (or deficit) for the year. This amount goes on line 18. We come back to line 19 in just a minute.

Part II includes lines 22 through 24, which is where you report your assets — cash, savings, or investments as well as property and equipment. (Equipment goes on line 24, other assets, with a description. Attach a page with an equipment list if you need to.) Total these figures for line 25.

Enter your total liabilities on line 26. They may include accounts payable, outstanding loans, and vacation time owed to employees, for example. Subtract line 26 from line 25, and you have your net assets or fund balance. Put this amount on line 27. If you pay off all your bills and sell all your assets, this amount is what's left over — in theory.

Notice that you need to report assets and liabilities for the beginning of the year and the end of the year. (If this 990 report is your first, you provide only end-of-year totals.) Refer to the form you submitted last year for these figures.

Now go back to line 19 in Part I. Enter your net assets from last year's form on this line. If an adjustment to your net assets was made during the year (usually done by an accountant), enter the figure for this adjustment on line 20 and attach an explanation. On line 21, enter the amount of your net assets at the end of the current year.

That's it for reporting your financial activities on the 990-EZ form. It was easy, wasn't it?

Parts III, IV, and V

Part III asks you to state your primary exempt purpose. This statement doesn't need to be long like the one you wrote for your Form 1023 application; a few words will do. You also need to describe your programs, say how many people you served, and give a total cost for each program. You find spaces for three separate programs, but if you have only one program, that's fine. If you have more than three, attach an additional sheet describing them.

Part III includes a space to report grants in each program area. This space is for grants made *by* your organization, not grants *to* your organization. You probably didn't make any grants, but if you did, report them here.

Part IV requires a list of your directors, with the board officers identified, and key employees and their addresses. The only key employee you need to report here is the executive director, if you have one. You also need to state how much time is devoted to each position each week and record any compensation received, including salary, retirement benefits, and expense allowances. If you have more than three people on your board of directors, attach an additional sheet. Because this information is public, most nonprofits use the organization's address for board members and staff, not home addresses.

Part V, the last part, hurrah! You're likely able to check no to the questions in this section or leave items blank. But several things may need your attention. Line 35 refers to income that may have come to your organization through

---

How the IRS decides that income is unrelated

The IRS definition of unrelated business income is based on three questions: Does the income come from a trade or business? Is it regularly carried on? Is it not substantially related to the organization's exempt purpose?

What do these questions mean? Consider an extreme example. The Juniper Avenue Young People's Club, a 501(c)(3) nonprofit with the mission of providing recreational opportunities, mentoring, and job skill training to adolescents, decides to open a shoe repair business. They rent a storefront space, purchase equipment, hire employees, and begin soliciting business. The shoe repair shop does very well. In fact, in the first year of operation, income exceeds expenses by $10,000. The club uses the money to pay some costs incurred in working with

young people in the neighborhood. The problem is that the shoe repair shop has no relationship to the club's charitable purpose. In this case, the club probably would be required to file Form 990-T and pay appropriate taxes on the $10,000. That's okay, however, because the club realized a profit that can be applied to some of its program costs.

However, what if the club opens the shoe repair shop with the purpose of providing training in the shoe repair trade to adolescents in the neighborhood? In that case, chances are good that any income from the business would be considered "substantially related to the organization's exempt purpose," and tax (known as UBIT) wouldn't be due on any proceeds.

activities not related to your charitable purpose. This is called *unrelated business income,* and if it totals more than $1,000, you must report it on Form 990-T. You may be liable for taxes on this income.

If you've amended your bylaws or articles of incorporation since you filed your last report, check that item and include a copy of the amended document when you send in the form.

Near the bottom of page 2, report who has custody of the organization's books and provide that person's address and phone number. The president or secretary of your board of directors should sign the form.

When to use the 990 report

If your organization had gross receipts over $100,000 in the last year, you must use the long 990 form. Don't despair. It's just a longer version of the 990-EZ form. We won't go through this form line by line. Refer to the detailed line-by-line instructions that come with your form.

If possible, work with an accountant to complete this form. Some of the financial reporting requirements are technical, and you're wise to seek professional assistance.

Your 990 needs to be postmarked on the 15th day of the fifth month after the close of your financial year unless you request an extension.

Reporting to Your State and Local Governments

You have reporting requirements for your state and possibly your local government, especially if you provide services under contract. Sometimes reporting to the state is as simple as completing a one-page form, attaching a copy of your 990, and paying a small fee.

More and more states (and some local governments) require registration for fundraising activities. Be sure to check local laws.

Some states require a separate financial form, although we think that most of them follow the federal form closely. You'll probably get all the needed reporting information when you ask for the incorporation packet, but if you didn't or you aren't sure, check with your state office that regulates nonprofit corporations. The contact list provided for Chapter 4 (CD0402) is a good resource here as well.

Part II
Managing a Nonprofit Organization

The 5th Wave   By Rich Tennant

In this part . . .

In this part, we introduce the major aspects of managing a nonprofit. The subjects — planning programs, devising sound budgets and financial oversight, choosing and maintaining facilities, attending to insurance, marketing your programs, and hiring and supervising employees — may sound familiar to anyone who has run a for-profit business. But some important skills are found only in the nonprofit sector: For instance, how many profit-making businesses depend heavily on volunteers to meet their goals? Part II answers that question, too.

Chapter 6

Building Your Board of Directors

In This Chapter

▶ Knowing what a board of directors does

▶ Recruiting board members

▶ Avoiding conflicts of interest

▶ Getting the most out of your board

Some boards of directors do miraculous things. Others just muddle through. But no nonprofit organization has an "ideal" board of directors all the time. We say this because you may get the impression that your board is so disorganized that you may as well close up shop and go fishing. But don't despair. Boards can always get better, and many nonprofits do excellent work with boards of directors that would send shivers down the backs of most nonprofit consultants. The purpose of this chapter is to help you understand how nonprofit boards work in a perfect world. (We don't live in a perfect world, though. Keep that in mind while reading.)

We're the first to agree that working with a board can drive you a little batty sometimes. Just doing all the work yourself may seem easier, but the strength and effectiveness of a nonprofit organization grows from its board of directors. What a group of people working together can accomplish is often surprising. You'll find building a good board and working with those members to achieve your mission worthwhile.

Understanding the Functions of a Nonprofit Board of Directors

A *board of directors* (which we refer to simply as "a board" from here on) is a group of people who agree to accept responsibility for a nonprofit organization. A board is responsible for ensuring that the nonprofit organization is fulfilling its mission and makes decisions about the organization, sets policy for the staff or volunteers to implement, and oversees the nonprofit's activities. Raising money for the nonprofit is also an important responsibility that many but not all boards assume. Board members almost always serve without compensation; they're volunteers who have no financial interest in the nonprofit's business.

A nonprofit organization doesn't have owners like a for-profit business does, but a board of directors guides and oversees the organization like an owner might. No one owns city, state, and federal governments, either, so citizens hand over the responsibility of running the government to elected officials. We expect those officials to govern the affairs of our city, state, and nation. The job of a nonprofit board is similar; in fact, it's referred to as *nonprofit governance.*

Key board role: Preserving public trust

A board's primary governance responsibility is *fiduciary,* or to uphold the public trust. Laws in the United States give special rights and privileges to nonprofits recognized by the IRS as public charities, primarily the right to exemption from corporate income tax and the right to receive contributions that are tax deductible for the donor. The government gives nonprofits this special status because they provide a public benefit. A board's leadership and oversight keep the organization's focus on that public benefit and make sure that these rights and privileges aren't abused.

Suppose that a nonprofit begins with a mission to rescue stray cats. People who support this idea make contributions to the nonprofit with the belief that their money is spent on programs to help the plight of stray cats. But, unknown to the donors, the nonprofit begins to spend its money on programs to support preschool education. Supporting preschool education is a worthy goal, but it's a long way from the original purpose of helping stray cats. So, in this example, even though the nonprofit is using those contributions for a good cause, they're not being used as the donors intended or to fulfill the organization's original purpose.

A nonprofit that collected funds for helping stray cats but instead used the funds for the personal benefit of the board members and staff would be even worse. This activity is serious and possibly a crime. Aside from potential felony fraud charges, such an activity violates IRS rules and could result in the revocation of the nonprofit's tax-exempt status.

Board members and staff — or anyone, for that matter — can't personally benefit from nonprofit funds except for compensation for services provided or reimbursement of expenses. In a for-profit business, net earnings (meaning profit) at the end of the year can be shared among the company's owners or stockholders. If nonprofit board members decide to divide surplus funds among themselves, it's called *inurement,* a big word that can be more or less defined as personal enrichment. A board must ensure that the nonprofit is doing what it set out to do, and it must make sure that funds are spent properly. If a board does nothing else, it must ensure these standards are adhered to.

Keep in mind that a board's responsibilities are legal responsibilities. BoardSource, a nonprofit organization providing information and services for nonprofit boards, outlines three duties for boards: care, loyalty, and obedience. Although they sound like vows one may take when entering a monastery, they actually describe established legal principles.

- ✔ The duty of care refers to the responsibility to be a prudent board member. In other words, board members must pay attention to what's going on and make decisions based on good information.
- ✔ The duty of loyalty means that a board member must put the organization's welfare above other interests when making decisions.
- ✔ The duty of obedience requires that board members act in accordance with the nonprofit's mission and goals.

Other board tasks

In addition to the legal and fiduciary responsibilities, a nonprofit board performs other roles, too.

Providing a guiding strategy

A board guides the overall planning and strategy of a nonprofit organization. At the most basic level, this job means reviewing the organization's mission statement and goals on a regular basis. Every nonprofit should have an organizational plan. Turn to Chapter 9 for more information on planning.

Hiring and working with the executive director

One role of a nonprofit board is to hire the executive director. Of course, many nonprofit organizations operate without paid staff, but if your nonprofit does have employees, finding the right executive director is one of the board's most important tasks. See Chapter 8 for information about hiring paid employees.

A board works with its executive director to set goals and objectives for the year. Board members shouldn't look over the director's shoulder every day. However, a board should have a good idea of the executive director's work plan and guarantee that her efforts are in line with the agency's purpose.

Overseeing the organization's finances

A board must see that the organization has the resources to carry out its goals. As part of this duty, many boards are active in fundraising. But a board also is responsible for reviewing the organization's budget and staying informed of the organization's financial situation. Nothing is more dismal than finding out, for example, that an organization hasn't been sending in its payroll taxes. Insist on good financial reporting. At a minimum, the board treasurer (or perhaps the executive director or bookkeeper, if you have one) should prepare quarterly financial reports and distribute them to your board.

Many people join boards because they care about and understand the nature of the service that the organization provides, but they may not be trained in bookkeeping and accounting. These board members should try not to let their eyes glaze over when the financial report is passed around at the board meeting, because part of a board member's job is to understand finances. If members don't understand the financial fine points, they should ask questions of staff and other board members and study Chapter 10 on nonprofit finances.

But maybe the problem is more than lack of comprehension. Maybe the financial information needs to be presented more clearly. If one board member doesn't understand the information, you can be sure that many other board members don't understand it, either. If your organization uses an outside accountant or bookkeeper to keep track of finances, boards can ask for a brief meeting with him to explain how he has presented the information. Many nonprofit service organizations (see Appendix A) offer affordable workshops on nonprofit finances and record keeping to assist board and staff members; others have organizations that place volunteers from businesses into nonprofits.

Working with an advisory board

Some organizations form *advisory boards,* which don't have governance responsibilities. Two types of advisory boards exist:

- Those advisory boards that have members who actually provide advice because of their professional expertise
- Those advisory boards formed so that prominent names can be listed on the organization's letterhead

We favor advisory boards that are asked for and give advice — even if it's only once per year. Some organizations use advisory board appointments as a way of getting to know potential board members.

Splitting and sharing responsibilities

Defining roles causes problems for a number of nonprofit organizations. Should the board of directors be involved in day-to-day management decisions? No, probably not. An executive director and her staff don't need board members to approve every management decision that comes along. The board must trust the staff to run the organization. To put it simply, the board sets the overall goals and policies, and the staff implements them.

But (and this is a big but) many nonprofits have limited staff or even no staff at all. What happens when the organization's work is done by the board and other volunteers?

In the case of volunteer-run organizations, board members must wear two hats. When they meet as a board of directors, they must see the larger picture and make group decisions that benefit the organization and its programs and clients. And, most important, they must exercise their fiduciary responsibilities. But when they have to do the hands-on work needed to provide the services and do the day-to-day tasks of running a nonprofit, board members must act as if they're employees. They may even hold regular, unpaid volunteer jobs with job descriptions and scheduled hours. Confusing, isn't it? Still, this distinction should always be in the minds of those who serve as both board members and staff.

In any organization, building practices that create checks and balances is a good idea. These practices are particularly important when board members also act as staff. For example, an organization has better financial oversight and control when one person approves bills for payment, a different person signs checks, and yet another person reviews the canceled checks and monthly bank statements. You don't *have* to use this system — it's just one way to make sure that everything is used and accounted for properly.

Titles are sounding more corporate

Although *executive director* is still the most common title for the top staff person in a non-profit organization, some nonprofits have begun to follow the corporate style and have given their executive directors the title of president and chief executive officer (CEO). In these organizations, the president of the board is called the *chairman of the board*. The acronyms float down in the organizational hierarchy. For example, the accountant may be called the CFO, for chief financial officer, and the CEO's right-hand person may be called vice president and COO, for chief operating officer.

The usual rationale for this change in titles is because it places nonprofit executives on more equal ground with corporate executives when the two groups meet to discuss sponsorships and joint marketing ventures. The titles your board selects should suit the structure, tone, and style of your organization. In other words, you can call yourself whatever you like.

Finding the Right People for Your Board

You don't want just anybody to serve on your board. You want the wealthiest, most generous members of your community who believe in what you're doing, will come to all meetings, be advocates for your programs, and sweep the floor on weekends.

But you won't find many board members who fit this description. Even so, two of these traits are critical to the success of the organization. Which two? *Believing in your mission and being a good advocate on behalf of your programs.* Sure, having rich members who will do the dirty work when it's needed is nice, but the most important thing is to find board members who understand and believe deeply in what you're doing. Showing up for board meetings is a nice habit, too.

You also should think seriously about the skills that board members bring to your organization. Do you need an accountant to help with financial statements? A public relations specialist to help with media campaigns? An attorney to help with legal matters? Yes, you probably do. But don't expect the

Encouraging someone to take the plunge

Many people think that a board member's primary role is to raise money. A popular slogan addressed to board members who aren't raising funds is "Give, get, or get off." Harsh, isn't it? But nonprofits can't fulfill their purposes effectively without money, and board members taking an active interest in the organization's financial vitality is important. But a board member's role is broader than fundraising. It includes staying well informed about the organization's work, selecting leadership, setting policies, planning, overseeing, and serving as an ambassador for the organization. Many highly skilled volunteers think that they shouldn't serve on boards because they aren't wealthy, and this misconception represents a real loss to nonprofit organizations.

Some people also are reluctant to serve on boards for other reasons, including personal and financial liability. Unpaid volunteers who aren't grossly negligent have some protection under the Volunteer Protection Act of 1997. If more information is needed about the possible liabilities of board members and other volunteers, we suggest you get in touch with BoardSource (www.boardsource.org) or your state's association of nonprofit organizations through the National Council of Nonprofit Associations (www.ncna.org).

Organizations can protect their boards by purchasing directors and officers' insurance (see Chapter 12). Generally, the organization's creditors can't come after its board members' personal wealth for payment. An exception is that the IRS can make board members financially accountable when organizations fail to pay payroll taxes. But even the IRS will work with an organization to develop a payment plan and schedule to catch up on taxes. People are right to take the responsibility of board service seriously, but nonprofit board work also can be fun and satisfying.

accountant to do your audit or the attorney to represent you in court. You need a disinterested professional to do that work.

Your board should reflect your organization's character and mission. A community organizing group dedicated to collective decision-making may want board members who work well together as a collective. A neighborhood development organization clearly wants board members from its neighborhood. A youth leadership organization may want to invest in future leadership by creating positions for youth members on its board. (***Note:*** Before adding young people to your board, you must check with an attorney about whether your state laws allow minors to serve on nonprofit boards. If your state prohibits minors from serving on nonprofit boards, you can consider inviting them to serve on advisory committees.)

Although having a friend or two on the board is fine, be careful about overloading the board with golfing buddies and carpool partners. Boards need diverse opinions and honest feedback from members.

Keeping the board fresh

Building a board should be a continuing process. Therefore, we highly recommend that your organizational bylaws specify terms of service. Two three-year terms or three two-year terms are the most common terms of board service. Almost always, bylaws allow reelection to the board after one year's absence. Limiting terms of service helps to keep fresh blood on the board. You want new ideas, which are more likely to come from people who are new to your organization.

To avoid having all your board members leave in the same year, stagger the years when terms expire. You can allow someone to serve an extra year or ask others to serve a shorter term.

If you're thinking about recruiting new members, drawing a grid is sometimes helpful. Along the top, list the skills you think you need on your board. Along the side, list your current board members and place checkmarks under the skills they bring to the board. This exercise helps you visualize the skills you need to fill when you're looking for new members. Check out CD0601 for a sample grid for planning board recruitment.

So, where do you find board members? Start with your organization's address book. Who do you know who might make a good member and be willing to serve? Ask your funders. Who benefits from your agency's work? Who are your agency's neighbors? Some cities have nonprofit support organizations that can help in this regard. Look at Appendix A for a list of these agencies.

Is keeping the same people on your board year after year easier than continually filling open positions? Sure, you certainly want some continuity from year-to-year. But if you don't turn over your board members, you run the danger of becoming a stagnant group that spends all its time doing things the way they've always done them. And, frankly, terms of service help you recruit new board members because they know that their time commitment is temporary.

Even if you don't specify board terms, continuously recruiting new board members is important. As time passes, board members' lives may change in ways that draw them away from your organization. Many nonprofit organizations lose vitality when their boards don't refresh themselves with new members.

Big boards, little boards, and medium boards

Opinions differ about the ideal number of board members. One school of thought holds that big boards are better because the members can divide work among more people, consider more diverse viewpoints, and reach into the community more extensively. Other people say that smaller boards are better because maintaining a working relationship with a smaller group is easier, and decision-making is better because the board has to consider fewer opinions. Those who support small boards also say that board members can easily become invisible in a large group, meaning that no one will notice if they don't do their share of the work.

We feel that there really isn't one right answer to the board-size question. Nonprofits vary widely in size, function, and type, so what works for one nonprofit may not work for another. Nonprofit board size is truly a case where the phrase "one size fits all" doesn't apply.

Following are some points to consider when setting board size:

- Start-up nonprofits tend to have smaller boards than more mature organizations. Start-up budgets tend to be smaller, and building a board of directors takes time.

- Boards that are actively engaged in major gift and special event fundraising tend to be larger because both fundraising techniques are fueled by personal contacts and friendships. The more board members you have, the more personalized invitations you can send to your next event. Some large cultural and arts institutions have 50 board members or more.

- Boards that govern nonprofits funded mostly by grants and contracts tend to have fewer members, perhaps an average of 10 to 18 members.

Selecting board officers and committees

Board officers are usually elected to two-year terms. Most nonprofit boards have a president, vice president, secretary, and treasurer. Sometimes the positions of secretary and treasurer are combined into one office. Seniority on the board, professional expertise, and skills at negotiating with and listening to others are common traits sought in a board's leaders. Ultimately, however, the board of directors chooses officers.

Table 6-1 outlines the responsibilities of board officers.

Table 6-1	Duties and Responsibilities of Board Officers
Office	*Duties and Responsibilities*
President	Presides at board meetings, appoints committee chairpersons, works closely with the executive director to guide the organization, and acts as public spokesperson for the organization (but also may assign this responsibility to the executive director)
Vice President	Presides at board meetings in the president's absence and serves as a committee chairperson as appointed by the president
Secretary	Maintains the organization's records, takes board-meeting minutes, and distributes minutes and announcements of upcoming meetings to board members
Treasurer	Oversees the organization's financial aspects, makes regular financial reports to the board, and serves as chairperson of the board finance committee

ON THE CD

Check out CD0602 for more detailed job descriptions you can use.

If the board has standing (permanent) committees, the board president appoints committee chairpersons. Typical standing committees are finance, development or fundraising, program, and nominating committees. Other possible committees that may be either standing or *ad hoc* — a temporary committee organized to deal with time-limited projects — include planning, investment, and facilities.

Table 6-2 outlines the responsibilities of common standing committees.

Table 6-2	Responsibilities of Standing Committees
Committee	*Responsibilities*
Development	Sets fundraising goals and plans fundraising activities for the organization
Finance	Assists the treasurer in overseeing financial reports and making budgets
Nominating	Recruits new board members and nominates board officers for election to their positions
Program	Oversees the program activities of the organization

Board committees make regular reports to the full board about the organization's activities in their particular areas. Board officer terms and the number and type of standing committees are written into the organization's bylaws.

If your organization is large enough to conduct an annual financial audit, your board may need to appoint an audit committee. In the wake of corporate accounting scandals, some states are passing or considering laws to require an audit for larger nonprofit organizations. Be sure to check the laws in your state.

Executive committees are standard groups on some larger boards of directors. Usually the members of the executive committee are the officers of the board. The executive committee may hold regular meetings to set the agenda for the meetings of the full board and to advise the board president, or it may come together on an as-needed basis. Sometimes an organization's bylaws empower the executive committee to make decisions on behalf of the full board in an emergency or other special circumstances.

Introducing new and prospective board members to the organization

Boards of directors exhibit all the characteristics of small groups, maybe even families: Friendships develop, alliances form, and disagreements occur. Over time, the group develops routines and habits that help make members feel comfortable with one another and help guide the board's work. When a new member joins the group or when a prospective new member visits, the existing members need to make that person comfortable and share the collective wisdom that they have accumulated.

Invite a prospective board member to observe at least one board meeting before electing her to membership. That way, the new member gets a chance to see how the board operates, and the current members have an opportunity to size up the new person. Encourage the prospective member to ask questions.

When asking someone to serve on your board, don't shy away from sharing a clear picture of the work to be done. You may be afraid that your prospect is going to say "no," if it seems like too much work. However, keep in mind that being asked is an honor, and contributing good work to a good cause is satisfying. (Also, if the person does decide you're asking too much of her, isn't it better to know now?)

If your nonprofit provides on-site programs, such as childcare, a health clinic, or a music school, new board members should take a tour either before or soon after they join the board.

A packet of background materials about the organization and board procedures helps the new member get up to speed quickly. The following information is useful in orienting new board members:

- ✔ Organization's mission statement
- ✔ Bylaws
- ✔ Description of board member responsibilities and expectations
- ✔ Board job descriptions
- ✔ Board minutes for the last two or three meetings
- ✔ Financial audit or financial statement
- ✔ Names, addresses, and phone numbers of other board members
- ✔ Organizational plan (if one is available)
- ✔ Description of programs
- ✔ Calendar of organization's events and scheduled board meetings
- ✔ News clippings about the organization

This information may seem like a lot of reading — and it is. But even if a new board member doesn't read everything from cover to cover, he at least has the reference material when he needs it.

We also suggest that the board president and/or the executive director meet with a new board member soon after she begins serving on the board, both to welcome her and to answer any questions.

Putting Staff Members on the Board

As a general rule, paid staff shouldn't be board members. The situation can just get too complicated. For example, *conflict of interest* is always a potential problem. Awkward moments are likely when board and staff have different priorities, such as when employees want raises, but the board says no.

Some exceptions to the rule do exist, though. In fact, many nonprofits have at least one staff member on their boards. In start-up nonprofits, for example, founders frequently serve as both board members and staff. This situation isn't surprising. Who's better suited to bring the vision and passion needed to create a new organization than the person who formed it in the first place? In many new nonprofits, of course, paying the staff isn't even possible; resources are so limited that all work is done on a volunteer basis.

If a founder or other staff member serves on the board, we recommend that he not be elected board president because it tends to keep all responsibility for vision and leadership in a single person's hands. Sharing that leadership can be an important first step toward broadening an organization's base of support.

Another example of an exception is an organization formed to support an artist or group of artists — a string quartet, for instance — where separating the artistic vision from the organizational mission is difficult. In this instance, including one or more of the artists on the board helps to illuminate that mission for others.

Laws vary by state, but, in many states, having a staff member on your board doesn't appear to be against the law. For example, under California nonprofit corporation law, up to 49 percent of the members of a nonprofit board of directors are allowed to receive compensation from the nonprofit. But the standards of philanthropy set forth by the Better Business Bureau Wise Giving Alliance say that a board should include no more than one paid staff member. Check out the state contacts list from Chapter 4 (CD0402) for a list of state offices where you can get information about nonprofit corporation law in your state.

Using the Board to Full Capacity

If you spend any time around nonprofit staff, you'll probably hear a few complaints about the board of directors. "I can't get my board to do anything." "I can't get them to face hard decisions." "I can't get them to raise money." Or, worst of all, "I can't get them to show up to meetings."

Motivating the board is an important part of any nonprofit leader's job. Keeping its members well-informed so that they can make thoughtful, appropriate recommendations is essential. Sometimes, most important is gently steering the board's attention back to the organization's mission and immediate needs.

Whether or not your nonprofit has paid staff, you can take steps to help the board do its work well.

If your nonprofit has an executive director, the working relationship between the executive director and the board president is key to having an effective board and an effective organization. Ideally, the relationship between these two leaders is one of respect and trust.

Getting commitment from board members

Getting members of a board to pull their weight sometimes seems like a problem that you can't solve. Every board member probably won't contribute equally to the work involved in governing a nonprofit organization. If everyone on your board shows up at every meeting, reads all the materials, studies the financial statements, and contributes to fundraising activities, consider yourself fortunate.

Here are some techniques that encourage full board member participation:

- ✔ **Board contracts:** Some nonprofits ask new board members to sign an agreement that outlines expectations for board service. The contract may include a commitment to contribute financially to the organization, attend all board meetings, and serve on one or more committees. Check out CD0603 for a sample board contract.

- ✔ **Bylaws:** Organizational bylaws can state the requirements for board participation. For example, a board member may face dismissal from the board if she misses three consecutive board meetings.

- ✔ **Job descriptions:** Just like employees, board members often do better if they know exactly what they're supposed to do. Creating job descriptions for officers, committee chairpersons, and individual board members may clarify responsibilities and make it easier to fulfill them.

- ✔ **Self-evaluation:** Sometimes encouraging a board to look at itself motivates board members (or encourages those who aren't pulling their weight to resign). CD0604 offers a sample board self-evaluation form.

- ✔ **Reliance on board members:** Solicit opinions from members between board meetings. Use their expertise and recognize their contributions.

Not all board members contribute equally to the work of the board due to time constraints, business travel, or just plain laziness. Give each member some slack. But if a board member's lack of participation impacts the full board, the decision is up to the board president (often in partnership with the executive director) to ask the member to reconsider his commitment to the organization.

To a great degree, each board member's board work reflects her commitment to the organization's mission. Board members who truly believe in what you're doing do everything they can to help you succeed.

Making board meetings effective

Most board work is done in meetings, either with the full board or in committees. We can't think of anything that damages board effectiveness more than poorly organized meetings that don't stay on topic and continue late into the night. Nonprofit board members are volunteers; they aren't being paid by the hour. The board president is responsible for ensuring that meetings are well organized and begin and end at a scheduled hour.

If the organization has an executive director, the president may delegate some responsibilities for setting up meetings. Ultimately, however, part of the president's job is to see that board members have the information they need to make good decisions and that they do so in a reasonable amount of time.

Getting the members to show up

Saying how often a board of directors should meet is impossible. The glib answer: as often as it needs to. But a meeting schedule really depends on the organization's needs and the amount of business conducted at board meetings. Some nonprofit boards meet only once a year, the bare legal minimum. These tend to be small but stable organizations with one or two employees. Most nonprofit boards meet more frequently than once a year; some meet quarterly, some meet every other month, and others schedule monthly meetings.

The advantage of having more frequent board meetings is that board members are more engaged in the governance of the organization. The disadvantage — especially if the agenda doesn't include much business — is that board members may be more tempted to skip meetings. Of course, the board president may call a board meeting at any time if the board needs to handle special business.

Some hyper-organized boards schedule board meetings at the beginning of the year for the entire year. By entering these dates in their appointment calendars months in advance, board members are less likely to schedule other events on the same days and are more likely to attend the meetings. For example, if you meet monthly, you may schedule your meetings for the second Tuesday of each month. If you're not this organized, always schedule the next meeting before the end of the present meeting. Doing so is much easier than trying to schedule a meeting by telephone or e-mail.

Some boards use a listserv or Yahoo! or MSN group to communicate between board meetings and to compile documents in an easily accessible place.

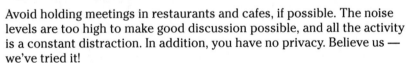

Having the best, most efficient meeting you can

Here are some tips to ensure good meetings:

- ✔ **Ten days to two weeks before a board meeting, send an announcement of the meeting to all board members.** Include the minutes from the last meeting and an agenda for the upcoming meeting. Also include any committee reports, financial statements, or background research that the board will discuss at the meeting.

- ✔ **Limit the length of meetings to two hours or less, if possible.** After two hours, especially if you're holding the meeting in the evening, attention begins to wane. If you must go longer than two hours, take a break. Offering refreshments is always a good idea.

- ✔ **Try to find a conference room for the meeting.** Holding a discussion around a conference table is much easier than holding one in someone's living room. The table offers a place to set papers, and people won't argue over who gets the recliner.

    Avoid holding meetings in restaurants and cafes, if possible. The noise levels are too high to make good discussion possible, and all the activity is a constant distraction. In addition, you have no privacy. Believe us — we've tried it!

- ✔ **Stick to the agenda.** Don't allow people to wander off the topic. Some agendas allow time for discussion after each item. You don't have to include discussion time, but if your meetings have been veering off course, this technique may work for your board. CD0605 and CD0606 are samples of common agenda types you can use as models.

- ✔ **Follow *Robert's Rules of Order*.** You don't need to be overly formal in your meetings (and many board meetings are very casual), but having a basic knowledge of when to make a motion and when to call the question is helpful.

Point of order!

Unless you're presiding over a very large and formal meeting, you probably don't need to delve too deeply into parliamentary rules. In fact, if you do find yourself in that situation, you should hire a professional parliamentarian to help keep the meeting in order.

In the 19th century, U.S. Army officer Henry Robert saw the need for a uniform set of rules to manage the give and take of meetings. He published the first edition of *Robert's Rules of Order* in 1876. The book is now in its 10th edition and is one of the best-known books in the United States (and available on the Web). It's also probably one of the least-read books.

For the purposes of most nonprofit board meetings, you only need a few basic rules:

✔ Calling a meeting to order simply announces the formal beginning of the meeting and the point at which you begin to record minutes. If you have a gavel, now is the time to use it.

✔ Making a *motion* is when a member suggests that the board vote on a policy or action. Another member of the group must second the motion. A motion made by committee doesn't need a second.

✔ If members need time to consider a motion, it should come after the motion has been moved and seconded.

✔ The board president usually signals when it's time to end discussion on a motion after ensuring everyone has had an opportunity to be heard. Then board members vote yes or no on the motion. Members may also abstain from voting if they desire. The abstention should be recorded in the minutes.

✔ To be strict, a motion is needed to adjourn the meeting. Most nonprofit boards don't follow this practice and adjourn the meeting when they reach the end of the agenda.

If this stuff really interests you, pick up a copy of *Robert's Rules For Dummies* by C. Alan Jennings, PRP (Wiley).

Chapter 7

Getting the Work Done with Volunteers

*V*olunteers are the lifeblood of the nonprofit sector. One government survey suggests that almost 30 percent of the population over age 16 performed some kind of volunteer work in the United States during 2003. That's a lot of people — more than 63 million!

Just about every nonprofit charitable organization uses volunteers in some capacity. In most cases, board members serve without compensation. For many nonprofit organizations in the United States, volunteers do all the work, from planting the trees to paying the bills. Even if your organization employs paid staff, volunteers still provide valuable service. Organizations depend on volunteers to staff telephone hotlines, lead scout troops, provide tutoring, coach youth sports teams, serve hot meals, organize fundraising events, and stuff envelopes. So if you're going to manage a nonprofit organization, you need to know how to work with volunteers.

Of course, you may be sitting in your office asking, "Where are these 63 million volunteers?" This chapter offers suggestions to help you decide what kind of volunteers you need, how to find them, and how to keep them happy after they arrive.

Understanding Why People Volunteer

The classic stereotype of a volunteer is someone who has lots of time to spare and is looking for something to do. Although this perception may have been true in the past when many women stayed out of the workplace and gave their energies to charity, the stereotype no longer fits. Women still volunteer more than men, and people between the ages of 35 and 44 are the likeliest to volunteer. Those members of the "likeliest group" also are likely to be balancing careers with raising families, not to mention taking care of aging parents, going to the gym, and keeping up with e-mail.

Why is it that people, even very busy people, volunteer their time? We think it's because more people have recognized the benefits of volunteering time to a favorite organization and because nonprofit organizations have become smarter about asking them.

Understanding why people volunteer makes it easier to find volunteers, organize their work, and recognize their contributions. Not everyone is motivated by the same factors. People volunteer for a variety of reasons, including their desire to

- **Help the community and others.** Helping others usually comes to mind first when people think of volunteers. But as you see when you read deeper in this list, their motives aren't always this simple.

- **Increase self-esteem.** Volunteering makes people feel better about themselves. Giving a few hours a week, or even a month, to an organization creates good feelings.

- **Help out friends.** Friends are often the first people we turn to when we need help. Volunteering also can create a great way to get together with friends on a regular basis.

- **Make new friends.** Volunteering is usually a social activity. People use this opportunity to meet interesting people who share their interests and values.

- **Try out a job.** People considering a job in the nonprofit sector often discover that volunteering is a good way to get a peek at what happens on the inside.

- **Polish their resumes.** Adding volunteer experience to a resume shows a commitment to helping others or to working in a particular field.

- **Develop new skills.** A volunteer job often gives people an opportunity to learn how to do something they didn't know how to do.

- **Enjoy something they love.** Many volunteer jobs come with intrinsic benefits for their participants. Ushers at the symphony get to hear the music. Gardeners removing invasive plants from a native plant preserve get to spend a day in a beautiful natural setting.

Keep this list in mind, and you'll realize that you don't have to focus your recruitment efforts exclusively on retired people or others who have a lot of leisure time. If you can provide an environment in which volunteers can bring their friends, meet others who share their interests, and learn new skills, you can lure even the busiest people into helping. Remember that you have no reason to be apologetic about asking for help: Volunteering benefits those people who step forward to assist you.

Designing a Volunteer Program

Most start-up organizations depend on volunteers because money to pay staff is unavailable. But a lack of resources isn't the only thing that drives a nonprofit to run with an all-volunteer staff. Some nonprofits make a deliberate decision to operate solely with volunteers to contain their costs and to achieve results with a collective effort among people who care deeply enough to contribute their time and effort.

Considering a volunteer coordinator

Although volunteers don't expect to be paid every two weeks, that doesn't mean they come without costs. Recruiting, training, managing, retaining, and thanking volunteers require effort from someone in the organization. We recommend assigning to someone the job of *volunteer coordinator,* a person responsible for overseeing or performing the following duties:

- ✔ **Recruiting:** Volunteers don't grow on trees. Depending on how many volunteers you need and the turnover rate of current volunteers, recruiting may be a more or less continuous process.

- ✔ **Training:** Volunteers don't come to work knowing everything they need to know. They can do any job for which they're qualified, but don't expect them to know the ropes until they're told what to do and how to do it.

- ✔ **Scheduling:** Volunteers need a schedule. Scheduling is even more important if your organization uses volunteers to staff an office or manage other tasks that require regular hours.

- ✔ **Appreciating:** Volunteers need to know that their work is valuable to the organization. This item is the last on our list, but it may be the most important. You don't have to pass out plaques, but we do recommend heartfelt acknowledgment. Saying thank you on a regular basis is essential.

If your organization depends heavily on or is staffed exclusively by volunteers, consider recruiting your volunteer coordinator from among board members or more-experienced volunteers. You can create committees to take responsibility for many jobs that need to be done, but some detail-oriented tasks — like scheduling or bill paying — are better managed by a single, responsible person.

Determining your need for volunteers

Look around your nonprofit organization and decide how many volunteers you need and what functions they can perform. We recommend creating (or helping your volunteer coordinator to create) a schedule of tasks to be completed — planning what needs to be done and how many people it will take to do the work. Table 7-1 lists the kinds of volunteer assignments you might jot down. By having such a list and prioritizing the tasks, you know what to do when an unexpected volunteer walks in the door.

Table 7-1	Sample Volunteer Task List	
Task	*Number of People*	*Time*
Data entry – donor list	1 person	3 hours per week
Bulk mailing	4 people	5 hours per month
Lawn cleanup	1 person	2 hours per week
Childcare	2 people	3 hours on Saturdays
Filing	1 person	2 hours per week

It's possible to have too many volunteers. Almost nothing is worse than asking people to help and then finding out that you have nothing for them to do. You may want to have both your chart of immediate tasks (like in Table 7-1) and a few "back burner" projects — like organizing press clippings in a scrapbook or taking inventory in the supply cabinet — in case you end up with more people than you need on a given day.

In the beginning, you may have to experiment before you know exactly how many volunteers you need for a particular job. For example, you may eventually discover that a 2,000-piece mailing takes about five hours for four people to complete. You may also find that hand-addressing envelopes takes longer than using labels, and preparing bulk mail takes longer than doing a first-class mailing.

Writing volunteer job descriptions

Volunteers perform better if they know what they're supposed to do. Preparing job descriptions for volunteer positions helps you to supervise better and to know what skills you're looking for in volunteers. (Take a look at Chapter 8 for detailed information on writing a job description.)

If anything, volunteer job descriptions should be even more complete than paid-employee job descriptions. If you can break jobs into small tasks; all the better, because volunteers often share the same job. For example, a different person may answer the office telephone each day of the week. In that case, keeping by the telephone a job description that includes a list of telephone procedures, frequently used telephone numbers, and other important information can bring consistency to the job.

See CD0701 and CD0702 for some sample volunteer job descriptions.

Organizing volunteers

Many nonprofits invite their volunteers to participate in committees. Committees allow volunteers to step forward and offer their best skills and the chance to learn to do new things. An advantage of forming committees is that it reinforces the social benefits of volunteering. As committee members get to know one another and figure out how to manage their tasks successfully, you or your volunteer coordinator can step back and let them take full responsibility.

Here's a fictitious example that gives you an idea of how to organize committees: A small nonprofit called the Sunshine and Health Project was organized to provide telephone referral and information sources for people seeking help with weight loss. It was started by three people who had lost weight and decided to help others do the same. A board of directors of ten people provides governance for Sunshine and Health and undertakes key volunteer roles in the organization. The board formed the following committees, each chaired by a board member but made up of individuals who provide volunteer services:

> ✔ **Telephone committee:** Sunshine and Health provides most of its services via telephone. The office receives about 60 calls each day from people seeking information about weight loss and referral to health clinics and counselors. The telephones are answered 12 hours a day, from 9 a.m. to 9 p.m., Monday through Friday. Two volunteers share responsibility for the phones in three-hour shifts. The nonprofit needs 40 volunteers each week to answer phones and provide information. Sunshine and Health also needs backup volunteers in case someone is ill or can't make his shift for some other reason.

✔ **Program committee:** This committee researches programs to which callers can be referred, maintains the database containing referral information, and provides training to telephone volunteers. Members of the committee include one physician and two registered nurses, all of whom provide professional oversight.

✔ **Publicity committee:** Sunshine and Health uses several methods to tell the public that its services are available. The publicity committee prepares and mails press releases and records and distributes public service announcements to radio stations. In addition, the committee operates a speakers' bureau of people who have benefited from Sunshine and Health's services. The committee also has developed a Web site that offers basic information about weight loss, maintains a directory of services in various cities, and invites its readers to sign up for a monthly e-mail newsletter.

✔ **Fundraising committee:** Sunshine and Health raises funds through a family-oriented walk-a-thon, appeal letters sent to people who have used its services, and gifts from businesses promoting a healthy lifestyle. Committee members plan and coordinate these events, write and send the appeal letters, and make personal calls on the business sponsors. They call upon all volunteers to make personal gifts, identify possible donors, and provide lists of contacts.

✔ **Administration committee:** Sunshine and Health receives individual donations from people who use its services, grants from foundations, and limited support from the health department in the city in which it's based. This committee is responsible for maintaining the organization's financial books, writing thank you letters to donors, and maintaining a database of past donors.

You may be able to think of other tasks that can be assigned to a volunteer committee. The kinds of jobs that need to be done vary, depending on the type of service your organization provides. The point to remember is that volunteer work needs to be organized (and supervised) in much the same way that paid work is organized.

In an all-volunteer organization, the responsibility for ensuring that the work gets done resides with the board of directors. The board must be committed to finding new volunteers and supervising their work. And board members must be ready to step in to do a job if no volunteers can be found.

Board members who also serve as program volunteers must remember to keep their roles as board members (governance and fiduciary) separate from their roles as program volunteers. In the latter case, the volunteers are operating like staff, not board members. There is a difference. See Chapter 6 for information about understanding and defining board members' roles.

Hunting for Volunteers

Most organizations are always on the lookout for volunteers. Volunteers move away, get tired, lose interest, or take new jobs with new hours. If your organization depends on volunteers, you probably need to maintain an ongoing recruitment process.

Using the tried-and-true methods

To cast a wide net, you want to use more than one method to find volunteers, and you don't want to spend much money on it. After all, you're looking for free help. Persistence matters: Good volunteer recruitment is like a healthy habit that you want to repeat. Here are a few of the most common and most successful methods for recruiting volunteers:

- **Announcements in the media:** Newspapers and radio and television stations often publish or air public service announcements for nonprofit organizations. Keep your press releases short — less than two pages for print media and less than 30 seconds when you read it aloud for radio and television. See Chapter 11 for more information about writing and distributing press releases.

- **Posters:** Use your word processing program to design posters calling for volunteers and display them wherever you can. Grocery stores, drugstores, churches, Laundromats, schools, and civic buildings often have bulletin boards where you can post announcements. Place them thoughtfully. For instance, put your call for foster homes for kittens at the pet food store and your community garden poster at nursery and home repair stores.

- **Word of mouth:** Encourage your current volunteers to recruit others. Have a "bring a friend" day with time for socializing. Ask your volunteers to post your posters in their places of business and don't forget to invite and coax your own friends and associates.

- **Schools and churches:** Both institutions often look for ways for students and members of the congregation to get involved in community service. *Service learning* — through which students learn about a topic by volunteering in their communities and then reflecting on what they have learned in their classrooms — is becoming popular at some schools, and many colleges and universities have campus centers for community relations and student volunteering.

Don't forget to reach out to the young people in your area. You benefit from their skills and ideas and contribute to training the next generation of volunteers!

✔ **Clubs and fraternal groups:** Many professional and social clubs include serving the community in their missions. From Kiwanis and Elks to the Junior League, Chamber of Commerce, or campus-based sororities and fraternities, clubs and membership groups can be an excellent volunteer resource.

✔ **Corporations and businesses:** In some communities, businesses look for volunteer opportunities for their employees. Different businesses encourage employee volunteerism in many ways: If they have a community relations, community affairs, or corporate giving department, it's likely to be a good place to begin asking about employee volunteers.

✔ **The Internet:** If you have a Web site and you're looking for volunteers, announce it on the site. You also can post your volunteer positions on some Web sites that exist just for that purpose:

- **ServeNet** (www.servenet.org), for example, provides a database of volunteer jobs. You can type in your zip code and find volunteer opportunities in your community.

- **Volunteer Match** (www.volunteermatch.org) invites nonprofits to set up accounts identifying the kinds of volunteers they need.

- **Idealist** is another widely-used tool (www.idealist.org).

- If your organization can use volunteers who aren't physically located near your office, have a look at the **Virtual Volunteering Project** (www.serviceleader.org/vv/). Maybe you can use online volunteers to answer questions via e-mail, help write grants and press releases, or get consultation on designing your Web site.

- If you're particularly interested in involving young volunteers in your work, **Youth Service America** (www.ysa.org) organizes an annual National Youth Service Day and other opportunities for volunteers between the ages of 5 and 25.

✔ **Local courts:** Some local court systems have community service programs for people working off parking fines or other minor violations.

Looking for volunteers at other nonprofits

No, we don't suggest that you steal volunteers from other nonprofits, but some organizations do exist to provide volunteer help. Volunteer centers, for example, make up a national network of organizations that recruit and place volunteers in nonprofits. You can find the volunteer center nearest you by following the links at the Points of Light Foundation Web site (www. pointsoflight.org/volunteercenters/volunteercenters.html).

Here's how some other organizations fill this need:

- Some United Way affiliates operate a loaned executive program.
- The Retired Senior Volunteer Project places retired people in volunteer positions.
- AmeriCorps (www.americorps.org) operates several programs, including Volunteers in Service to America (VISTA) volunteers, who receive stipends from the federal government to assist in antipoverty programs across the country.
- The Arts and Business Council, Inc. (www.artsandbusiness.org/bvahome.htm), operates programs in 11 states matching business people with arts organizations.

Sometimes your nonprofit competition won't mind sharing their contacts who are loyal to a particular kind of activity. In our city, for example, several organizations put on film festivals once each year and some volunteers who love to see the films volunteer to work in box offices, press rooms, and other capacities, migrating from one festival to the next. Rather than detracting from their contributions to one organization, their "migrant volunteering" makes them more knowledgeable and strengthens their public relations skills. When recruiting for short-term volunteer assignments, don't be afraid to ask your "competition" if you can invite some of their great bird watchers, marathon runners, brownie bakers, and scarecrow makers.

Finding volunteers with special skills

If you're looking for volunteers with special training or experience, spend some time thinking about where you can find them. Target your recruitment efforts to places where you're most likely to identify the people with the talents you need.

Suppose that your organization is seeking someone with accounting experience to help you maintain your books. Local accounting firms, corporate offices, and public school administration offices may be good recruiting ground for someone who can assist with bookkeeping. In some states, the professional organization of certified public accountants (CPAs) links its members to nonprofit volunteer assignments.

And don't forget other nonprofit organizations in your community. A more established nonprofit may have staff members who are interested in your cause. You may be able to get some experienced help in setting up your fundraising plan, your computer network, or your publicity materials. Just because someone works at another nonprofit doesn't mean that she won't find it gratifying to apply her skills for you as well.

Hiring interns

Interns are specialized volunteers who come to you as a part of an education or training program. In most cases, a student intern's goal is developing practical, hands-on work experience.

Sometimes internship programs require the nonprofit to pay a fee or to provide the intern with a modest stipend.

As with employees and volunteers, you should provide the intern with clear expectations about job duties, attendance, and so on. If you decide to go this route, be ready to spend time supervising and evaluating the intern's job performance. Don't forget that the intern's experience is part of his grade.

Interviewing and Screening Volunteers

If you're placing volunteers in sensitive jobs, such as working with children or providing peer counseling, screen the applicants carefully. Screening, including a fingerprint check, is sometimes required by law, licensing requirements, or your insurance carrier. Some states also require a test for tuberculosis. Check with local authorities about the requirements in your area.

While the authorities do the fingerprinting and criminal background checks, you can do some screening of your own. Require volunteer applicants to fill out a job application just as if they were applying for paid work. Ask for references and check them. Review resumes and conduct formal interviews. (See Chapter 8 for information about job interviews.) Avoid paranoia, but don't discount your gut feelings, either.

If you're using volunteers in professional roles, such as accounting, check their qualifications just as you check the qualifications of an applicant for a paid position. Again, it's possible that this process may offend potential volunteers, but it's far better to make sure the person can do the job, even if she's doing it for free.

See CD0703 for a volunteer intake form.

We realize that screening can be a delicate issue. You're walking a tightrope between the rights of individual privacy and the rights of the organization to be sure that no harm will befall clients. Some potential volunteers may be offended by background checks. Explain to them that the procedures aren't directed at them personally but are in place to ensure that clients are protected. Also, treat all volunteer applicants the same. Don't pass up screening someone just because she's a personal friend.

A cheat sheet for the FAQs

Be prepared to answer questions when people call to volunteer. If you're already using volunteers to answer the telephone, prepare a list of common questions and their answers, and place that list near the telephone. On the Internet, lists of questions and answers are known as FAQs, which stands for Frequently Asked Questions. Here are some sample FAQs that the Sunshine and Health Project, a fictional nonprofit discussed in the section "Organizing volunteers," may need:

What are the hours I would be needed? We answer the phones five days a week from 9 in the morning until 9 at night. We ask people to work a three-hour shift once a week.

How will I know what to say? All volunteers receive one day of training. Training is offered once a month, almost always on Saturday.

What kind of advice can I give? Our volunteers can't give medical advice or advice on specific diets. We refer callers to existing services and professionals. We ask volunteers to be positive and to offer general support to all callers.

How do I know where to refer people? We have a complete database of weight loss and related counseling services. It's a simple matter of looking through a loose-leaf notebook or our computer database to find the appropriate phone numbers.

What if I get sick and can't cover my shift? We have volunteers on standby to cover unexpected absences. If you aren't able to volunteer on a regular, weekly basis, you might consider being a backup volunteer.

Are we asked to do any other work? Sometimes we ask volunteers to help with mailings between phone calls.

Will you pay my auto (or public transportation) expenses? We're sorry, but our budget doesn't cover reimbursing volunteers for expenses. Some expenses may be deductible on your income tax, however. You should check with your tax specialist.

Can I deduct the value of my time from my income taxes? No, the IRS doesn't allow tax deductions for volunteer time.

These questions and answers also can be printed in a brochure and mailed to potential volunteers who request more information. Also include background information about your organization.

Managing Your Volunteers

Just like managing paid employees, working with volunteers requires attention to management tasks. Volunteers need training and orientation, as well as clear, written lists of responsibilities and expectations. Basic expectations for volunteers are easily outlined in a volunteer agreement form. You want to maintain records of the time and tasks they contribute to your organization, and you should consider whether to include them in your insurance coverage.

See CD0704 for a sample volunteer agreement form.

Providing adequate training

The degree and extent of training volunteers depends on the type of job you're asking them to do. Volunteers who answer telephones, for example, may need more training than those volunteers who stuff envelopes for the publicity committee. They need to know the background information about the program or service, information about the types of services available, proper telephone etiquette, and emergency procedures, just to name a few.

If you need to provide a full day's training or training over a longer period, we suggest consulting with a professional trainer to either provide the training or help you to design the curriculum. Although you may be concerned about investing too much of volunteers' valuable time in training, remember that key motivations for volunteering include meeting people and doing things with friends. Trainings can be great opportunities to introduce volunteers to one another and build camaraderie among them.

Putting it in writing

In addition to on-site training, you should give volunteers written materials that restate the information covered in the training. Include with these materials attendance requirements, whom to telephone in case of illness, and other necessary information that volunteers may need to know when carrying out their tasks.

Larger organizations that use many volunteers sometimes publish a *volunteer handbook*. Such a handbook doesn't need to be an elaborately printed document; it can be several typed pages stapled together or a simple loose-leaf notebook. The more information you provide, the better your volunteers can perform.

Keeping good records

Keep records of your volunteers and how much time they spend doing work for your organization. You may be asked to provide a reference for a volunteer who's working to develop job skills or providing a service through an organized volunteer program. You may also need to dismiss a volunteer who is unreliable, and having clear, written records of hours and tasks can justify that difficult act.

If you use professional volunteers to perform tasks that you'd otherwise have to pay for, you may want to include the value of the volunteer time as an in-kind contribution on your financial statement. See Chapter 10 for more information about financial statements.

Insuring your volunteers

Typically, nonprofit organizations carry liability and property insurance. Almost all states require that workers' compensation insurance be in place to cover on-the-job injuries to employees. Beyond this basic insurance, coverage depends on the type of services provided and the degree of risk involved. We discuss insurance for nonprofits in greater detail in Chapter 12.

Keep in mind that volunteers usually aren't liable for their actions as long as they work within the scope of the volunteer activity to which they have been assigned, perform as any reasonable person would perform, and don't engage in criminal activity. Unfortunately, people have become more eager to file lawsuits at the drop of a hat. If someone sues you or one of your volunteers, you have to legally defend the case even if it's without merit. One advantage to liability insurance is that your insurance carrier takes on the responsibility of defending the suit.

Workers' compensation may or may not be available to volunteers in your state. If you can include volunteers under your state law, consider doing so, because a workers' comp claim usually precludes the volunteer from filing a suit for damages against your organization, and you want your volunteer to be covered if she sustains an injury.

Insuring volunteers is a subject of debate in the nonprofit sector. Some people take the position that insurance agents and brokers try to convince you to insure anything and everything. Others believe that liability insurance and, in some cases, workers' compensation insurance should be provided. As is the case with all insurance questions, evaluate your risks and decide whether the cost of insuring against risks is a good investment. This process is called *risk management*. To find information about risk management for nonprofit organizations, contact the Nonprofit Risk Management Center at www.nonprofitrisk.org.

Getting rid of bad volunteers

If you work with lots of volunteers, especially volunteers who perform complex and sensitive jobs, you may discover one or more volunteers who don't have the skills or personalities to perform at an acceptable level. We hope you never face this situation, but if you do — for example, maybe someone is giving bad information or acting rudely — you shouldn't ignore the situation.

Discussing the problem behavior with the volunteer is the first step. Treat this meeting as if you were counseling a paid employee whose job performance was below par. This is another reason why written job descriptions for volunteers, written standards for performance, and records of volunteer time and contributed tasks are important.

Exercise caution when meeting with a volunteer about her unacceptable behavior, especially if you don't have clearly written performance guidelines. Volunteers who are released have been known to sue the nonprofit agency. If you have concerns about this possibility, consult an attorney before you do anything.

Talking to someone, volunteer or not, about poor work is never pleasant. However, if someone working for your organization is being disruptive, giving bad information, or otherwise causing potential harm to your program or the people you serve, you have a responsibility to correct the problem.

Saying Thank You to Volunteers

Volunteers give their time and, in many cases, expertise to help your organization succeed. It's only right that you thank them and thank them often. Thank them in the hallway after they've completed their work for the day, and also formally recognize their contributions. Here are some standard ways of recognizing volunteers:

- ✔ **Annual recognition event:** This kind of event is the most formal (and probably the most expensive) way of thanking volunteers. Some organizations have a sit-down dinner or wine and cheese reception once a year to say thanks and give awards to volunteers who have made extraordinary contributions.

- ✔ **Gifts:** Although "tokens of appreciation" may be very deserved, we recommend caution when giving gifts to volunteers. Don't spend lots of money buying them presents because you can bet that some of them will ask why you're spending scarce nonprofit money on something that isn't necessary. If you can get a local business to donate gift certificates or other items, that's a better way to go.

- ✔ **Admission to performances or events:** If your organization presents plays, musical performances, lectures, or readings, consider offering free admission to some events.

✔ **Public acknowledgment:** You can identify the names of your volunteers in your newsletter or Web site. An alternative is an annual newspaper ad that lists the names of your volunteers.

✔ **Thank you letters:** Don't underestimate the power of a simple thank you note. Unless you have hundreds of volunteers, make sure you write your notes by hand. Most people appreciate a handwritten note more than a typewritten form letter.

In addition to thank you letters and recognition events, you can increase volunteer satisfaction (and retention) by treating volunteers well on a day-to-day basis. Here are some easy tips to keep volunteer satisfaction high:

✔ **Don't make volunteers work in isolation if you can avoid it.** Many volunteers give their time because they enjoy socializing with others.

✔ **Vary the job to avoid boredom.** You may need help cleaning the storeroom or hand-addressing 1,000 envelopes, but try to assign jobs that offer more mental stimulation as well.

✔ **Pay attention to the work done by your volunteers.** Your interest in what they're doing adds value to their work and recognizes that many of them are volunteering to develop new skills.

✔ **Help volunteers understand your nonprofit's work.** If they've been answering the telephones in the front office, give them a behind-the-scenes tour or a chance to observe or participate in other activities of the organization.

✔ **Bring in pizza or doughnuts once in a while as an impromptu thank you.** Food can provide a great break from a monotonous job or celebration of a major task's completion.

✔ **Talk to your volunteers.** Get to know them as friends of your organization who are committed to its work.

Chapter 8

Getting the Work Done with Paid Staff

Some nonprofits have paid staff from the very beginning. For example, nonprofits that start out with grant funding to operate a program may have paid staff. Other nonprofits may start more slowly, with the board of directors and other volunteers initially doing all the work and hiring paid employees later. And many nonprofits never have paid staff. These organizations may use consultants or temporary employees to help raise money or catch up on filing, but they never have the money to support regular full-time employees.

No rules exist about when a nonprofit organization should employ paid staff. You probably aren't going to wake up one morning and say to yourself, "Hey, it's time to hire some staff." The organization must determine whether it has enough work to justify a paid staff and whether it has the resources to pay salaries and associated expenses. New nonprofits often begin by hiring part-time staff or consultants before bringing on full-time employees.

Hiring your first staff member should be cause for celebration. It means that your nonprofit has reached a milestone in its development. But it also means that the organization (and the board of directors) will have more responsibilities to raise funds and ensure that proper personnel policies are in place and followed. This chapter covers the details.

Deciding That You Need Help

Knowing when to take the leap from being an all-volunteer group to being a boss or a paid employee isn't easy, and it's not a leap to take without looking at where you're about to land. Hiring employees creates responsibilities for the board, not the least of which is paying a salary every two weeks. You also need to pay payroll taxes and provide a workplace, equipment, and — don't forget — guidance and supervision. Expect to have more bookkeeping duties and more complex financial reports, because you need to keep track of payroll records, vacation time, and sick days and decide which holidays your organization will observe. (The last one should be a snap, right?)

To ease into the transition, a nonprofit may begin by hiring an independent contractor to handle a specific task, such as bookkeeping or grant writing, and then go from there. (We discuss working with independent contractors and consultants at the end of this chapter.)

A variety of situations, such as the following, may signal that it's time to hire your first employee:

- ✔ The work has been done solely by board members and volunteers, but people are getting tired and the work isn't getting done as well as it should.

- ✔ The demand for your organization's services has increased to the point that volunteers need a consistent point person who can coordinate its complexity or focus on administrative details.

- ✔ The organization's founder has been paid irregularly for work on specific projects. Resources have increased to the point that you can now pay a regular salary.

- ✔ The organization is starting a new activity that requires someone with a specific professional license or degree and no member of the board or volunteer group is appropriately qualified.

- ✔ The nonprofit receives a major grant that both provides more resources and requires significant record-keeping and program management.

Hiring salaried employees should be a long-term commitment. For this reason, the organization needs to have sufficient cash flow to ensure regular payment of salaries, benefits, and payroll taxes.

A crisis can sometimes take place when a volunteer-run organization hires its first staff member. Knowing that they're now paying someone to be responsible, board members may decide to sit on their hands and let others do the work. Bringing on a first staff member is a good time to honor board and volunteer contributions to the organization (to keep motivation high) and to invest in a board retreat or training that reminds everyone of the work ahead and the board's important role in it.

Readying Your Nonprofit for Paid Employees

Before you start writing a job description, or placing a classified ad, you need to invest time in some upfront prep work, readying your organization to take on paid employees. This preparation includes writing personnel policies, setting up payroll systems, and deciding on benefits.

Developing your personnel policies

Personnel policies and procedures outline how an organization relates to its employees. They're essential for both supervisors and employees because they provide guidelines about what's expected in the workplace and on the job. They ensure that all employees receive equal treatment, provide the steps necessary for disciplinary action if it's needed, and lay out expectations for employees.

Many start-up and small organizations that have only one or two employees give personnel policies a low priority. Frankly, you may have more important things to deal with, such as how to find the money to meet payroll next month. We suggest, however, that you begin early to formalize your rules in the form of an employee handbook. Doing so really doesn't take much time, and it can save you headaches down the road.

You must follow federal and state labor laws when establishing personnel policies. If you're uncertain about whether you can require certain behavior or work hours from your employees, consult an attorney.

When forming policies, begin with the easy stuff. Decide on your organization's office hours, holidays, vacation policy, and other basic necessities.

Determining work and off time

Most organizations follow the lead of others when setting holiday and vacation policy. Although you find a lot of variation, many nonprofits in the United States grant two weeks' vacation per year to new employees. Employees typically receive more vacation time after a longer period of service, such as three weeks after three years, and four weeks after five to eight years. The most common sick leave policy is ten days per year. While you're at it, you want to give some thought to bereavement and maternity leave policies.

Paid vacation time is a benefit to both employees and employers. Employees return from vacation rested and ready to give their best efforts to the organization. For this reason, you should encourage people to take vacations during the year in which they earn the vacation. Most organizations and businesses don't allow employees to accrue vacation time beyond a certain amount. This policy ensures that employees use vacations for the purpose for which they're intended. Such a policy also controls the amount of liability to make a cash payment for unused vacation time if the employee resigns or is terminated.

Employees must be given paid time off for jury duty and voting.

Consider reviewing the personnel policies of other nonprofit organizations in your area. To get started, the Minnesota Council of Nonprofits has sample personnel policies on its Web site under Human Resources at www.mncn.org. A few telephone calls to other executive directors may help answer questions that arise as you refine your policies.

See CD0801 for sample personnel policies.

Other important items

In addition to vacations and holidays, you have other basics to cover in your policies:

- ✔ A statement that the board of directors may change the policies

- ✔ A statement of nondiscrimination in employment, usually presented as a policy established by the board of directors — especially important if your organization is seeking government grants or contracts

- ✔ A statement about parental leave and long-term disability policies

- ✔ A statement of hiring procedures and the probationary period (see "Evaluating your new hire's progress" later in this chapter)

- ✔ A statement of employment termination policy, including a grievance procedure

Many organizations also include the following few items to help new employees understand the organization:

- ✔ A statement of the organizational mission

- ✔ A statement outlining the history of the organization

- ✔ A statement of the values held by the organization

When you add paid employees to your organization, you assume legal responsibilities that begin with the recruitment process. We recommend that you consult *Human Resources Kit For Dummies* by Max Messmer (Wiley) to be sure that you cover all the bases.

Setting up a payroll system

When an organization begins employing workers, it first must establish a payroll system. The organization needs to decide how often to distribute paychecks, for example. You can disburse paychecks on any schedule you choose — weekly, biweekly, semimonthly, or monthly. (*Biweekly* means every two weeks and results in 26 paychecks per year; *semimonthly* means twice a month and results in 24 paychecks per year.) In our experience, semimonthly is the most common schedule for payment, but the decision is up to the organization.

Although in-house staff can handle payroll, contracting with a payroll service is a better option. Most banks either provide payroll services or can recommend one. Payroll services are inexpensive — they're almost always cheaper than assigning a staff person the job of handling payroll. They make the proper withholding deductions based on income level, number of dependents, and state laws; make tax deposits; and maintain a record of vacation and sick leave. Usually when you contract with such a service, they require that you keep enough funds on deposit with them to cover two or three months of salaries and benefits.

If you decide to handle your own payroll, be sure to make tax deposits on time. Failure to pay federal and state payroll taxes is probably the quickest way to get your organization in serious trouble.

Typical deductions include the following, although state tax laws show much variation:

- ✔ Federal income tax withholding
- ✔ Social Security tax (matched by the employer)
- ✔ State income tax withholding
- ✔ State unemployment and disability insurance

Providing benefits and perquisites

You make the decisions about some of your employee benefits — such as sick leave, vacation time, and holidays — when writing your personnel policies.

Health insurance is a benefit that your organization may or may not be able to provide. The cost of health insurance decreases based on the size of the group to which you belong. If your organization has only one employee, purchasing health insurance may be costly unless you can join a larger group. Check with state associations for nonprofit organizations or your local United Way office to see whether they have a health insurance program that will cover your employees. For more on insurance, see Chapter 12.

Preparing to Hire

After you write your policies, put your payroll systems in place, and decide on your benefits, you're finished with the groundwork needed to hire 1 or 100 employees. You're probably just hiring one person for now. To set off on that path, you want to clearly describe what that job entails, consider salary levels, and announce the position. This section walks you through those important steps.

First things first: Writing a job description

One of the first things you should do when looking to hire a paid employee is to write a job description for the position you want to fill. Going through this exercise helps to clarify the skills needed for the job, guides you in selecting among applicants, and serves as a job blueprint for the new employee.

A job description usually includes the following information:

- ✔ A short paragraph describing the job and the work environment
- ✔ A list of duties and responsibilities
- ✔ A list of skills and abilities needed for the job
- ✔ Experience and education required
- ✔ Special qualifications required or desired

We include several standard job descriptions on the CD. See CD0802 for an Executive Director job description, CD0803 for a Development Director job description, and CD0804 for an Office Administrator job description.

When writing your job description, keep in mind that work in nonprofit organizations can be split into three broad areas:

- ✔ **Services:** Services are the reason the organization exists in the first place. They may include developing protected open space on a coastal mountain range, providing home visits and hot meals to seniors, or organizing after-school activities for children. This list is almost unlimited.

- ✔ **Administrative functions:** These functions include bookkeeping and accounting, office management, property or building management, marketing, Web design, clerical services, benefits administration, and contract management. You can add to this list as needed.

- ✔ **Fundraising:** This area falls under various names, including *resource development* and *advancement.* Depending on the size of your organization, one person may be in charge of all aspects of raising money or different people may specialize in writing grants to foundations and government, creating sponsorships with corporations, or raising money from individual donors.

The larger these areas (or departments) are, the greater the specialization within them. But when you're looking to hire your first staff member, that one person may have job responsibilities in more than one area, perhaps even in all three areas. It may seem like too much to describe in a single document, but that complexity and the high level of responsibility this person will have make it particularly important to create a job description that's crystal clear.

Considering necessary qualifications

Some nonprofit jobs require various levels of formal education and special training. If you're hiring someone to provide counseling services, for example, that employee probably needs to meet certain education and licensing requirements in order to provide the services legally. If you're hiring someone to work with children, the applicant may need to pass various background checks, depending on the laws of your state.

Professional and business associations can provide helpful information about job qualifications. For example, if you need specifics about the qualifications that a speech pathologist should have, contact the American Speech-Language-Hearing Association (www.asha.org). The American Society of Association Executives (www.asaenet.org) may help you find appropriate national or local associations.

In addition to any degrees and certifications, you may want to specify that applicants have a certain amount of experience in doing the work you're going to ask them to do. (If you do so, be prepared to pay a higher salary to fill the position.)

You can't, of course, require that an applicant be of a particular ethnic background, race, age, creed, or sexual preference. You can't deny employment to a woman because she's expecting a child. You also can't refuse employment to a person with a disability as long as he can perform the job with reasonable accommodations.

Deciding salary levels

Deciding on a fair salary isn't easy. Compensation levels in nonprofits range from hardly anything to six-figure salaries at large-budget organizations. (Keep in mind, however, that large nonprofits represent only a small percentage of active nonprofits.)

Considering factors that affect salary

Although exceptions always exist, the following list outlines some factors that determine salary levels:

- ✔ **Geographic location:** Salary levels differ from place to place due to the cost of living. If your nonprofit is in a major metropolitan area, expect to pay more to attract qualified staff than if you're located in a rural area.

- ✔ **Education and experience:** Someone with ten years of experience can command higher compensation than someone just beginning his career. Education levels also affect salary, as does having specialized knowledge or skills. Jobs requiring a master's degree or a PhD pay more than those jobs that don't.

- ✔ **Job duties and responsibilities:** Employees who direct programs and supervise others typically earn more than employees who have fewer responsibilities.

- ✔ **Nonprofit type:** Compensation levels vary from one nonprofit to the next. Organizations providing health services, for example, typically have higher salary levels than arts organizations.

- ✔ **Union membership:** Labor unions set standards for salaries and benefits in many fields, from classical musicians to nurses and educators.

- ✔ **Organizational culture:** This category, which is harder to define, is connected to the organization's traditions and values. For instance, nonprofits with boards of directors filled with business and corporate members often offer higher salary levels than organizations with boards that don't have the corporate perspective.

Finding out salaries of comparable positions

A salary survey, which you can conduct by phone or mail, is a good way to assess the current salary levels in your area and for your nonprofit type. Telephone surveys probably should be done from board president to board president because most people are reluctant to reveal their own salaries. Mail surveys can be constructed so that respondents remain anonymous.

The simplest method of finding salaries of comparable positions is to look at job listings in the newspaper and on the Internet. Not all ads list salaries, but those ads that do can give you a general idea of what others are paying for similar work.

Some nonprofit management organizations conduct annual or biannual surveys of salary levels in the areas in which they work. More often than not, access to the surveys requires payment, but it's probably a good investment because these surveys tend to be the most complete and up-to-date. A good place to inquire about salary surveys is through your state association of nonprofits (see the National Council of Nonprofit Associations Web site at www.ncna.org). They list 41 state and regional associations, and more are on the way.

Using a search firm can be helpful, especially if the position requires a national search. Be prepared to pay a hefty fee, however. Fees are often based on a percentage of the first year's salary.

Announcing the position

After you decide on the qualifications and skills needed for the job, advertise its availability. Here's a list of ways to publicize your job opening:

- **Professional journals:** If you're hiring for a professional position, professional journals are the place to advertise the job. Use your favorite Web search engine to track down the addresses of appropriate journals.

- **Classified ads:** Putting a classified ad in a newspaper is the usual way to seek applicants for a job. Frankly, we've never had much luck with ads in general publications, and ads can be expensive, especially in high-circulation dailies. Sometimes you get a better response from smaller neighborhood and ethnic weekly papers.

- **Bulletin boards:** Posting job announcements on bulletin boards at colleges, universities, other agencies, job centers, and even grocery stores is an inexpensive approach. In addition, you can put as many details as you want on a small poster at no extra cost.

- **Web sites:** The Internet has become a valuable marketplace for job seekers. Search for job listings in the occupation category you hope to fill. Also, look for local Web sites that carry job listings. Many Web sites charge a fee for posting a job opening. OpportunityKnocks (`www.opportunitynocs.org`) is a good online site.

- **Word of mouth:** This is a tried-and-true method. Spread the word to other nonprofits — especially those in your field — churches, and anywhere else people congregate. Don't forget to e-mail the announcement to colleagues and to Internet mailing lists, often called *listservs,* read by people in your field.

Although it's up to you, we recommend stating the salary level in your ad because doing so helps screen out applicants for whom the compensation may be too low.

Making the Hire

Now comes the time to make the big decision. Sifting through resumes, conducting interviews, and deciding on an employee can be a daunting task. Sometimes the right choice jumps out at you; other times, you have to choose between two or three (or 20!) candidates who have equal qualifications. That's when making up your mind gets hard.

Looking at resumes

Resumes and cover letters give you the first opportunity to evaluate candidates for the position. Respond quickly with a postcard or an e-mail to let applicants know that their materials have arrived. If possible, give a date by which they can expect to hear from you again. Doing so reduces the number of phone calls you get asking whether you've received the resume and when you plan to make a decision. It's also the polite thing to do.

Resumes come in various formats, and we don't really have an opinion as to which one is the best. Regardless of how the resume is organized, here are the questions we ask ourselves when reviewing a resume:

✔ **Is it free of typographical errors and misspellings?** A typo may be excused if everything else appears to be in order, but more than one or two errors implies that the candidate is likely to be careless in her job.

✔ **Is the information laid out in a logical, easy-to-follow manner?** The relative clarity of the resume can give you insight into the applicant's communication skills.

✔ **Does the applicant have the right job experience, education, and licenses, if needed?** We like to give a little slack on experience because sometimes highly motivated and effective employees are people who have to "grow into" the job. Also, nonprofit organizations often receive resumes from people who are changing careers. They may not have the exact experience you're looking for, but maybe what they learned in their previous jobs easily transfers to the position you're trying to fill.

✔ **How often has the applicant changed jobs?** You can never be guaranteed that an employee will stay as long as you want him to, but you have to ask yourself, "If I hire this person, will he pack up and move on even before he finishes job training?" At the same time, don't automatically let higher-than-average job switching turn you off to an excellent candidate. Maybe he has an explanation. Ask.

Cover letters also can be good clues to an individual's future job performance. For one thing, you get an idea of the applicant's writing abilities, and you may even get some insight into his personality. Some job announcements state that a cover letter should accompany the resume, and some even go so far as to ask the applicant to respond to questions such as "Why are you well suited to this job?" or "What do you think are the major issues facing so-and-so?" It's up to you as to whether asking a list of questions enables you to more easily compare applicants to one another.

You'll probably reject at least half the resumes out of hand. We never cease to be amazed by how many people apply for jobs for which they don't have even the minimal qualifications. We understand that searching for a job is difficult and frustrating, but we also wonder whether applicants read our "position available" ads as closely as they should.

Separate your resumes into two piles — one for rejected applications and one for applications that need closer scrutiny. Send the rejected candidates a letter thanking them for their interest. From the other pile, decide how many candidates you want to interview. Reviewing the resumes with one or two board members to bring several perspectives to the choice is often helpful. One technique is to select the top three applicants for interviews. Reserve the other applicants for backup interviews if the first three aren't suitable or if they've already accepted other jobs.

Interviewing candidates

Now that you have chosen the top three or five or eight resumes, it's time to invite the applicants in for an interview. Interviewing job candidates is a formidable task. Big companies have human resource departments with trained interviewers who spend their days asking questions of prospective employees. We're neither human resource specialists nor trained interviewers, but here are some tricks we've learned over the years:

✔ **Prepare a list of three or four standard questions that you ask all applicants.** Doing so enables you to compare answers across applicants. The interview shouldn't be so formal as to make the candidate (and you) uncomfortable, but standardizing it to some degree is good. Here's a short list of typical questions:

- Why are you interested in this position?

- What do you see as your strengths? As your weaknesses?

- How would you use your previous work experience in this job?

- What are your long-term goals?

✔ **Group interviews with three or more people can give interviewers good insight into how the applicant will perform in board and community meetings.** Also, different people notice different things about each applicant. Avoid making the candidate face a large group, which can make her unnecessarily nervous.

✔ **If this employee isn't your first and the job to be filled is for a director or supervisor position, arrange for each finalist to meet at least some of the staff he'll be supervising.** Giving staff members a chance to meet their potential new boss is courteous, and their impressions are helpful in making the final selection.

You can't ask an applicant personal questions about his age, religious practice, medical history, marital status, sexual preference, or racial background. You can't ask whether he has been arrested or convicted of a felony without proof of necessity for asking. You also can't ask whether he has children. Nor can you ask about any physical or mental conditions that are unrelated to performing the job. For good information about interviewing and other human resource matters, see HR ProOnline (www.hrproonline.com/ehome.htm).

Taking notes during the interview is acceptable, and you also may find preparing a checklist on which you can rate the applicant in different areas to be helpful. If you do, try to rate the applicants discreetly. Job interviews are stressful enough without letting the applicant know that you rated him a 3 on a scale of 1 to 10.

Digging deeper with references

We assume that no one would include a "bad" letter of recommendation in an application packet, so we don't pay that much attention to prewritten letters of recommendation. We do think that checking references by telephone or even in a personal meeting, if possible, is necessary.

But sometimes even talking to references doesn't provide much useful information. A job applicant wants to put her best face forward, so naturally she chooses people with favorable opinions as references. Also, employment laws are such that speaking to a former employer often yields little more than a confirmation that your applicant was employed between certain dates.

If you have the opportunity to have a good conversation with the candidate's former employer, pay close attention to what they're not saying as well as attending to their description of the candidate's abilities. Some typical questions ask what duties the applicant handled in her previous jobs, what her strengths and weaknesses were on the job, whether the candidate had a positive attitude toward work, and whether or not the reference would rehire the candidate.

We've included a sample reference-checking form — CD0805.

Often, the grapevine is the best way to get information about a candidate. Using the grapevine is easier if the candidate has been working in your community, of course, but even if the applicant hails from another city, you can call other nonprofits to get information. You may be able to find people who have knowledge of the candidate's previous work. (Of course, be wary if you come across an informant who has a personal grudge against the applicant. It's not always easy to know whether this is the case, so don't depend on a single source.)

You can conduct formal background checks of education credentials, criminal history, and other information as long as you get the applicant's permission. If you feel that this type of research is necessary, we suggest hiring a reputable company that specializes in this sort of work.

The degree to which you go to collect information about an applicant depends on the magnitude of the position. If you're hiring someone to lead a large and complex organization, you likely want to dig deeper into a candidate's background than if you're hiring a data entry clerk. We do know of several instances when people were hired for big jobs after less-than-stellar performances in their previous positions. We're not suggesting that people shouldn't be given a second chance; we are saying, however, that you should know as much as possible about an individual's previous job performance before hiring her.

Making your decision

We can't tell you how to make the final decision about whom to hire. You have to weigh qualifications, experience, poise, and desire. These decisions can be difficult, and frankly, you may not be certain that you've made the right choice until the new employee has performed on the job.

If possible, get more than one opinion. If qualifications and experience are equal, intangible factors come more into play. Will the candidate fit well into

Hiring the founder

Many organizations that have the opportunity to hire their first employees skip over the job postings and interviews and hire the obvious person at hand: their founder. After all, the founder had the original idea for the organization and did all the hard work to plan and incorporate it. She may have even read this book! Wouldn't she be the best person for the job?

In many cases the answer is "yes." Founders can make excellent, charismatic nonprofit staff leaders, but that doesn't mean that the board (and the founder) should skip over every step that goes into the hiring of an "outside" person. For example, developing a detailed job description clarifies expectations for everyone involved; and the board, not the founder/employee, should set the salary level. What if the founder doesn't have all the skills required of an executive director? Many founders have strong program skills but haven't previously managed others or done bookkeeping. The board should recognize any shortcomings and work with her to develop a professional development and training plan or to delegate certain roles to a qualified volunteer or consultant.

Sometimes when founders become the directors of nonprofits, the board may be reluctant to

criticize a less than stellar performance in an employee review or to recognize when the organization's needs have outgrown the founder's skills or knowledge. Some founders are great at starting things but less talented as day-to-day managers.

Hiring founders is a tricky arena in nonprofit management. It requires a candid, trusting relationship between the founder and the board. Keep in mind some of the basic principles of board responsibilities and board-staff relations, such as the following:

✔ At their essence, nonprofit organizations don't have owners but rely on the voluntary leadership of their boards. No founder may be treated as if she "owns" the organization.

✔ The board must not abdicate its responsibility to conduct reviews of the founder/director's performance.

✔ The board and founder share responsibilities for decision making — the board at the level of overall direction, planning, and policy, and the founder/director at the level of management and implementation of programs.

the organizational culture? Will the candidate's style of work fit with the organization's management style? Do the applicant's professional goals fit with the organization's goals? If this employee is going to be your first, is the candidate a self-starter type or does he need active supervision to do a good job?

Be cautious when making a personnel decision based on intangible factors. A candidate who's charming may be a treat to have around the office, but that doesn't always mean that he'll do the job well.

Make sure that you document your reasons for making a personnel decision: They should be based primarily on the candidate's performance in previous jobs and experience that's relevant to your position.

Bringing the New Hire Onboard

Much hard work is behind you when you make the hiring decision, but any employee's first days and months are challenging, and you want to give careful attention to helping your new staff member make a good start.

Confirming employment terms in writing

After the new employee accepts the position orally, it's common practice to send a letter to put the details in writing. Enclose a copy of the personnel policies (see the section "Developing your personnel policies," earlier in this chapter) and place a signature line near the lower right corner of the letter so the new hire can acknowledge receipt of the letter and the personnel policies. Ask the employee to return a copy of the signed letter to you, and keep the letter in the employee's personnel file.

The letter should include the employee's starting date, job title, and salary, as well as other information that you agreed to in the prehire discussions held between the organization and the employee. For example, you may include a brief statement about the employee's responsibilities. (We put a sample hire letter on the CD — CD0806 — so that you can get a better idea of what we're talking about.)

Getting your new hire started on the job

In the United States, one of the first things a new employee must do is complete a W-4 form (for income tax withholding) and an I-9 form (to show proof of the employee's legal right to work in the country). These forms are required by law and are available on the IRS Web site (www.irs.gov).

After all the necessary paperwork is out of the way, you need to spend some time getting your new hire acclimated to the working environment. New employees don't begin producing at top form on the first day of work. Absorbing the details of the organization and figuring out the ins and outs of new job duties take time. This fact is particularly true when the person hired is the organization's first employee and has no model to follow.

Whether you're a board member for an organization that's hired its first employee, or the director of an organization bringing someone new onto the staff, here are some ways to ease an employee's transition to a new job:

- ✔ **Provide good working conditions.** You may think that a reminder to purchase the basic furniture and tools someone needs to perform his work is too basic, but we've heard about new employees who didn't even have a desk on their first day.

- ✔ **Show the new person around.** Provide a tour of the office and programs, and introduce him to volunteers and board members. Review office emergency procedures on day one. Oh yeah, and don't forget to show the new employee where the bathroom is!

- ✔ **Give the employee information about the organization.** Make available the organization's files and records. Reading board minutes, newsletters, solicitation letters, donor records, and grant proposals will steep him in the organization's work.

- ✔ **Answer questions.** Encourage new employees to ask questions, and provide the answers as soon as possible. Particularly if he's the organization's one and only employee, board members should check in regularly, making themselves available as resources. Being a one-person staff can be lonely and overwhelming.

- ✔ **Offer special training.** A new employee may need special training — for example, about a computer software program or laws and regulations specific to your nonprofit — in order to perform his job. Sometimes you may have to send the employee to a workshop; other times, he can be trained by a board member, volunteer, or another staff member.

Evaluating your new hire's progress

Most organizations establish a period, usually three to six months, when new employees are "on probation." During this time, new employees learn their jobs, and managers can observe them at their work. Although we don't especially like the term *probationary* because it conjures an image of misbehavior, this period is important for both the new staff person and her manager. Be honest with yourself and the employee. If it becomes apparent that the person can't do the job, making a personnel change during this period is easier than after she becomes a permanent employee.

Be sure you have included an explanation of your probationary period in your personnel policies and that the new employee is aware of the policy.

Conduct a performance evaluation at the end of the probationary period. The evaluation should be written (and added to the employee's personnel file) and discussed in a meeting with the employee. Rating employees on a number scale on various aspects of the job was once the common format. Today, a narrative evaluation that addresses performance in achieving previously agreed upon goals and objectives is much more helpful.

Many employees are happier in their jobs if they have ongoing opportunities to learn new things and develop new skills. An annual employee review is an excellent opportunity to review professional development goals with the employee. It's also a good time to review ways — through workshops, training, or trying on new roles — he may continue to grow in the job.

Managing Employees

Much of this chapter focuses on small organizations that are hiring their first staff members. In these organizations, the board oversees the staff member, and someone taking on the coordinator role — either board or staff — oversees the volunteers.

What if your agency has grown more complex? Everyone needs a boss. In nonprofit organizations, the board assumes that role for the executive director who, in turn, provides supervision to other employees, either directly or through a management team. The common way to visualize these relationships is through an *organizational chart,* a schematic drawing showing the hierarchical management relationships in an organization.

A chart such as the one in Figure 8-1 may be overkill for your nonprofit, especially if you're the only employee, but for larger organizations, charts help to delineate management responsibilities and who reports to whom.

Understanding what a manager does

The responsibility of management to employees includes the following aspects:

- ✔ **Planning:** Planning happens at levels from the board of directors, which carries the responsibility for overall organizational planning, to the custodian, who plans how best to accomplish cleaning and maintenance tasks. It's best if managers work closely with those employees they're managing to develop department and individual goals.

✔ **Leading and motivating:** You may want to add inspiring to this category. We believe that good management grows out of respect and cooperation. Be sure that staff members are familiar with the organization's goals and that they know how their work helps to achieve those goals.

✔ **Gathering tools and resources:** Don't ask someone to dig a hole without giving him a spade. In other words, you can't expect employees to do a good job if they don't have the means to do it. Time, equipment, proper training, and access to information are necessary.

✔ **Problem solving:** This is one of the most important aspects of good management. You can bet that problems will arise as you manage your organization and employees. Be understanding and creative in solving these problems. Ask for help in the form of ideas and suggestions from those employees you supervise.

✔ **Evaluation:** Employees should receive formal evaluations once each year. Effective evaluation begins with goal setting, and you want to help subordinates set clear goals and objectives.

Communicating with your staff

We can't say enough about the importance of good communication. If your nonprofit has only one or two staff members, your job is easier than if you need to communicate with 50 or more employees, but good communication is always important.

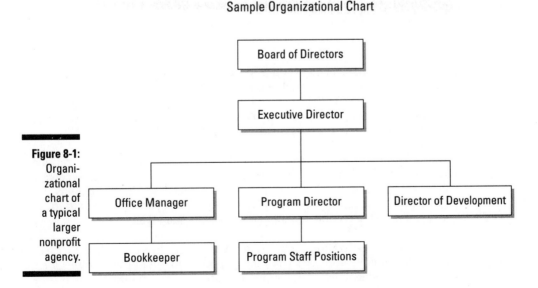

Sample Organizational Chart

Figure 8-1: Organizational chart of a typical larger nonprofit agency.

Of course, confidentiality is important in some matters. For example, if the organization is contemplating a major change, such as a merger with another organization, some information needs to be withheld from the staff. On the other hand, letting rumors circulate about changes that may affect staff can create worse problems than being forthcoming about the details of potential change. Give people as much information as you can, and be sure that they have a chance to tell you how they feel.

Communication is a two-way street. A good manager keeps an open ear and devises ways to ensure that his employees have a way to voice complaints, offer suggestions, and participate in setting goals and objectives.

Holding regular staff meetings

Too many meetings can be a waste of time, but having regularly scheduled staff meetings is a good way to transmit information to employees and give them an opportunity to offer input and feedback and to keep everyone working toward the same goal. Keep these points in mind when arranging staff meetings:

- **Try to schedule the meetings at a specific time on a regular basis.** Hold meetings no more often than once a week and no less often than once a month, depending on the needs of the organization.

- **All meetings should have an agenda.** Nothing is worse than going to a meeting that has no point and no direction.

- **Keep to a schedule.** Unless you have big issues to talk about, one hour is usually long enough to cover everything you need to cover.

- **Provide time on the agenda for feedback.** Be sure that everyone has a chance to speak.

Writing memos to staff

Use memos to introduce new policies and other important information so that you don't have any misunderstandings. By putting the information in writing, you can clearly explain the situation. If the policy is controversial, distribute the memo shortly before a scheduled staff meeting so that employees have an opportunity to respond.

Some larger organizations create a staff newsletter that covers organizational programs and achievements. People sometimes work better if they receive recognition for their work. Stories about client successes, gains made by the organization, and announcements about staff comings and goings help to instill feelings of accomplishment and organizational loyalty.

For very large organizations, a dedicated Web site or intranet that's accessible only to employees can transmit information and offer opportunities for staff to provide feedback and to communicate with one another.

Talking around the water cooler

Although formal written communication is important, nonprofit leaders also need to communicate informally by being accessible to staff in the hallways and around the water cooler. Some people are able to communicate concerns better in an informal setting than in a staff meeting. Managers who sit behind closed doors all the time often have a hard time relating with their staff.

Don't force the camaraderie. Let it develop naturally. Being accessible for informal conversations is the best way to do so.

Getting away for staff retreats

From time to time, especially if the organization is facing big changes, you may want to arrange a half-day or full-day retreat to address issues, do department or organizational planning, or provide specialized training. A retreat needs an agenda that's flexible and developed with the help of participants. Every retreat should have an objective and be led by a competent group facilitator.

Letting a staff member go

Some people enjoy barking, "You're fired!" We don't. We've spent sleepless nights before and after terminating an employee who wasn't right for a job. Although you may not lose sleep over letting an employee go, it's obviously not something to take lightly.

When do you need to consider cutting ties with an employee? Sometimes the employee isn't producing the quality of work required by the job or isn't producing work in a timely manner. Other times the employee may be fired for inappropriate behavior, such as not following your organization's guidelines for appropriate interaction with clients.

If you're a boss and facing the likelihood or need to terminate an employee, we recommend that you

✔ **Review the written personnel policies that you have provided to all employees.** Document in writing the employee's poor performance or inappropriate behavior and make clear the connection between your complaints and those policies.

Many people deserve an opportunity to improve. Sit down with the employee and speak candidly and firmly about the level of improvement or change in behavior that you expect. Set written goals for an improved performance and a date for a follow-up consultation.

> ✔ **Respect the employee's privacy.** Don't share your complaints with others except, if necessary, your board chair.
>
> ✔ **Encourage them to leave as soon as they're terminated and "walk them to the door."** Disgruntled former employees can damage your organization's records and documents in a few days, hours, or even minutes.

Wrongful discharge lawsuits are common and can be very expensive. If you need to terminate an employee and aren't sure how to proceed, consult with a human resources expert or an attorney. The up-front investment may save you much time, expense, and trouble later.

Sometimes organizations have to let employees go because they no longer have sufficient money to pay their salaries. If you're the employee's boss in this situation, try to do the following:

> ✔ **Give them as much warning as possible about the date of their termination.** Don't keep it quiet while pulling out all the stops to raise money to save their positions. Surprising them with the bad news is inconsiderate.
>
> ✔ **Try to plan ahead and provide some severance pay to help them while they seek a new job.** Although you may want to keep them on the job until the last possible minute, good employees deserve good treatment. If they leave your agency with good feelings, you're in a better position to hire them back in the future.
>
> ✔ **Offer to serve as a reference or to write letters of recommendation.** If the money isn't coming in, and you can't find a way to keep the employee on, this gesture is one of the best things you can do.

Using Independent Contractors

Maybe your organization isn't quite ready to take the leap into the employment waters. If work needs to be done that volunteers can't do, working with an *independent contractor* may be a way to accomplish some organizational goals.

According to employment and tax laws in the United States, you can hire people in two ways: as salaried employees or independent contractors. Rarely do you say to yourself, "I need an independent contractor to design my Web page," or "I need an independent contractor to write more grants for us." More commonly used terms are *consultant* or *freelancer,* or titles these specialists use for the jobs that they do. For example, small organizations may contract with an accountant or bookkeeper to maintain financial records and prepare financial reports.

Independent contractors aren't just a resource for small organizations: Large-scale, well-heeled nonprofits also use them. A good organizational consultant, hired as an independent contractor, can bring a fresh perspective to assessing an organization's work, a depth and breadth of experience the organization hasn't yet developed, and focused attention to a project — say the writing of a new strategic plan — that staff can't give while managing day-to-day operations.

Differentiating an independent contractor from an employee

Technical differences between employees and independent contractors are reflected in how you hire, pay, and manage them. Independent contractors are almost always paid a flat fee or hourly rate for their work, ideally on a schedule that's set out in a contract that specifies the work to be done and the fee. Although you don't have to withhold federal and state payroll taxes, you need to file an IRS Form 1099 that records the amount paid over a full year (usually a calendar year) and the contractor's Social Security number or federal tax ID number (EIN).

Proceed with caution, because there's often a thin line between an independent contractor and an employee. Just because someone works a limited number of hours each week doesn't mean that she should be an independent contractor. The IRS doesn't look kindly on trying to pass off employees as independent contractors. Here's a short list of factors that differentiate an independent contractor from an employee:

- ✔ **Independent contractors are just that — independent.** Although setting time parameters for the job is fine, contractors should be free to set their own schedules and work with little direction from the organization. They should provide their own offices and equipment.

- ✔ **If you have to provide extensive training for the contractor to do the job, chances increase that the contractor may be considered an employee.** In hiring an independent contractor, you're supposed to be engaging someone with specific expertise.

- ✔ **If a contractor is working only for your organization and is putting in many hours each week, he may be considered an employee.** If you hire a contractor with the idea that the relationship will continue indefinitely, rather than for a specific project or period; or if that contractor provides services that are a key part of your regular business activity, the IRS believes that you likely have the right to direct and control that worker's activities. To the IRS, this association looks like an employer-employee relationship.

If you think that you may be pushing the envelope on this question, consult an attorney or tax specialist who can give you proper advice. Authorities are giving increasing scrutiny to the distinction between regular employees and independent contractors.

The IRS has defined "Common-Law Rules" for determining whether someone is an employee or an independent contractor. Check the IRS Publication 15A: Employer's Supplemental Tax Guide for definition of these rules. The publication is available on the IRS Web site at www.irs.gov.

If you want to hire someone for a short-term assignment or a limited number of hours but if the work is taking place in your offices, using your equipment, and requiring your regular supervision, consider using a temporary employment agency. The agency handles the employee's benefits, including their employment taxes, and re-assigns the employee if he's a poor fit for the job. Although using a temp agency may cost more than hiring the person directly, the agency can help you find someone who is qualified.

What can an independent contractor do for you?

Independent contractors can help you with just about any aspect of your organization, from personnel matters to hooking up a computer network. But nonprofits most commonly bring them in to help out with

- ✔ **Fundraising.** Fundraising consultants help with grant writing, planning for fundraising, special events, direct mail, and major gift and capital campaigns, among other methods of raising funds.

- ✔ **Organizational development.** Organization development consultants may guide your board and staff through a planning process or help you develop tools needed to evaluate your organization's work to name just two examples.

- ✔ **Marketing and public relations.** Consultants can help you spread the word about your organization's good work by handling a public relations campaign directed at the media, developing your Web site, creating compelling brochures and newsletters, creating short promotional films, and many other strategies.

- ✔ **Evaluation and assessment.** Evaluators can take an in-depth look at an organization's programs, bringing specialized skills to that assessment and the value of an unbiased point of view.

Have a clear idea of what you want to accomplish before you seek help. Sometimes you don't know exactly what you're aiming to accomplish, but you should still try to articulate as clearly as possible what your aim is in hiring a consultant before you go looking for one.

Grant writers won't do it all for you

Don't expect a hired grant writer to solve all your funding problems. Hiring grant writers is fine, but understand that they need to work with your programs, financial statements, brochures, and so on. Grant proposals are really a group production; they depend on input from program and management staff, among others. And although a well-written grant proposal is important, writing alone won't nail down the grant. You need to have a solid program or project, a well-thought-out argument for why it deserves funding, and a solid financial plan.

Organizational consultants can't solve all your problems; they don't carry magic beans in their pockets. They make recommendations, but quite likely it's going to be up to you to carry them out and push your agency forward.

Finding a consultant: Ask around

We don't have a single best way to find consultants. You can certainly look in your local yellow pages or search the Web for nonprofit consultants who work in your area, but we think that the best way is to use word of mouth, if possible. A few calls to other nearby nonprofits may provide some leads. You also may be able to find a consultant through a nonprofit support organization. For example, the Alliance for Nonprofit Management also maintains a national database of nonprofit consultants at www.allianceonline.org.

We prefer consultants who have more than one way of doing things. Not all nonprofits are alike, and what works for one may not work for another. Some consultants have either accepted a particular school of thought or have developed their own tried-and-true methods. Be cautious when a consultant tells you that there's only one way to do something. Also, as your project evolves, you may find that you need a different kind of help than you originally imagined. Believe us, these kinds of things happen all the time. Ask the consultant whether she's willing to consider revisiting the project goals along the way and adjusting her approach if the need arises.

Some consultants work as sole practitioners; others work in consulting companies. Working with a company or consulting group may give you access to more varied expertise. On the other hand, consultants working alone tend to have lower overhead expenses so their fees may (and we stress *may*) be lower.

Interviewing consultants

Interviewing a consultant is similar to interviewing a regular job applicant. You want to review the resume carefully to see whether the candidate's experience and expertise match your needs. Don't be intimidated just because the person sitting across the table from you has more experience than you do. She'll be working for you. Ask any questions that you feel are necessary so that you can be sure you've chosen the right person.

Interview more than one person before you make your decision. As with interviewing for staff positions, having more than one person present at the interview is important because it lets you see how the prospective consultant interacts with a small group and gives you multiple perspectives on the consultant.

You may have the opportunity to use a volunteer consultant provided by a program that provides free or low-cost assistance to nonprofits. Interview these individuals just as you would a paid consultant. Remember that you'll be investing time in working with this person and you need to be certain that she's right for your organization.

Ask interviewees to describe their method or approach to the problem or project that you're seeking to solve or complete. Don't expect them to give you a full-blown plan in the interview, but they should be able to give you a good picture of how they plan to approach the issue. Also, if your project culminates with a written report, ask the applicant for writing samples.

Don't expect a consultant to solve your problem before you enter into a contract. Although finding out whether the consultant has the ability to do the job is important, expecting him to give you all the answers before you agree to pay for the work is unreasonable.

Signing the contract

You need to have a signed contract with every consultant with whom you work. These points should be clearly stated in the contract:

  ✔ **The scope of work and expected results.** You can include more or less detail here depending on the type of project the consultant is performing. If you're hiring the consultant to facilitate a one-day retreat for your board of directors, be sure that the contract includes the preparation time needed. Also, will the consultant be writing a report following the retreat? Try to touch on as many details as possible. The more specific, the better. Sometimes if the scope of work is very detailed, that detail is included as an attachment to the main part of the contract.

✔ **Fees, of course.** Some consultants charge an hourly rate plus expenses; others charge a flat rate that may or may not include expenses per project. The contract should state that you must approve expenses over a certain amount. Or you can write into the agreement that expenses are limited to a certain sum each month. Consultant fees vary, just like salaries, from one geographic area to another and depend on the type of work to be done and the experience of the consultant.

We don't recommend paying fundraising consultants a percentage of money raised. Although some consultants, grant writers, and, in particular, telemarketers work under this arrangement, percentage payment isn't considered good practice by most fundraisers and nonprofit managers. See the Association of Fundraising Professional's Code of Ethics for more information about this issue; read the "Ethics" page at www.afpnet.org.

✔ **The schedule of when you'll pay the fees.** Some consultants who work on an hourly basis may send you an invoice at the end of the month. Consultants working on a flat-fee basis may require advance payment on a portion of the fee. This is fine. It's protection for the consultant, who probably has as many cash-flow problems as you do. The final payment shouldn't come before the project is completed. Be sure to ask the consultant for an estimate of their out-of-pocket expenses and how they plan to bill you for such costs.

✔ **Special contingencies.** What if the consultant gets sick? What if your organization faces an unforeseen crisis and you don't have time to work with the consultant? What if you've chosen the wrong consultant? You should include a mutually agreed-upon way to end the contract before the project is completed. A 30-day cancellation notice is common.

✔ **A timetable for completing the work.** You and the consultant need to negotiate the timetable. Have you ever had remodeling work done on your house? You know that contractors can get distracted by other work, right? That's why having a schedule is so important.

✔ **The organization's role in the project.** If the consultant needs access to background materials, records, volunteers, board members, or staff, you must provide this access in a timely manner so that the consultant can complete the job on schedule.

✔ **Required insurance.** What if your consultant injures someone in the course of working on your project? If she's not insured, the liability could become your organization's responsibility. Just to be on the safe side, many consultant contracts include standard language about the consultant's responsibility to carry liability insurance and to pay workers' compensation insurance and other legally required benefits if they have employees who will be working on your project.

✔ **Ownership of the finished product.** This point doesn't apply to every consulting project, but if yours focuses on developing a study or a report, specify in the contract whether your organization, the consultant, or both have the rights to distribute, quote, and otherwise make use of the results. Often the organization has the right to publish and produce the report if it gives proper credit to the author, and the consultant owns the copyright and has permission to make use of lessons learned in articles or future studies. Sometimes you agree to seek approval from one another before using the work. Think this through carefully. What if, for example, you hire a consultant to produce a candid study of a project that isn't going well? Does your organization want something highly critical to show up on the consultant's Web site?

Don't assume that because your organization has paid for a writing project, it will own the copyright on the finished product. See `http://copylaw.com/new_articles/wfh.html` for a guide to current copyright laws.

We think having the consultant prepare the contract is a good idea. It's the final chance to make sure that he understands what you want done. You may suggest changes when you see the first draft.

Chapter 9

Planning: Why and How Nonprofits Make Plans

*T*he word *planning* can be intimidating. It brings up images of daylong meetings in stuffy conference rooms with outside experts wielding marker pens. Of course, not all planning takes that sort of effort — perfectly good plans can be made with a pencil on the back of an envelope, or even just imagined in your head. People make plans all the time, from organizing a vacation to deciding how to get all the errands done on a Saturday afternoon.

Organization planning, however, requires more effort. It's a group project that calls for research, brainstorming, discussion, and, in the end, agreement on a goal and the strategies and tactics needed to reach that goal. Simply put, organizational planning is deciding where to go and how to get there. The planning process helps to ensure that everyone is headed in the same direction.

In this chapter, we cover planning for nonprofit organizations in all its forms, from strategic plans to program plans to work plans. Plan to join us!

Why Spend Valuable Time Planning?

No organization has unlimited funds. Even the largest, wealthiest nonprofit needs to decide how to allocate its resources effectively. Planning helps you make decisions about how to spend your organization's money by answering questions such as "Is now the best time to invest in a new program?" and "Is it better to hire another staff person for the fundraising department, or should we hire a consultant?"

A nonprofit organization undertakes planning for the following reasons:

✔ To create a <u>structure</u> that guides its activities in pursuit of its mission.

✔ To allocate organizational <u>resources</u> in the most effective way.

✔ To create a <u>framework</u> against which the organization's <u>performance</u> can be evaluated.

✔ To reach agreement among board, staff, and supporters on desirable <u>goals</u> for the organization.

Think of a plan as a <u>blueprint</u> or scheme describing what needs to be done to accomplish an end. In an ideal world, if your organization completes every step of its plan, you achieve your goals.

The _act_ of <u>planning is equally important</u> as the final plan itself because, in theory, the planning group's decision-making process ensures that everyone understands what needs to be done and agrees that it's worth doing.

Making Your Organizational Plan

Organizational planning is what people usually think about when they think about planning. Many funders, for example, ask whether you have a long-range or strategic plan, and some ask you to include it with your proposals. <u>An organizational plan, usually covering a three- to five-year period</u>, sets <u>goals for the organization and describes the objectives that must be accomplished to achieve those goals.</u>

The steps for successful organizational planning are as follows:

1. **Decide whether it's the right time to plan.**

2. **Look at your mission.**

3. **Assess the external and internal situation.**

4. **Hear from stakeholders.**

5. **Make decisions.**

6. **Write the plan.**

Planning is an ongoing activity. A formal effort to develop a long-range or strategic plan may occur only once every three to five years, but planning for the purposes of accomplishing objectives, creating a budget, and developing fundraising programs goes on all the time.

Getting ready

Make no mistake: A full-bore, all-out organizational planning effort requires considerable time, energy, and commitment from everyone involved. Some nonprofits spend a year or more developing an organizational plan.

Don't jump into the process without understanding that it will add to your workload and complicate your life for a period of time. Also, you can't plan by yourself. If you're the executive director of a nonprofit organization who thinks that planning is needed, but the board of directors doesn't agree with your assessment, don't try to start the process on your own. Take a couple of steps backward and begin the work of persuading board members that planning is worth the effort.

Don't start the planning process if your nonprofit is in a crisis mode. It's tempting, for example, to launch a strategic planning effort if you just lost a major source of funding. But you have more immediate concerns to deal with in that situation. Delay organizational planning until you see a period of smooth sailing.

If you have the support, and foreclosure isn't hanging over your agency's head, the best way to get started is to form a planning committee. This small group of board members, staff, and one or two outside people can take on the role of guiding the planning process and, in the beginning, pull together the facts and observations that you need to make your planning decisions.

Working from your organization's mission

Reviewing the organization's mission statement is one of the first tasks facing an organization beginning the long-range planning process. (Chapter 3 covers mission statements.) Ask yourself these questions:

✔ Is the problem we set out to solve still a problem?

✔ Can we fine-tune the mission statement to make it more specific, or is the mission statement too specific?

✔ Does the mission statement contain enough flexibility to allow the organization to grow?

Keep your mission statement in mind throughout the planning process. At every turn, ask yourself: "If we do this, will we be true to our mission?" "Will this new program we're considering help us accomplish what we want to do?"

Assessing the external situation

Early in the long-range planning process you need to collect information about external factors that influence the nonprofit's operation. Someone, or a subcommittee of the planning committee, should find the answers to the following questions and distribute them to everyone on the committee before the formal planning meetings begin:

✔ Are other nonprofits providing similar services in the community? If so, how are our services different?

✔ What are the demographic trends in our area? Will they have an impact on the number of people who may need or use our services?

✔ What are the trends in the professional area in which our nonprofit operates? Are new methods being developed? Will there be a shortage of professionally trained staff?

✔ How stable are the funding sources on which we depend? What about changes in government funding? Can we find new potential sources of funding?

The decisions you make are only as good as the information on which you base them. Therefore, it's important to find the best and most up-to-date data available that may have an impact on your organization and its programs.

You may want to collect information from the general public or a particular constituency of your nonprofit. Questionnaires and focus groups are two ways to get input from the public. Before you undertake either of these techniques, however, spend some time thinking about what you want to find out. Write a list of questions for which you want answers.

If possible, consult with someone experienced in preparing surveys, because the phrasing of questions affects the answers you get. Look for expertise in this area at local colleges and universities. If you can't get expert help in this area, consider doing a series of one-on-one interviews with fewer people.

Bad information leads to bad decisions. Or, put another way, garbage in, garbage out. So, when gathering background information to guide planning decisions, take the time to get the most accurate, up-to-date facts available.

Assessing the internal situation

In addition to surveying the environment in which the organization operates, you need to expend some effort assessing the organization itself. Consider the following factors when doing an internal analysis:

- ✔ Is the board of directors fully engaged with organization? Should any weaknesses on the board be filled? Is the board engaged in fundraising?

- ✔ What are the capabilities of the staff? Does the organization have enough staff to implement changes in how it operates? Is staff training needed?

- ✔ What are the organization's major accomplishments? What are its milestones?

- ✔ Has the organization operated within its budget? Is financial reporting adequate? Are appropriate financial controls in place?

- ✔ Does the organization have adequate technology? What are its future equipment needs?

- ✔ Does the organization have a variety of funding sources? Are funding sources stable?

Hearing from all your stakeholders

Unless you have a very small organization, you probably can't include every single person in the planning process. You do need to include all stakeholder groups, however. A *stakeholder* is someone who has a reason for wanting the organization to succeed. Paid employees and, presumably, members of the board certainly qualify. But although these two groups may be the most closely connected to the nonprofit, they're by no means the only people who have a stake in the organization's success.

In our view, you should include all the following groups in planning:

- ✔ Board of directors
- ✔ Staff
- ✔ Users of services
- ✔ Volunteers

> ✔ Donors
> ✔ Community leaders

Some organizations make the mistake of leaving planning only to the board of directors. Although the board does hold the final responsibility for guiding a nonprofit, the staff, clients, and donors have different perspectives on the nonprofit's operation that should be included when considering the organization's future.

If you don't have a client representative on the board (and you probably should), organize a client advisory committee and empower the members to appoint one or two people to the planning committee. The same holds true for staff. Although we don't recommend that paid staff members serve on the board of the nonprofit that employs them, they should be involved in the planning process. Staff members often have information about the organization and the environment in which it operates that's crucial to the making of a good plan.

Check out the sample planning retreat agenda (CD0901) for some guidance in organizing your planning retreat.

One purpose of organizational planning is to bring stakeholders together in pursuit of a common goal. People work harder to achieve the goals when they're asked to help set the goals.

Studying your organization's pros and cons

Be objective when looking at the pros and cons of your organization. It's tempting, for example, to put the best face on the activities of the board of directors. They're volunteers, after all. How much time do they really have to govern the organization? But if you don't identify important deficiencies because you don't want to hurt someone's feelings, your planning efforts will be handicapped by bad information.

The same advice holds true when evaluating staff strengths and weaknesses, and when assessing your external situation. For example, pointing out that the executive director needs more training in staff supervision may not be easy, but if you aren't honest, you can't identify problems, and positive change can't occur.

Guard against bias. Sometimes people get so close to the situation they're evaluating that they can't see the true picture with an objective eye. Include outside people who have no history with the organization and have no personal stake in the outcome.

Also, don't assume that all the people you interview know what they're talking about. Accepting statements without verification can lead to bad decisions. For example, if someone says that getting a grant to pay the costs of a program start-up is a piece of cake, check with potential funders before you agree that it's an easy task.

Yes, honesty can create conflict. Be prepared for it. Set some rules when going into planning meetings. Make sure that all the participants have a chance to state their case. Demand that all the participants show respect for one another. Arguments can be productive if they don't disintegrate into shouting matches. Always place the emphasis on the organization, not on personalities.

Calling in the SWOT team

One common way to analyze the information you've collected is to perform a SWOT analysis. *SWOT* is an acronym for Strengths-Weaknesses-Opportunities-Threats. SWOT analysis is usually done in a facilitated meeting in which the participants have agreed upon ground rules. If you prefer, however, stake-holders can complete their version of the analysis individually and then come together to discuss the results as a group.

For example, the results of a SWOT analysis for an organization providing counseling services to families may look something like the following:

Strengths

- ✔ The program staff is highly qualified and committed.
- ✔ Clients rate the program services as high quality.
- ✔ The organization has a surplus equal to approximately three months of operating expenses.
- ✔ Program costs are largely funded by government grants.

Weaknesses

- ✔ The cost per client is higher than in similar programs.
- ✔ Most revenues are from government sources; contributed income is low.
- ✔ The programs aren't well known in the general public.

Opportunities

- ✔ Population trend predictions indicate that the client base will increase over the next ten years.
- ✔ Review of news coverage suggests that the media are showing increasing interest in covering issues important to nonprofit organizations.
- ✔ The organization has cash reserves to invest in growth.

Threats

- ✔ Local government (the primary funding source) will face a budget deficit during the next fiscal year.
- ✔ Over the past five years, program costs have increased at a rate of 3 percent a year.

A review of this SWOT analysis reveals an organization that has been successful in providing quality services and getting those services funded by government contracts. However, the responses also make it clear that the program's future may be in jeopardy if organizational change doesn't take place. Depending on a single source of income for most costs is troublesome, especially because the funding entity apparently needs to make budget cuts in the next few years. Even if the program continues to be funded by government, cost-of-living increases may cease because of tight financial needs. Over time, as program costs increase and funding remains stagnant, the organization runs a risk of not being able to get reimbursed for the full costs of its programs.

On the positive side, this organization has time and resources to begin to diversify revenues. Little effort has been made to interest donors in supporting the organization's work; in fact, the programs are more or less invisible in the community. One strategy to increase revenue is to develop an annual campaign led by the board of directors and, at the same time, to work toward getting coverage of the nonprofit's programs in the local media.

As this example shows, one or more items often can be listed as both a strength and a weakness. Here, for instance, you see the fact that programs are largely funded by the government as a strength, but it's also a weakness because it has created a situation in which the organization relies on a single source of funding.

Pulling it all together

After the research, analysis, and discussion, it's time to determine future directions and put the results into a final plan. Ideally, the plans of the organization will become apparent after sifting through and discussing the material assembled. If the planning group can't reach a consensus, more discussion (and perhaps more data) is needed.

We recommend using a professional meeting facilitator. A facilitator brings a neutral viewpoint to the proceedings and can be very effective in helping a group arrive at a consensus about organizational goals.

Making sure your goals make sense

Organization goals need to be specific, measurable, and attainable within a set period of time. Don't set a goal like "In five years, the XYZ Tutoring Project will be the best tutoring program west of the Mississippi." You have no way to evaluate whether the organization is the best tutoring program west of the Mississippi, and even if you could determine the "best" program, the goal is so general and vague that you can't set objectives to achieve it.

Instead, an organizational goal for this program may be something like, "In five years, the XYZ Tutoring Project will provide tutoring services that are recognized by classroom teachers as effective in improving student performance." This goal can be measured. It's also attainable through implementing a series of strategies that may include better training for tutors, improved communication with classroom teachers to determine student needs, acquisition of computers to aid in tutoring sessions, and so on.

Itemizing the parts that form your plan

When you reach a consensus about your organization's goals, assemble a written plan. The components of the plan include the following items:

- ✔ An executive summary
- ✔ A statement of the organizational mission (and vision and values statements if you have them)
- ✔ A description of the planning process, including the groups represented
- ✔ Organizational goals
- ✔ Strategies to achieve those goals
- ✔ Appendixes that contain summaries of the background material used to determine the plan

Have a look at the sample outline for writing an organization plan (CD0902) for some help in getting started.

Assign the task of drafting the document to your best writer. When he finishes the draft, the planning committee should review it to ensure that the plan is stated clearly. Submit the final draft to the full board for approval.

Don't chisel your plan in stone

Although having a plan is important, flexibility in its implementation is just as important. Things change. Reviewing your plan is an ongoing activity; probably

Clear and simple language is your friend

A common failing of planning documents (and grant proposals, for that matter) is the use of jargon and vague language. An organizational plan that uses such wording and lacks clarity does nothing to increase your credibility with your constituents or your funders. You don't want readers to ask, "What is it that they're going to do?"

If you have a choice between a five-syllable word and a one-syllable word, choose the one-syllable word. Don't try to impress people with your vocabulary. Clear, simple language is better than complex language.

Monitor your use of jargon. People working in a particular field or area develop special meanings for words that their colleagues understand. In a way, these words are a sort of shorthand that makes communication easier and faster. But avoid using these "professional" terms when writing a document for general consumption. If you have no other alternative, be sure to define all terms.

once a year, you should submit your organizational plan to a formal review by the stakeholders who developed it.

Your plan should be flexible. For example, suppose that your organization has decided through the planning process to begin offering after-school tutoring services but later discovers that another agency plans to do the same thing. In that case, don't move ahead until you consider the consequences of entering into competition with another nonprofit. If you face this situation, we recommend talking with the other nonprofit to find a common solution. Maybe a joint program is called for, or maybe you find that the other group is in a better position to offer the program. Don't force your decisions. If circumstances change, change your plans.

Putting Plans into Action

Unfortunately, too many well-crafted plans end up in a drawer or on a bookshelf. Participants may have expended great effort to create the document, and board and staff may have formed close bonds during the planning process. But if the decisions made during that wonderful board/staff retreat at the charming lakeside inn aren't translated into goals, objectives, and outcomes, what's the point besides camaraderie?

No matter what sort of plan you create — organizational, fund-raising, marketing, program, or a plan to help an employee structure his work — you need to break the larger, all-encompassing goals into smaller pieces so you can achieve your goals one step at a time.

Defining and setting goals, strategies, objectives, and outcomes

Getting lost in all the terminology is easy. Goals, strategies, and objectives have been a part of planning for many years. Only in the past ten years or so have planning specialists put more emphasis on outcomes.

Here are brief definitions of the four terms:

✔ *Goals* are things your organization hopes to achieve. Goals can be set at the organizational level, the program or department level, or the individual employee level. Using a road trip as an analogy, a goal is traveling from Chicago to New York.

✔ *Strategies* are approaches or ways to achieve goals. Usually, more than one option exists. You can travel to New York by several methods: plane, train, automobile, or on foot. After considering the costs, your schedule, and your hiking ability, you decide to travel by car.

✔ *Objectives* are smaller steps that one must accomplish to reach a goal, and they're always stated in a way that can be measured. So on a trip from Chicago to New York, an objective may be to drive 325 miles on the first day. When you pull into the motel parking lot, you can check your odometer to see whether you've achieved your objective for the day.

✔ *Outcomes* describe the result of reaching a goal. In the example of driving from Chicago to New York, the outcome is clear — you're in New York, not Chicago. Like objectives, outcomes should be measurable or in some way testable. In New York, you look out the hotel window and see the Chrysler Building. Yep, you're in New York.

To see how all four terms come into play, look at the example of a plan in Table 9-1. Reading from top to bottom, you have the whole plan, from organizational goal to outcome.

Table 9-1	Organizational Goal to Outcome
What We Call It	*What It Is*
Organizational goal	Diversify income
Strategy	Increase individual contributed income
Strategic goal	Develop annual campaign
Objective 1	Compile prospect list

(continued)

Table 9-1 *(continued)*	
What We Call It	*What It Is*
Objective 2	Create appeal letter
Objective 3	Mail appeal letter
Outcome	Organization is less dependent on a single funder

Don't get bogged down in terms. How you label the different steps in the planning process doesn't really matter all that much. The important thing is to understand that goals, strategies, objectives, and outcomes are a good way of talking about what you're trying to accomplish and how you're going to do it.

Creating a work plan

You can see in Table 9-1 that the objectives are still general. You can add a way of measuring them by stating how many prospects you want to acquire, how much the appeal costs to produce, and how many appeal letters you plan to mail. But each objective in Table 9-1 requires several steps. Here's where *work plans* come into play. Work plans break tasks into small steps so they can be easily managed.

Work plans grow out of organizational and program goals and are the nuts and bolts of planning. They're also called *action plans.* They contain specific objectives associated with a deadline for completion and a notation as to who's responsible for completing the task.

Sometimes grant proposals, especially proposals for government funds, require specific objectives described in a work plan. Individual employees also can develop work plans, either at their supervisor's request or simply as an exercise to help the employees organize their work. People also use work plans to deal with an organizational crisis or rapid organizational change. They can also use them as management tools.

Think of a work plan as a blueprint. It provides a way to keep on top of what has to be done and when it needs to be completed. An action plan contains the answers to the following questions for each objective:

- ✔ What is the end result? (If possible, quantify the results. For example, three grant proposals will be submitted.)
- ✔ How long will it take to do the job?
- ✔ Who will be responsible for doing the job?
- ✔ What resources are needed?

A typical work plan may look like Table 9-2.

Table 9-2	Sample Work Plan			
Objective	*By When*	*By Whom*	*Resources Needed*	*Date Completed*
Research three potential foundation funders	April 30, 2007	Allen	Foundation directory, Web search	April 28, 2007
Prepare three grant proposals	July 30, 2007	Allen	Program objectives, budgets	July 21, 2007
Follow up on proposals	September 15, 2007	Allen	None	September 10, 2007

Work plans require that a job be broken down into smaller tasks. In Table 9-2, for example, the three objectives can be split into even smaller tasks. The objective to complete three grant proposals can be divided into the individual steps for writing a grant (covered in Chapter 17):

✔ Assembling background information and support materials

✔ Developing the budget

✔ Writing the first draft

✔ Revising and rewriting

✔ Proofing and assembling the proposal

✔ Submitting the proposal by the deadline

Be aware that you can take the creation of a work plan to a point of absurdity. For example, you can split the job of submitting a proposal into even smaller steps, such as finding the envelope, affixing proper postage, walking to the post office, and dropping the envelope in the mail slot. You see what we mean. Don't make work plans so detailed and specific that writing the plan takes more time than doing the work the plan specifies.

Planning for Programs

Program planning is such an important part of nonprofit work that we think it needs its own section. Nearly all nonprofit organizations provide a service of one sort or another. The organization provides services through programs.

A small nonprofit may have only one. Larger nonprofits may have dozens. No matter how many programs you have, you may be thinking of adding a new one or changing the ones you have.

Assessing needs

A needs assessment is an important part of program planning. If you're thinking of starting a new program, for example, a needs assessment to determine whether the program is necessary should probably be the first step you take.

A *needs assessment* is more or less a research project. You don't necessarily need to hold to the strict requirements of scientific inquiry, but just as you do when collecting information to help guide organizational planning, you should do everything possible to ensure that the information is accurate and free of bias.

Determining the questions to be answered

You probably already have a general idea of what you need to find out in your needs assessment. The most basic question is whether the program is needed. But in order to answer that question, a needs assessment should evaluate the answers to the following questions:

- ✔ **Are other programs providing the same service?** Obviously, you don't want to duplicate services if another organization is already doing the job. If you believe that your competition isn't doing a good job, that's another question. Jump to the second point.

- ✔ **How many people might use the service?** Getting a good estimate of the number of people the new program will serve is important. Doing so helps you justify establishing the program and helps you to plan for staff needs.

- ✔ **Can and will people pay for the service?** If so, how much? This question brings us to how to fund the program. Can you expect 25 percent of your clients to pay the full fees for the service; 25 percent to pay 75 percent; 25 percent to pay 50 percent; and 25 percent to need full subsidies?

- ✔ **Do any special requirements for providing the program exist?** Does it need to be near good public transportation? Is parking important? Will people come to the neighborhood where you're providing the services?

- ✔ **What are the trends?** Will the number of people using the service increase or decrease in the future? Is the population in your community increasing, decreasing, or staying the same? If you begin with 25 clients, how many clients do you expect to have in three years?

Finding the right data

Just as when you collect information for organizational planning, your goal is to get the most accurate, unbiased data available. Don't depend on only one source of information. Here are some ways to get it:

- ✔ **Talk to colleagues in your community.** Ideally, you have relationships with the people and organizations that provide similar services. Ask their opinions about your ideas for new programming.

- ✔ **Look at census data.** The best sources for population information are the numbers collected through a census (`www.census.gov`). Some municipal and regional planning groups also publish population growth projections. These projections are estimates, but census data doesn't represent an absolutely accurate count of the people in your community, either. Get all the numbers you can get.

- ✔ **Get information from potential users of the service by distributing questionnaires and holding focus groups.** The questions you ask in large part determine the answers you get. If possible, find someone who has experience in preparing survey questions to give you a hand.

- ✔ **Look at similar programs in other communities.** Although you can't always depend on the experience of others fitting exactly with your particular situation, examining what others have done is always wise.

We've put together a needs assessment questionnaire (CD0903) as an example of a simple survey.

Some people say that they don't want to share an idea with others because they're afraid someone may steal it. Although you can't rule out the chances of this happening, we believe that it's a rare occurrence. In almost all cases, being open about your plans is a good idea.

Going beyond the needs assessment

Just because a new program is needed doesn't necessarily mean that your organization should be the one to start it. You need to take other factors into account before taking the leap into starting a new program. Consider the factors in the following sections when assessing your ability to start a new program.

Paying attention to the budget

A new program is almost always going to add expenses to your organizational budget. If we thought about it long enough, we could think of an example in which increased program costs aren't a factor, but we don't have all year. To

Expanding the Elmwood Tutoring Project

Consider the case of the imaginary Elmwood Saturday Morning Tutoring Project, a five-year-old volunteer tutoring program serving 50 children ages 8 to 14. Volunteers tutor children in 30-minute sessions. Supervised activities and refreshments are available from 9 until noon on Saturdays during the school year. The program has one paid staff person: a volunteer coordinator and trainer who sometimes writes grant proposals. A board member does the bookkeeping. Eight members of the 12-member board also volunteer as tutors. The nonprofit doesn't charge fees to families. The $75,000 annual budget covers the costs of the single staff person's salary, supplies and refreshments, and insurance. Elmwood receives grants of $25,000 a year from the school district and $30,000 from the city. The organization raises the remaining $20,000 from small foundation grants and contributions from board members, volunteers, and parents. The program takes place in the Methodist church basement, the use of which is donated to the program.

The Elmwood board of directors is considering expanding its programs to offer after-school tutoring one afternoon per week from 3:30 to 5:30 p.m. The directors decide that the following questions need to be answered:

✔ Do parents express interest in additional tutoring and activities for their children? If so, how many? Are parents able and willing to provide transportation to and from the tutoring program on a weekday afternoon? Do they prefer a day of the week?

✔ What are the enrollment trends of the school district? Is the number of students increasing or decreasing? If so, at what rate?

✔ Are other organizations, or is the school district itself, considering establishing an after-school tutoring program?

✔ Will volunteer tutors be willing to increase their time commitment to provide tutoring in the afternoon program? Are other members of the community willing to become tutors?

✔ Will the church basement be available during this time?

✔ How much additional administrative work will the new program require?

✔ Will funders support the program's expansion by increasing their financial support?

Not all these questions require a needs assessment, of course. For example, discovering whether the church basement is available is probably a simple matter of a single phone call. The Elmwood board president can speak to the school district and city government about the chances of increased funding. Additional scheduling and volunteer training will be needed. Elmwood determines that enough additional work will be created to warrant the hiring of one half-time assistant for the volunteer coordinator and trainer. Hiring an additional staff person will slightly increase the bookkeeping needed.

The other questions, however, should be addressed by completing a needs assessment. Elmwood decides to go about it this way:

✔ Elmwood receives permission from the school district to mail a questionnaire to parents of third through seventh graders. The questionnaire begins with a short description of the proposed program and questions about interest, time, and transportation. Volunteers also pass out questionnaires to parents whose children are enrolled in the Saturday program. Elmwood board members who serve as tutors discuss the proposed program with parents who use the Saturday morning program.

✔ Elmwood acquires population trend projections for the next ten years for the community from the city government. It secures school district projections from the principal's office.

✔ Elmwood board members make contacts with social service agencies in the community to determine whether a similar program is being considered.

✔ Elmwood polls tutors about their interest and availability for an afternoon program.

Through these activities, Elmwood discovers that parents are interested in the program. By comparing the results of the returned questionnaires and discussions with parents, it's estimated that an average of 30 children may be enrolled in a program on Tuesday afternoons. Parents can provide transportation to and from the program, and the church basement is available. Both the school district and the city indicate that additional funding is a possibility, and the school population is projected to increase slowly but steadily over the next ten years. No other agencies are planning to start tutoring programs.

So far, so good. Parents and the school district appear to be interested. Increased funding is a definite possibility, and space is available.

One problem, however, arises. Only two volunteer tutors are available on Tuesday afternoons from 3:30 to 5:30. Other volunteers have either work or family commitments that don't allow them to add time to their volunteer activities.

Elmwood needs to secure more tutors before the program can proceed. Before Elmwood commits to the program, it has a local radio station air public service announcements calling for volunteer tutors. A short feature article about Elmwood appears in the local newspaper. It also sends out a call for more volunteers. Within a week, Elmwood has received 20 phone calls from people expressing interest in volunteering for the project. Elmwood assumes that if half these people actually become tutors, it will have sufficient volunteers to carry out the new program.

Voilà! The pieces have fallen into place. Perhaps a bit too neatly for the real world, but you get the idea.

---

be sure that you don't get yourself into a financial hole, carefully project the extra costs you'll have from additional staff, increased space, equipment, and insurance.

After you have solid expense projections, you have to project where you're going to find the added revenue needed to pay these costs. If you're sitting on a surplus, be careful about tapping into this money for new program expenses. Program expenses recur every year; your surplus funds may not be there next year.

Evaluating organizational and staff capability

Does your organization have the knowledge and expertise to provide the program services? This question may not be a concern if the proposed program is merely an extension of what you've been doing. If your organization is branching out into new areas, however, be sure that you or someone in the organization has the credentials to provide a quality program.

Also pay attention to hidden staff costs. For example, consider whether your current program director will have sufficient time to provide adequate supervision for the new program.

Remembering special requirements

Check whether you need additional licensing or accreditation to provide the program. This issue is especially important for human services programs. For example, if you've been working with teenagers and want to expand to elementary and preschool children, find out whether your program space must meet additional code requirements in order to serve a younger client group.

Arts organizations also should be aware that adding new programs can create problems with building codes. For example, suppose you have a visual arts gallery that typically serves no more than ten people at a time. If you decide to hold poetry readings every Tuesday night and expect audiences of 50 or more, your building may not have enough exits.

Fitting it into the mission

From time to time, we're all tempted by the idea of doing something new. Gee, wouldn't it be nice if we could sell goldfish in the front lobby? But you have to ask yourself what selling goldfish has to do with your organization's mission. If you go too far afield, you'll be exploring unknown territory.

You can change your mission, of course, but you shouldn't do so without considerable thought. Altering a mission statement just to justify a new program probably isn't reason enough to do so.

Thinking long term

An idea that looks good today may not look good next year or the year after. Don't forget that costs rise year after year. Your staff appreciates raises occasionally, and the overall cost of doing business increases. Try to imagine where the program will be five and ten years into the future.

Doing program planning as a team

As with organizational planning, program planning should be done as a group exercise. It doesn't have to be as extensive as the organizational planning process, but you get more acceptance of the new program and guard against omitting important details when you work with others to develop new programs.

To explain your program, take a tip from the business sector

If you were starting a new business and looking for investors, one of the first things you'd do is create a business plan. Nonprofits are wise to follow this model when developing a new program. A business model is useful in explaining the program and can form the basics of grant proposals when you seek funding.

Business plans should include the following information:

✔ An executive summary that covers the main points of the plan.

✔ An explanation of the need for the program and who will use it. (This information is comparable to the market analysis in a for-profit business plan.)

✔ A description of the program and your strategies for implementing it.

✔ Resumes and background information about the people who will provide and manage the program services.

✔ Three-year projections of income and expenses for the project, including an organizational budget for the current year.

Hindsight: Evaluating How You Did

Planning helps you move toward the future in an orderly fashion, but the goals and objectives that result from the planning process also encourage a nonprofit organization to look backward and evaluate its performance and (we hope!) its successes.

Evaluation is particularly important to nonprofit organizations because, unlike for-profit businesses, nonprofits can't evaluate their performance by showing a profit at the end of the year or increasing the value of their stock. Foundations almost always require that grant-funded projects be evaluated, and of course, you yourself will want to know how you're doing.

Selecting the right kind of evaluation

Evaluations come in many varieties. Sometimes they're as simple as documenting that the program did what it was supposed to do; more in-depth evaluations may test whether some anticipated change occurred as a result of the project. Elaborate and complex evaluations often require an outside professional evaluator.

Nonprofit organizations are concerned with three basic types of evaluation:

- ✔ **Process evaluation:** Did the project do what it was supposed to do? Often, this answer requires no more than simple counting. "This series of school concerts will have a combined audience of 1,500 children." To complete the evaluation of this statement, all you need to do is to keep audience attendance figures.

- ✔ **Goal-based evaluation:** Did the project reach its goals? Depending on the goal you're evaluating, this type of evaluation can be either simple or complex: "Establish an AIDS awareness program in the southeastern quadrant of the city that reaches 500 individuals during its first year." Determining whether a program was established is simple; figuring out how many people the program actually reached is a little more difficult. This answer depends, of course, on what method the project is using to reach people. In other words, you must define what you mean by "reach" before you start the program.

- ✔ **Outcome evaluation:** Did the project have the desired outcome? For example, if you oversee an AIDS awareness program, a desired outcome may be a reduced risk of contracting HIV. Evaluating such an outcome requires an in-depth study of the population in that section of the city to determine whether behavior changed in a way that reduces the chances of HIV exposure. The evaluator needs to collect or have access to baseline data about HIV exposure before the program begins in order to evaluate this outcome adequately.

Sometimes we use more than one type of evaluation on a project. Combining process- and goal-based evaluation is very common, for example. The type of evaluation you use depends on the requirements of your audience for the evaluation. For whom are you evaluating the program? Yourself? Donors? Funders, for example, may request that one or all of the above types of evaluation be carried out on a project they're supporting. A board of directors may want to know whether your program is accomplishing its intended outcome. Ideally, every project is evaluated in all the ways mentioned above. In reality, evaluations take time and cost money that you may not have. Outcome evaluations in particular can be very difficult to accomplish.

Planning for evaluation

Setting up an evaluation framework after a project has started isn't impossible, but it's certainly more difficult. Under the best circumstances, you should determine what you're going to evaluate and how you're going to evaluate it upfront during the program design. For instance, many, if not most, evaluations require that data be collected during the life of the project. So if the plan is to ask clients to evaluate the services they receive, you should be ready to hand over a questionnaire to the first person who walks in the door.

Planning for evaluation also helps you to set program goals and objectives. Just ask yourself: Can it be measured? Here are some other questions to ask yourself when planning for evaluation:

✔ **For what purpose is the evaluation being done?**

✔ **Which of the following people will read the evaluation?**

- Foundation program officers

- Board of directors

- Managers and supervisors

- Professional colleagues

- Yourself

- The public

✔ **What is the method of evaluation?** Evaluations can be done in several ways. Decide which of the following methods or combination of methods is best for your purposes:

- Questionnaires and surveys

- Review of project documentation

- Interviews/focus groups with users of the program

- Program observations

- Pretesting and post-testing

Choosing evaluators: Inside or outside?

Some projects require an outside evaluator — someone who's familiar with the program area, has experience as an evaluator, and isn't associated with your organization. In other words, you're looking for a person who has nothing at stake in the results of the evaluation. Projects that need this in-depth analysis are usually large and complex. If a funding agency requests an outside evaluator, expect the agency to pay for the evaluation as part of project expenses.

Internal staff members do most evaluations. Though not as expensive as hiring a consultant, even an internal evaluation involves costs. Project budgets should reflect the staff and materials costs that result from evaluations.

Telling the truth

Honesty and forthrightness are important in evaluations. You may be tempted to fudge the results of attendance figures or the number of clients the program has served, but in more cases than not, the truth comes out in the end. An organization can damage its reputation among its peers and funders if someone discovers that evaluations have been falsified.

Programs do fall short of their goals. We wish this didn't happen, but it does. Remember, you're evaluating against a set of goals and objectives that were projections, maybe as long as three years earlier. The best approach is to provide honest numbers and explain why or how the results are different than those results you expected at the beginning of the project.

Chapter 10

Showing the Money: Budgets and Financial Reports

· ·

In This Chapter

▶ Preparing a budget for an organization

▶ Constructing additional budgets on a smaller scale

▶ Using your budget

▶ Anticipating revenue and expenses

▶ Putting your financial statement in order

▶ Understanding financial statements

▶ Adopting good financial practices

· ·

*N*onprofit organizations are expected to spend cautiously and honor the trust placed in them by their donors. As a result, they need to be especially good at budgeting and living within their means.

Designing budgets is a critical part of program planning, grant writing, and evaluation. Maintaining a financially stable organization is one of management's most important tasks. And asking the right questions about financial reports is one of the board's key responsibilities.

M-O-N-E-Y . . . frankly, there's no getting away from it. No money, no program.

Making a Budget = Having a Plan

Because a budget is composed of numbers and because most people were taught that arithmetic is an exact science, you may panic when faced with making a budget. What if you don't get it absolutely right?

Relax. Making a budget is yet another form of organizational planning (the topic of Chapter 9). Often it's done hand-in-hand with other types of planning. It estimates how you intend to gather and disperse money on behalf of your organization's mission. In the course of a year, the cost of utilities or postage may rise, and the cost of airline flights and computer equipment may fall. You're not expected to employ extra-sensory perception in making a budget — just to be reasonable and thoughtful.

If your organization doesn't spend more than it takes in, and if it holds onto a little emergency money at the bank, why does it need a budget? We propose that while writing and agreeing upon a budget is an important process for your staff or board, even more important is working with the budget after you've created it. After you've written your budget, write down all the actual amounts that relate to the income you hoped for and expenditures you planned. It's a discipline that makes you watchful and keeps your organization on solid ground.

Beginning with zero

Zero is a hard place to start when you're making a budget, but it's where every new organization begins.

A budget has two key sections — income and expenses. (See Figure 10-1 for typical line items.) Because dreaming up expenses that exceed your organization's means is easy, we suggest that you begin with income, making conservative estimates for what you may earn and what you may attract in contributions. As you work on the contributed income estimates, you also may want to look at Chapter 13, which discusses developing a fundraising plan.

Examining income

It's common to separate your income statement into two general categories, "earned" and "contributed," also called "revenue" (contract or fee income) and "support" (contributions), respectively.

Here are some common questions to ask yourself as you begin budgeting the income section of your budget:

- Will you offer services or products for which you'll charge money? How many services and how often? How many people are likely to use them? What can you reasonably charge?

- Can you charge membership fees to people and give them a premium or discount in exchange for paying those fees?

✔ Are the founders and board of your organization able to contribute some start-up funds? Are they able to talk to their friends and associates about contributing?

✔ Is your organization well-positioned to receive a grant or grants?

✔ Are you capable of sponsoring a fundraising event?

✔ Could you provide visibility to a business sponsor in exchange for a contribution?

Anatomy of a basic budget

INCOME
Earned Income
    Government contracts
    Product sales
    Memberships
    Interest from investments
       Subtotal
Contributed Income
    Government grants
    Foundation grants
    Corporate contributions
    Individual gifts
    Special events (net income)
       Subtotal
       TOTAL INCOME

EXPENSES
Personnel Expenses
    Salaries
    Benefits @ _% of salaries
    Independent contractors
       Subtotal personnel
Non-personnel Expenses
    Rent
    Utilities & Telephone
    Insurance
    Office supplies
    Program materials
    Local travel
    Printing
       Subtotal non-personnel
       TOTAL Expenses
       Balance (the difference between total income and total expenses)

Figure 10-1: Showing how expense items usually are named.

Evaluating expenses

In anticipating expenses, start with anything concerning payment of people. That list may include the following:

- ✔ **Salaries for employees, both full-time and part-time:** On your budget, list each position by title and identify the full-time salary and the percent of full time that person is working for you.

- ✔ **Benefits for salaried employees:** In most states, at a minimum, you need to pay approximately 12.5 percent of salaries to cover legally required benefits such as employment taxes. Your organization also may provide health insurance or a retirement plan to its employees. If so, you want to compute those costs as percentages of your total salaries and include them in your budget as benefits. Benefits come immediately after your salary expenses.

- ✔ **Fees for services to consultants or service agencies:** You may hire a publicist, grant writer, evaluator, or other consultant to handle important tasks. Such consultants are responsible for paying their own tax and insurance costs. Show fees paid to consultants directly after salaries and benefits in your budget.

At this point, compute a subtotal for all your personnel costs.

Next, identify all the nonpersonnel expenses, beginning with ongoing operating costs that allow your organization to offer programs. These expenses may include the following:

- ✔ Rent
- ✔ Utilities
- ✔ Telephone and Internet expenses
- ✔ Office supplies
- ✔ Printing
- ✔ Insurance

New organizations often have special start-up costs for the first year. They may need to purchase desks and chairs, computers, signs, shelving, office cubicles, and even playground equipment; and they may need to pay for first and last months' rent, telephone and Internet hook-up costs, and a photocopier or postage machine lease. Finally, do you have costs associated with the specific nature of the work of your organization? These costs range widely but can include diagnostic tests, carpentry tools, classroom supplies, and printed materials.

As much as possible, keep notes about the estimates you made in drafting your budget in your budget files. For example, if you're planning to print a catalog or book, indicate the quantity and dimensions and note whether you want it printed in color. Thinking through such details helps you draft a more accurate budget, and keeping your budget worksheet helps you to remember your assumptions and follow your budget when it comes time to place your order with a printer.

We present three different organization budgets on the CD with this book — CD1001, CD1002, and CD1003. Two of the examples show how organizations compare budgets to actual costs.

What's a good budget?

In a good budget, the income and expenses are equal to one another, or you have somewhat more income than expenses. That's what people mean when they say that a budget is "balanced."

Having said that, organizations' budgets vary widely, and no one right model exists. As a general rule, your budget looks healthy when you show multiple sources of income and a combination of contributed income and earned revenue. Why? Wouldn't it be easier to keep track of one or two major grants and contracts? Or one annual special event?

The reason is based on the adage "Don't put all your eggs in one basket." What if a power outage strikes on the night of your gala? What if one of your major granting or contract sources changes its guidelines? Your programs could be jeopardized.

Another sound concept is "saving for a rainy day." Many organizations slowly develop a *cash reserve,* money put aside in case unexpected expenses arise. If they need to use their cash reserves, they take care to replace them as soon as possible. Often their board sets a policy for how large a reserve they want to keep and how quickly expended reserve funds must be replaced.

Onward and upward (or downward)

As your first year passes and your organization develops programs, it also develops a financial track record. After you have a financial history, anticipating the future can be easier. You need to analyze every assumption you make, but at least you have a baseline of revenues and expenses from the first year.

Here are some questions to consider in drafting future years' budgets:

- ✔ What are your earned income trends? Are they likely to continue or change? Do you face any new competition or opportunities?

- ✔ How many of your current year's grants or contracts may be renewed and at what levels?

- ✔ How likely are you to increase individual giving or special events revenues in the coming year?

- ✔ What is the duration of all employees' employment periods? Anticipate the scheduling of possible annual raises.

- ✔ How does your personnel policy affect your budget? Do you offer benefits that kick in after an employee has worked with you for three months or six months or five years? If so, don't forget to include these increased costs.

- ✔ When does your lease obligate you to pay for rent increases or taxes?

- ✔ Have rate increases been scheduled for utilities, postage, or other services?

What do you show if you don't have to pay for it?

Some nonprofit organizations benefit from donated goods and services rather than or in addition to contributed and earned cash. Suppose, for instance, that a local business provides office space for your organization so that you don't have to pay rent, 50 volunteers contribute labor to your organization each week, and a major advertising firm sponsors a free marketing campaign to promote your work.

These gifts of goods and services are called *in-kind contributions*. How can you show these valuable resources in your organization's budget?

First, we encourage you to make the effort. If you don't show these contributions, you don't truly represent the scope of your agency in your budget and you're underplaying how much the community values its work. On the other hand, mixing the in-kind materials and services with the cash can make following and managing your budget confusing.

So what's the solution? We prefer creating in-kind subheadings within the budget or summarizing all the in-kind contributions at the end of the cash budget in a separate section.

In showing the value of a volunteer's time, identify the value of the labor contributed. In other words, if a surgeon volunteers to drive a bus for you, the value of that time is at the rate of a bus driver's salary, not a surgeon's.

Making Budgets for Programs or Departments

If your organization focuses on a single service, you can skip ahead to read about projecting cash flow, but many nonprofit organizations manage several programs or departments. Each of these programs has a budget that must fit within the overall organizational budget. Often in applying for a grant, you're asked for a project budget and an organizational budget.

Suppose that when your nonprofit organization begins, you offer only one program — an after-school center that provides tutoring and homework assistance for low-income children. The program really clicks, and more and more children begin showing up after school — some because they need tutors but others because their parents are at work and the kids need a safe place to go. To serve these new needs, you add art classes and a sports program.

So now, instead of one program, you have three. Each has its own special budgetary needs. A volunteer coordinator trains and recruits the tutors and purchases books, notebooks, and school supplies. The art program requires an artist's time, supplies, space for art making, and access to a kiln. To offer a sports program, your agency rents the nearby gym, hires four coaches, uses a volunteer coordinator to recruit parents and other assistant coaches, and purchases equipment.

The specific costs of a program — books, art supplies, coaches — are called its *direct* costs.

But each of your three programs also depends on materials and services provided by other people, such as the full-time executive director of your agency, the part-time development director, and the bookkeeper. Those people work on behalf of all programs. Each of the three after-school programs also uses the agency offices, utilities, telephones, and printed materials.

The costs that the various programs share — such as the executive director's salary, bookkeeping services, rent, and telephone bills — are called *indirect* costs. You can think of these shared costs as the glue that holds the agency together.

When you prepare a program or department budget, you want to include both direct costs and indirect costs.

Dealing with indirect costs — the "sticky" part

Direct costs are pretty straightforward. For example, you know what you have to pay your tutors per hour, and you know how many hours they work. But indirect costs can be sticky, and we don't mean because they're the organizational glue. They're sticky to deal with because determining how to divide them accurately among your organization's activities is hard. Many grantmakers are reluctant to pay true indirect costs associated with programs and, if your organization depends heavily on grants, that reluctance can put you in the awkward financial position of being able to pay for a famous basketball coach but not to turn on the lights in the gym.

When your organization is relatively small with just a few programs, you may be able to keep accurate records for how staff members spend their time, how many square feet in a building a program uses, even how many office supplies your staff checks out of the supply cabinet, and, based on those records, estimate fairly your indirect costs.

As it grows in complexity and number of programs, you may compute indirect costs using a formula you derive based on your direct costs. We outline sample formulas and steps to derive them in Table 10-1.

Table 10-1	Indirect Cost Formula for After-School Center
First, add all of your direct costs:	
Program	**Direct Costs of Each Program**
Tutoring and homework assistance	$ 46,000
Arts and crafts	$ 60,000
Athletics	$164,000
Total direct costs:	$270,000
Then compute the percentage of total direct costs that each program represents:	
Tutoring and homework assistance	$46,000 ÷ $270,000 = 17%
Arts and crafts	$60,000 ÷ $270,000 = 22%
Athletics	$164,000 ÷ $270,000 = 61%

In many cases, you can reasonably assume that the indirect costs of a program correlate to its direct costs, or that a program that's more expensive requires more oversight of staff, more volunteers, and more use of office space. In the case of the After-School Center, all the indirect costs — which include a salary for the director, a contracted bookkeeper, rent, utilities, telephones, and printing — total $85,500.

Using this figure, we can put together the direct and indirect costs into a true financial picture of each program by dividing the $85,500 in indirect costs according to the formulas we developed for direct costs in Table 10-1. We outline the proposed allocation in Table 10-2.

Table 10-2	Allocating Indirect Costs for After-School Center	
Program	*Formula*	*Indirect Cost Amount*
Tutoring program	$85,500 × 17%	$14,535
Arts and crafts program	$85,500 × 22%	$18,810
Athletics program	$85,500 × 61%	$52,155

Sometimes organizations write a project budget by identifying all the direct costs in detail and then showing the indirect costs as one lump sum at the bottom of the list of expenses. But some funding sources balk at paying for indirect costs when they're shown this way. The funders want to know what actual expenses contribute to those indirect costs. We recommend that you integrate the indirect costs with the direct costs.

CD1004 shows the tutoring program budget with the indirect costs integrated alongside the direct costs. This shows a true picture of the project's needs.

Isolating general administrative and fundraising costs

Another common and slightly different method is to assume that some of the organization's administrative costs are "purely administrative" and some of its fundraising costs are "purely development." If a bookkeeper or accountant prepares a financial statement for you about the fiscal results of the past year's activities, he likely will make this assumption. IRS Form 990 that most nonprofits file annually asks organizations to present their expenses in this way. (See Chapter 5 for more about preparing a 990.)

You may think, for example, that your executive director spends 80 percent of her time attending to the needs of the organization's different programs. She spends another 20 percent of her time negotiating leases, hiring a payroll service, or meeting with new board members, along with other activities serving the overall organization that are very hard to assign to programs. If you make this assumption, "shave off" the 20 percent for what's called "general and administrative" before applying your indirect cost formulas.

Some people believe in thresholds or standards limiting the costs for administration and fundraising. Most donors like to see their money going toward programs rather than paying for overhead. We can't blame them. But frankly, setting a clear standard for reasonable overhead can be hard. "Reasonable" depends a great deal on an organization's age, mission, and point of development as well as on its primary sources of income. Piloting a new activity often is more expensive than sustaining it after you work out the kinks. In fundraising, writing a grant proposal is likely to cost less than producing a costume ball or conducting a direct mail campaign. If you believe that your management and fundraising costs may be considered high in comparison to your overall budget, be prepared to explain your situation or consider reorganizing and streamlining your efforts.

A growing number of Web sites about charitable giving analyze the percentage of nonprofits' expenses dedicated to management and fundraising and use this information as a means of identifying which organizations make efficient use of charitable contributions. Stay abreast of how these sites analyze your organization, and communicate with them if you feel they judge you unfairly.

Working with Your Budget

Your budget isn't capable of getting up and walking out of the room, but it needs to be an "active document." If you simply create it once a year to keep in a file folder and submit with grant proposals, it doesn't do you much good. A good budget is crumpled, coffee-stained, and much scrutinized. A good budget guides and predicts.

Numbers in your budgets are meant to be compared. One critically important comparison looks at actual income and expenses alongside the original projections you made in your budget. Most organizations create a spreadsheet that includes columns for:

- ✔ Annual budget
- ✔ Year to date income and expenses

✔ Current month's budget (½ of the annual budget)

✔ Current month's income and expenses

Pay close attention to where you're exceeding your budget and where you're falling short. Use your progress as a guide to adjust your fundraising or your expenditures.

The CD accompanying this book demonstrates two ways of tracking actual income and expenses in comparison to budgeted income and expenses. See CD1005 and CD1006.

To take a critical, long view of your financial progress, use CD1007, the Five Year Trend Line.

Other useful exercises to make sure your budget is "living and breathing" include the following:

✔ Involve your staff (paid and volunteer) in the early stages of drafting the coming year's budget. When you can't afford all their dreams, involve them in setting priorities.

✔ Three months before the beginning of your new fiscal year, meet with a small committee of board members to review and refine a budget draft after you've met with your staff. Present the draft with options and recommendations to the entire board for discussion and formal approval.

✔ If your organization's situation changes, prepare and adopt a formal budget revision. Budget revisions are time consuming, but don't try to proceed with a budget that doesn't reflect the size and scope of your organization. You don't want to try to find your way through Colorado with a map of Utah.

✔ Provide copies monthly or quarterly to your entire board or board finance committee. Encourage your board treasurer to summarize the organization's financial situation and invite questions and discussion at each meeting.

✔ Keep notes in your budget file about changes you recommend for years ahead.

Check out CD1008, "Monthly Information Every Nonprofit Board Needs to Know," another tool to keep your budget "living and breathing."

Because we know that revenues aren't earned, grants aren't received, and expenses aren't incurred at the same levels every month throughout the year, along with these practices, we recommend that you project your cash flow (see the following section).

Projecting Cash Flow

A *cash flow projection* is a subdocument of your budget that estimates not just how much money you will receive and spend over the course of a year, but *when* you will receive and spend it. It breaks down your budget into increments of time. Some organizations create quarterly (three month) projections, some monthly, some weekly. Although grantmaking organizations and major donors are likely to want to see your budget (and may want to see the version that compares projections to actual amounts), your cash flow projection generally is a document for you, your board, and possibly a loan source.

If you think of a budget as the spine of an organization — supporting all its limbs — the cash flow statement is its heart and lungs. A good cash flow statement is in constant movement, anticipating and following your every move. Based on the careful way you developed your budget, you may know that you're likely to have enough revenue to cover your organization's expenses in the coming year. The cash flow helps you figure out whether you'll have that money at hand when you need it.

You can map out a cash flow statement at various levels of detail. Our personal preference is to tie cash flow planning to the frequency with which you pay employees. Often this pay period is every two weeks.

Constructing your cash flow projection

To set up a cash flow projection, begin with a copy of your budget and add details to the names of all of the various categories. For instance, under "Foundation Grants," write down the names of every foundation from whom you now receive money and of any from whom you anticipate receiving a grant. Add the same kinds of details for your expense categories. For example, under "Utilities," add separate lines for each bill you receive such as water, electricity, gas, or sewer service.

We recommend that you project forward by going backwards. Sounds contradictory, doesn't it? Create columns for the most recently completed three months of your year. Go through your records while you fill out your form. Put any income received into the appropriate periods, and write down all your expenses in the right categories and time periods. If you've forgotten any categories, you have a chance to add them. Having these actual figures for the recent past helps you see patterns of income and expense and to be realistic about your expectations.

Now, begin projecting: Go back to each line item and write down the estimated amount that's due during each two-week period. Begin with the "easy" items — like the rent that's a constant amount due on a certain day each month or the employer's share of federal payroll taxes.

Next, look at the consistent bills that change a little bit over time. If your utility bills are high during winter months because your agency is using the furnace more, don't forget to project that increase. If you hold a phone-a-thon twice a year that causes unusually high usage rates, figure that in.

As you get into the flow of making predictions, it's easy to become too optimistic about your anticipated income. If you've applied for a grant that you're just not sure about, don't put it into your cash flow projection. If your annual fundraising event raises between $25,000 and $32,000 each year, project $25,000 in income. The reason? You probably won't have any problem knowing what to do when you have more money than anticipated, but you may have a problem making up a shortfall! Your cash flow projection is supposed to help keep you from falling short.

You're almost finished at this point. As a next step, look back at your financial records to see how much money you had at the beginning of the first two-week period of your cash flow projection. Place this figure in a "Balance Forward" row as the first income item for your first two-week period. Add it to all the income for those two weeks and subtract those two weeks' expenses. The difference gives you the next "Balance Forward" amount that belongs at the top row for the next column of income for the *next* two-week period. And keep going. The balance for each two-week period is steadily carried over to the top.

Table 10-3 shows a highly simplified sample of a cash flow projection:

Table 10-3	Simple Cash Flow Projection		
Income	1/1–1/14	1/15–1/28	1/29–2/11
Balance Forward	$21,603	$14,684	$52,795
Government Contract		$50,000	
Williams Grant	$5,700		
Power Company			$2,500
Board Giving	$2,000	$750	
Total income	$29,303	$65,434	$55,295

(continued)

Table 10-3 *(continued)*

Expenses	1/1–1/14	1/15–1/28	1/29–2/11
Payroll	$11,197	$11,197	$11,197
Health Benefits	$447		$447
Payroll Taxes			
Rent	$2,500		$2,500
Electric Company	$475		$475
Telephone			$875
Office supplies		$120	$120
Travel and Transportation	$1322	$8,700	
Total expenses	$14,619	$12,639	$24,314
Balance:	$14,684	$52,795	$30,981

See CD1009 and CD1010 for a detailed sample cash flow projection and for a blank form you can use to begin your own cash flow statement.

What if you don't have enough?

You probably won't have more income than expenses in every single two-week period throughout the year. During some periods, you get ahead, and at other times, you fall behind. Your goal is to sustain a generally positive balance over the course of time and to be able to cover your most critical bills — payroll, taxes, insurance, and utilities — in a timely manner.

Some government agencies and foundations pay grants as reimbursements for expenses after you've incurred them. You may need to prepare for cash flow problems while waiting to be reimbursed.

We want to promise that you'll always have enough resources to sustain your organization's good work. But some times will be lean. Then what?

First, your cash flow projection should help you to anticipate when you may fall short. It enables you to plan ahead and solicit board members who have not yet made gifts in the current year, send letters to past donors, cut costs, or delay purchases.

We also recommend being proactive about contacting your creditors. If you think you can't pay a bill on time, call and ask for an extension or explain that you're forced to make a partial payment now with the balance coming in a few weeks. Your ability to do business depends upon your earning and sustaining other people's trust. If you can't have perfect credit, being honest and forthright is the next best thing. It's hard to do, but important.

Don't "hide" behind your bills, thinking that if you don't say anything, nobody will notice. If you're facing a period of debt, call anyone to whom you owe money and explain the situation and your timeline for paying your bills. Among other things, your honesty helps them with *their* cash flow. And when your expenses are exceeding your income, always try to cover your federal, state, and local tax obligations. Fees and interest on unpaid taxes add up quickly. If that's not possible, don't forget to call those agencies. Setting up a payment plan, both over the phone and in writing, can prevent your assets (or a board member's) from being frozen.

Borrowing to make ends meet

Another route to managing cash shortfalls is to borrow the money you need to cover your bills. Your cash flow statement can help you plan the size and duration of the loan you need. Here are some of your options if you need to borrow money:

- ✔ **Ask a board member for assistance.** If the board member can help, you can probably secure the loan quickly and at a reasonable interest rate (or no interest rate).

- ✔ **Ask local foundations whether they know of a loan fund for nonprofit organizations.** Some associations of grantmakers and government agencies offer such loans at low interest to their grantees who face cash flow problems. Such a program is likely to be more sympathetic to your needs than a commercial lending institution may be.

- ✔ **Apply for a small business loan at your bank.** Foundations sometimes make this process easier by guaranteeing bank loans of nonprofits.

- ✔ **Check to see whether you qualify for a line of credit from your bank.** A *line of credit* allows you to borrow up to a certain sum for a certain period of time. When the organization repays the borrowed amount, often it can't borrow from its line of credit again for a designated period of time. Your organization may want to apply for a line of credit even if it doesn't expect immediate cash flow problems. Doing so can provide a safety net for emergencies.

- ✔ **As a last resort, borrow the money from a staff member's (or an organizational) credit card.** Do this only if you're positive that you can repay the loan quickly and cover the interest.

Some nonprofit directors have taken out second mortgages on their homes to cover their organizations' debts, but we don't recommend doing so. Dedication is worthy, but drastic steps can lead to resentment and job burnout, which may be more destructive to an organization than owing money.

Borrowing money rarely occurs without financial or emotional costs. Borrowing from a board member may erode the board's confidence in the organization and trust in its leadership. Borrowing from a foundation-supported loan fund draws potential funders' attention to your organization's cash flow problems. Borrowing from banks involves paying interest. Credit card borrowing is fast, but the interest charged is high. However, borrowing is better than incurring penalties and interest charges — particularly on tax obligations.

Preparing Financial Statements

If a budget is a document about the future, a financial statement is about history. Nonprofit organizations prepare a financial statement at least once a year, at the end of the fiscal year. (See Chapter 4 for more information on a fiscal year.) Many organizations also prepare monthly or quarterly "in progress" versions of their annual financial statements.

Preparing and interpreting financial statements is a special area of expertise that goes beyond the scope of this book. Many nonprofits seek outside professional help for this essential task. If hiring such assistance is beyond your organization's means, we recommend that you become acquainted with *Accounting For Dummies,* 3rd Edition, by John A. Tracy (Wiley). If you do choose to prepare your own financial statements, you may want to hire an accountant at year's end to review them for accuracy.

The information in your yearly financial statement closely resembles the Form 990 financial report that your organization must submit to the IRS if it's received $25,000 or more in the past year. You can find more information about filling out a 990 in Chapter 5. You'll also be including your financial statement in your board orientation packets and with requests for funding. Some organizations publish it in an "Annual Report" of activities.

You can find a copy of Form 990 at www.irs.gov.

Your organization may choose to have its books audited by a certified public accountant or firm. This service involves a formal study of its systems for managing its finances, a review of the accuracy and format of its financial statement, and commentary about its relative financial health.

In hiring a certified public accountant to conduct your audit or financial review, make sure the person has knowledge about or expertise in nonprofit organizations. Nonprofits use some accounting terms and bookkeeping methods that differ from profit-making businesses.

Some states have adopted or are considering legislation that requires organizations of a certain size to have their books audited. The federal government is considering similar requirements. In California, for example, organizations with annual income of $2 million or more must have their books audited. Check the offices that regulate nonprofits in your state to see whether they have created specific audit guidelines. Some of your funders also may require audited statements from applicants. Even if it isn't required, your board may decide that it's a good idea to have the books examined by an outside auditor.

If you're reading an audit

In addition to a statement of your organization's financial position and of its activities — or income and expenses, an audit also contains an analysis of cash flow over the course of the year, a statement of functional expenses, a cover letter, and several pages of footnotes.

Looking at the statement of functional expenses (if your statement has been formally reviewed or audited), analyze the percentage of the organization's total expenditures that you spent on general and administrative costs and fundraising. Discuss among staff or with board members whether you believe they're appropriate to the age, size, and kind of organization you're managing.

Reading the narrative sections includes the following:

✔ The cover letter from the accounting firm that prepared your audit should include a standard phrase indicating that the professional who prepared the audit believes that it "presents fairly in all material respects . . ." the position of the organization. This phrase means that the organization's systems for keeping its financial records were good and the auditors believe their opinions are sound.

✔ Read the footnotes to the audit. You may encounter in them points of concern — like building leases that are about to end or balloon payments that are soon going to be due for the organization's mortgage — that aren't obvious when you read the numbers.

✔ Ask to see the management memorandum if the auditor prepared one. This memo includes recommendations for changes in the way the organization manages its financial decisions or its record keeping systems. The board and executive director should take steps together to implement the recommended changes or, if the recommendations exceed the organization's capacity, write a memorandum responding to them and asking for changes in the auditor's memorandum.

Although your organization can learn a great deal from an audit, the practice isn't appropriate or necessary for every nonprofit. The process is expensive and time consuming. Two rigorous but less expensive options are having a formal "financial review" conducted by a CPA firm or having your organization's books audited every other year.

Many nonprofits wonder whether they should seek pro bono audits from accounting firms or ask a board member's firm to audit their books. Although we're big fans of contributed services, a pro bono audit is a bad idea and asking a board member for assistance is a very bad idea. An auditor is supposed to be neutral about your organization: An audit, to have value, should be prepared independently of the organization's staff and board. It loses its value as the voice of outside validation when provided as a gift.

Reading Your Financial Statements

Audited or not, prepared by you or by a bookkeeper or accountant, your organization needs to produce financial statements, and it's critically important for you to understand how to interpret them.

You'll encounter two standard systems for writing about your organization's financial history: cash and accrual. Here are some details about each system:

- ✔ **A cash system closely resembles the way most people keep their checkbooks.** You enter income into the books when you receive and deposit a check or cash. You enter expenses when you pay a bill. Many find a cash system to be a comfortable approach because it's straightforward. When your books show a positive balance, you have money in hand or in the bank.

- ✔ **An accrual system recognizes income when it's promised and expenses when they're obligated.** Suppose that you receive a grant award letter from a foundation promising your organization $60,000 over a two-year period. This grant is going to be paid in four checks of $15,000 each. In an accrual system, you enter the entire $60,000 as income in your books when you receive the grant award letter — when that money is promised. On the expense side, you enter your bills into your books when you incur them — which may be before they're due.

Each of these approaches has possible disadvantages:

- ✔ In cash books, your organization may owe money in unpaid bills, but those debts aren't apparent because they aren't on your books until they're paid.

- ✔ In cash books, your organization may have been awarded a large grant but look poor because you haven't received the check.

✔ In cash books, it's harder to tell whether you owe payroll taxes.

✔ In accrual books, you may have been promised a large contribution but not yet received it. You may have no cash in hand, but your books look as if you have surplus income.

Keeping books by an accrual system is standard accounting practice these days, recommended by the Financial Accounting Standards Board, but small organizations often can get by with a cash system.

Parts of a standard financial statement

Because accrual systems are standard practice for nonprofits, we focus the rest of this section on financial statements that are based on an accrual system. Nonprofit financial statements include two important "sub-statements":

✔ **The *statement of position* (also called a balance sheet) provides an overview of what an organization is worth.** It outlines how much money is available in bank accounts and other investments; the value of property, furniture, and equipment; immediate bills; and other debts and liabilities.

✔ **The *statement of activities* outlines "Revenues, Gains, and Supports" and "Expenses and Other Losses," which tell you how much money the organization received in the past year, its sources for that income, and how it spent that income.** Statements of activities divide an organization's income and expenses into three categories:

- **Unrestricted funds** were available to the organization to spend in the fiscal year covered by the statement.

- **Temporarily restricted funds** were promised or awarded in the year covered by the statement but they were given to the organization for it to spend in the future or for a specific task that isn't yet completed.

- **Permanently restricted funds** were given to the organization for permanent investments — such as endowments. They may not be spent on current activities.

They also contain a statement of *functional expense,* which details expenses spent on programs and those expenses that were exclusively for general and administrative costs and for fundraising costs.

Many staff and board members are drawn to nonprofit organizations because they're knowledgeable about the services they provide and their eyes glaze over when they're faced with financial statements. This lack of interest in finances is understandable but can be dangerous: The board and staff are stewards of the organization's resources and responsible for its financial health.

We include a sample of an audited financial statement on the CD, CD1011, that you can use to become familiar with the terms used and the organization of information.

Asking the right financial questions

At the year's end, when you've completed the financial statement, we suggest reviewing the following points either as a board or within the board's finance committee. You can ask different questions about the statement of position (or balance sheet) and the statement of activities. The answers will arm you with a clear understanding of your organization's financial health.

Looking at the statement of position, ask:

- ✔ **Do the cash and cash equivalents exceed the accounts payable?** If so, the organization has enough cash in the bank to pay its immediate bills to vendors.

- ✔ **Do the total current assets exceed the current liabilities?** If they do, the organization has enough money readily at hand to cover all its immediate obligations, such as bills and taxes, employee benefits, and loan payments.

- ✔ **How much of the assets are made up of property, equipment, or other durable goods the organization owns and what is the nature of those assets?** Some organizations can appear to be financially healthy because their total assets are high, but all those assets are made up of things that would be hard for them to sell.

- ✔ **In the current liabilities section, is the amount of payroll taxes payable a high figure?** If so, the organization may be delinquent in paying its taxes. (Many taxes are paid quarterly, so don't expect a zero figure for the "payroll tax" item.)

- ✔ **In the liabilities section, do you see an item for a refundable advance or deferred revenue?** If you see this item, it means money for a service was given to the organization before the organization provided that service (such as subscription income theater goers pay in advance of attending performances). Make sure that the organization has sufficient resources to provide the services it's promised.

- ✔ **Has the organization borrowed money?** If so, the amount appears in the liabilities section as a loan or line of credit. Compare its total net assets to the total amount borrowed. If the numbers are similar, the organization may have cash at hand but all of it must be repaid.

✔ **Do the assets exceed the liabilities?** Your total assets and liabilities will add up to the same number, but look at how they compare in the temporarily restricted column. If the assets are higher than the liabilities, the organization has promises for future revenues or money in hand that it can use to cover the costs of future activities. That's good!

✔ **Does your organization's statement have a column for permanently restricted funds?** If so, that likely means that it has an endowment. Take a look at that column. Is all the money that needs to be legally held as an endowment shown as a positive figure in that permanently restricted column, or has the organization borrowed from it? If you owe money to the permanently restricted column, the amount borrowed is shown in brackets. Ask about plans for timely return of restricted funds.

The financial statement will be dated, and the answers to the questions you have just asked should give you a good picture of the health of your organization over its entire history leading up to that date. Now it's time to look at the statement of activities, which illustrates what happened in the past year. Two simple questions will summarize that story. Look to the bottom of the page to see:

✔ **Is the change in net assets a negative or positive number?** If it's negative, the organization lost money in the previous year. If the loss is a high number, ask why it took place. If it's a modest amount, ask whether it's part of a downward trend or something that occurs occasionally.

✔ **Is the number shown for total net assets a positive number?** If so, the organization is in a positive financial position (even if it lost money in the past year). That's good news!

Managing Financial Systems

Even in a small organization, you want to establish careful practices about how you handle money and financial documents. If you have a one-person office, creating all of the following controls may be impossible, but you should try to implement them as far as possible:

✔ Store checkbooks, savings passbooks, blank checks, financial records, and cash in a locked, secure place.

✔ Regularly back up financial records that you keep on computers and store a copy off-site in a safe location.

✔ Assign to different people the separate functions of writing checks, signing checks, reconciling bank accounts, and checking the canceled checks that return from the bank. If you can arrange for three different people to perform these tasks, great. If not, maybe a board member can double-check canceled checks. Look for accuracy and for anything that looks fishy, such as checks made out to vendors you don't recognize, checks canceled by people or businesses other than those to whom they're written, or canceled checks that are missing from bank statements. Embezzlement is rare but possible, and taking these steps is a way to detect it. Trust us, we've discovered such a case!

✔ Require two signatures on checks or bank transfers over a certain amount, often $1,000. (You can adopt this requirement as an internal policy, and your bank often monitors larger transactions to make sure that the policy is followed.)

✔ Retain in organized files all paperwork that backs up your banking documents. These documents may include personnel time sheets, box office or other records for tickets sold, receipts, and invoices.

✔ Keep an itemized list of any furniture or equipment you purchase or receive as donations (including computers), noting the date they were purchased or received and their value.

Chapter 11

Marketing: Spreading the Word about Your Good Work

In This Chapter

▶ Attending to everyday basics

▶ Looking at who you are and who you serve

▶ Building your publicity machine through mass media

You may think that marketing has no place in the nonprofit sector. After all, if an organization's work isn't driven by the dollar, and if its focus is entirely on meeting a community need, why does it need to sell its services? If your motivation is to do good, isn't it crass to toot your own horn?

But wait. Marketing — the process of connecting consumers to services and products — is just as critical to the success of nonprofit organizations as it is to commercial enterprises. Both nonprofit and commercial organizations depend on getting the word out, and the message from both is the same: Here we are, and here's what we can do for you. Come and check us out.

You can go far if you have the "goods" — good planning, good stories, good will, and good luck. And persistence.

Taking Care of the Basics

Before you begin tackling client surveys and media releases, you need to spend a little time making sure you have a few basic communication tools in place. These tools help you tell your clients, audiences, donors, and the general public who you are and what you do.

In this section, we provide some tips for the most basic communication tools that every nonprofit — large or small, new or old — should have.

Selecting letterhead

Your letterhead should include the following:

- ✔ Your organization's name
- ✔ Address
- ✔ Phone number
- ✔ Fax number
- ✔ E-mail address and Web site (if you have one)

Many organizations also list their board members on the letterhead. Doing so is a great way to highlight the board members' affiliations with your organization, but if your board is rapidly changing and growing, you may be reprinting the letterhead every few weeks. You may also want to include a tag line, briefly identifying what your organization does, like *Feeding the hungry in Tuborville.*

In selecting letterhead, choose paper that makes clear, readable photocopies (avoid dark papers or those with lots of flecks and spots).

Printing a background sheet or brochure

A *background sheet* is a one-page typed overview of your organization's purpose and programs. You can enclose it with press releases, grant proposals, and fundraising letters. Place copies in your lobby or reception area for visitors to read.

As you grow, your organization may want to get a little bit fancier and move beyond a simple typed sheet to invest in a folded brochure with photographs or drawings. A good brochure clearly conveys the essence of your organization.

Saving money at the printer

Printing costs can eat a hole right through your nonprofit's wallet. If you print postcards, odd-sized announcement cards, bookmarks, or other smaller marketing pieces, talk to a local printer about including your job around the edges of a larger piece being printed or on odd-sized paper trimmed from larger jobs. This type of printing can be very inexpensive.

Talk to other organizations that print materials on a similar schedule to yours (such as calendars of events that get printed every month). By processing your print jobs at the same time and using the same paper, you may be able to save money for all parties.

You want it to be inviting and readable. Visual elements, if you can afford them and they're appropriate, help to make a more attractive document and tell your story in fewer words.

Designing a logo

A good logo suits the tone of your organization. Many people remember pictures more vividly than words. They may remember your logo more easily than they remember your organization's name! You don't want to grow tired of your logo or have it confused with the logo of another group in your community.

If you need to create a logo, try not to resort to standard computer font symbols or clip art. Do you know a graphic artist or a printer with a good eye who can help you create something original? If not, we recommend a simple solution: Choose an attractive typeface in which to present your name. You can get fancier later.

If your organization is small and your resources are limited, don't design a logo that has to be printed in more than one color of ink. Using just one color helps to control your printing costs.

Posting your sign

How do people find your physical location? An attractive sign can be an important part of your image. In some cases, banners can be printed more easily and cheaply than other kinds of signs. Consider all the options for price, image, durability, flexibility, and visibility — awnings, quilts, stencils on glass, neon, flags.

When you post your sign, consider its placement. We once had a great sign behind an enormous oak tree. Nobody could find our organization.

Creating a Web site

Most nonprofit organizations feel that having a presence on the Web is as important as being listed in the telephone book or printing a brochure. A basic Web site need not be difficult to create. You may want an overview of your agency on the home page, and a few additional pages where people find out about your organization's leaders and programs. As you grow, you can add more bells and whistles.

An unattended Web site leaves a bad impression. Broken Web links and out-of-date information tell the reader that your organization isn't paying attention to important details. If you're going to have a Web site, assign someone in your organization the task of maintaining and updating it regularly. If your budget allows, consider hiring a Web design firm or Web savvy individual to create and maintain your site.

Producing an annual report

Begin producing an annual report after your first year of operating. The report may be a letter, brochure, pamphlet, or even a book. Usually, the annual report includes a financial statement for the year, along with an overview of recent accomplishments. It may also include letters from the president and executive director of your organization.

Issuing a newsletter

A newsletter offers background stories and information about your organization. You can have it printed, "print" it on a copy machine, or publish it on the Web. Issuing a newsletter is a great way to keep in touch with your organization's constituents, and it can take them behind the scenes of your organization. You may use it to profile members of your staff, board, and constituents; alert followers to coming events; summarize research; and announce news about your organization's work.

Taking care of customers — your best marketing tool

If your constituents, audiences, patients, clients, volunteers, and board members aren't treated well, you can make major investments in advertising and public relations but still struggle to find new customers and keep your old ones. Small adjustments in customer service can make a big difference to your organization's image.

The trick is to attend to service in little ways all the time. Every staff member and volunteer needs to be aware of the importance of customer service. We offer five key areas to address to improve (or maintain) your service levels.

On the telephone

Talk to all staff and volunteers about how to answer the phone politely and otherwise use it to maximum effect. Provide a cheat sheet with lists of extensions, instructions on how to forward calls, and any other useful information.

Simple additions to a greeting, like, "May I help you?" or telling the caller the receptionist's name can set a friendly, professional tone.

Make a rule for yourself to return all calls within 24 hours or, if that's not possible, within one week. Let callers know, through your voice mail greeting, when they may expect to hear from you.

If you're selecting a voice mail system, make sure it's user friendly for your callers. We prefer a small number of transfers within the system and options for modifying standard recorded announcements with more personal and pertinent messages.

If your agency is likely to receive calls from people requiring counseling or emergency assistance, make sure that everyone answering the phone is thoroughly trained in how to calm a caller and provide a referral.

At the door

Someone needs to (cheerfully) answer the door. If you're in a small office without a receptionist and the interruptions are frequent, you can rotate this task among staff members or volunteers.

If visitors must use a buzzer or pass through a security system, try to balance the coldness of that experience with a friendly intercom greeting and pleasant foyer.

Before and after the sale

If you have something to sell, make it easy to buy. Accepting only cash is far too restrictive. The banker managing your business account can help prepare you to accept credit card orders. Also, consider selling over the Web; more and more sites are available on the Web to assist small businesses with Web sales.

If a customer isn't satisfied with your product or service, invite the customer to give feedback and listen carefully. Offer a partial or complete refund. Doing so wins loyalty.

With a note

Keep some nice stationery and postcards handy so that writing personal notes is easy. Hand-written notes are more personal and often make a stronger impression than formal, typed letters.

Write thank you notes within a few days of any contribution.

If your organization receives *things* — like a theatre group that receives play manuscripts or a natural history museum that accepts scholarly papers for publication — have prestamped postcards ready that acknowledge the item's receipt and state when the person submitting it can expect to hear from you.

In the details

An old saying suggests that the devil lurks in the details, but that's also where you find the heart and soul of hospitality and service. Keep notes in a database or on file cards about the interests, connections, and preferences of your board members, donors, and frequent customers. Learn the names of your board members' significant others and be prepared to greet them personally at events and on the phone.

Discovering Who You Are: First Steps to Marketing

You've put your basic tools in place and your programs are up and running, but you sense that something is wrong. You know that you're addressing a need and that your agency is highly regarded. Why aren't your programs full? How can you engage more people in the important work that you do?

If a marketing program is what you need (and we believe it is), the first step is understanding your current situation — what you do, who you serve, who admires your work, and who is willing to support it. When you know the answers to these questions, you can begin to build marketing strategies that are tailored to all your key audiences — the people who walk through your doors every day to receive your services, your board members and staff, your donors and volunteers, and the community at large. Blend in your budget constraints (we all have to do that!), and you're ready to roll.

Your A to Z references on marketing and public relations

Whole books — hundreds and hundreds of whole books — have been written on the topic of marketing and the related field of public relations. Our job in this chapter is to take you on a quick fly-over of marketing for nonprofit organizations so that you get the big picture and know where to turn for details. And for all the details on marketing plans, surveys, public relations, press releases, and related topics, we recommend three other books from Wiley: *Marketing For Dummies,* 2nd Edition, by Alexander Hiam, MBA; *Marketing Kit For Dummies,* 2nd Edition, by Alexander Hiam, MBA; and *Small Business Marketing For Dummies,* 2nd Edition, by Barbara Findlay Schenck.

Defining your current market

If you want to improve the way you reach your public, you first need to know how your current marketing works. Who are your customers? How did they find out about your organization? Why do they make use of your programs?

Surveying your customers to gain important info

You may never discover who reads about your organization in the newspaper or sees your sign every day on the bus, but some people — those with whom you directly communicate — can be identified. Start by defining your core group — your most important constituents — and work out from there.

Suppose that your organization is a small historical society that organizes exhibits and panel discussions at three libraries in your town, publishes a quarterly newsletter, and maintains a Web site featuring news and information about its collection. Your current customers (or stakeholders, if you want to use a common nonprofit term), working from the core to the outer boundaries, include the following:

- Your board and staff (and their friends and relations)
- Your docents and volunteers
- Families and organizations that donate materials to your collection
- Local library staff and board members
- Persons signing up for your mailing list at panel discussions
- Schools and other groups visiting your exhibits
- Scholars and other archivists writing to ask about your holdings
- Patrons of the three libraries
- Subscribers to your quarterly newsletter
- Persons visiting your organization's Web site

Drawing up this list of interested persons is easy enough. But for marketing purposes, you need to know as much as possible about the characteristics, backgrounds, and interests of each group. Some things you can do to collect this sort of information include

- Creating a database of your supporters by gathering names and addresses from every possible source within your organization — items like checks from donors, subscription forms from newsletter subscribers, and sign-up sheets from volunteers. Enter these names and addresses in a computer database or word processing program that can sort them by postal or zip code. (Many mailing list, database, and even word processing programs have sorting options. Filemaker Pro, Microsoft Access, Microsoft Word, and Corel Word Perfect are all widely available choices.) Review the zip codes appearing most frequently on this list. If you're in the United States, you can visit the United States Census Bureau Web site (`www.census.gov`) and get demographic information about residents in those zip code areas.

✔ Asking the three libraries if they collect demographic data when visitors apply for library cards and whether they can share that information with you. (Also, some public agencies have information about their constituents on their Web sites.)

✔ Interviewing schools or other groups when they call to sign up for a tour. You can ask them a few questions over the phone as part of the registration process. Find out how they heard about your program, why they want to visit it, and whether they have other needs you may be able to address.

✔ Inserting clearly worded and inviting surveys in the programs at your public events. At the beginning and end of an event, make a brief public pitch explaining why it's so important for people to respond to the surveys. Make pencils or pens available. Create incentives for completing the form, like a free museum membership for a person whose survey is drawn at random. Include the same survey as part of your mailed newsletter. Provide a return envelope to make it easy for readers to respond. Make it easy for visitors of your Web site to provide their e-mail addresses, and send a brief survey to them by e-mail.

Be aware that the way questions are worded can influence the answers you get. If you want to seek help in developing your survey, check with local colleges and universities for faculty members or graduate students who understand survey techniques and who may be willing to give you some guidance. Also, the Web site `zoomerang.com` provides assistance with online surveys; and you can find many sample surveys on the Web that give you ideas about wording questions.

You can find two sample surveys (CD1101 and CD1102) that may suggest wording for your survey questions on the CD that accompanies this book.

Organizing and interpreting the responses

After you have survey results, you can create a simple check sheet to compile the responses. Or you can use database and word processing programs mentioned earlier in this chapter to create a record for each person who responds or for each event at which surveys are gathered. You may discover that you serve several distinct groups of people. Low-income students use the library after school and visit your exhibits while they are there. Middle-income mothers from the immediate neighborhood bring their toddlers to the library for afternoon stories and take advantage of your programs. And

Designing a useful survey

Developing a picture of your current clients is critically important to creating a marketing plan, and a good survey can be your camera.

If you're going to go to the effort to conduct a survey, it needs to have a purpose and be based on questions you want to explore, such as why the people who currently use your services find them worthwhile. If you can get to the root of why others value you, you've figured out a lot about how to talk about your work to your future constituents.

If you make the survey too long, some people won't complete it. You probably want to include some multiple-choice questions, but be sure to have one or two open-ended questions so people have a chance to speak their piece. Explore different kinds of information by asking how convenient and appealing your events and services are, and by asking your patrons what other kinds of programs they would enjoy. Also, ask your current consumers how they found out about you. The answers tell you which forms of your current marketing are effective and begin to suggest how you may most effectively spread the word further about your programs.

wealthy older adults volunteer as docents, serve on your board, and attend your organization's panel discussions.

With this valuable information, you may be able to recognize ways to reach more people who resemble the ones you're already serving. The more challenging task is to reach and entice new groups of people.

Do people gather at your organization's programs but you don't know who they are? Sponsor free drawings in which contestants compete for prizes by filling out forms with their names, addresses, and phone numbers.

If you discover that your clients like your program offerings but find the times you offer them inconvenient, do you want to experiment with new times and formats? For instance, do consumers find Sunday afternoons (when the library is closed) to be more convenient? What other barriers inhibit their involvement? Maybe mothers with toddlers want to come to your lectures but need childcare. Perhaps you charge a modest admission fee for lectures but students find that charge to be too high.

One of your hardest marketing tasks is analyzing the very basis of what you do and how you do it. You may feel that your historical society's close working relationship with libraries is its greatest asset, but the surveys may point out that those libraries are cold and musty during winter months. You may do better by taking over a neighborhood restaurant, creating a "warmer" atmosphere — even offering hot gingerbread and beverages.

To succeed at reaching and serving more people, you want to keep an open mind, be observant, and test your hunches.

Defining who you want to reach and how

Armed with information about the people who already know about your non-profit, you're now ready to extend your reach by defining target groups you want to serve and learning how best to reach them. In general, it's wisest to begin with your current constituents and work to expand within their demographic group or to others who are similar to them.

As you shift your attention to reaching new groups, be cautious. You may alienate and lose current followers. The more different demographically your new target groups are from the people you now serve, the more difficult and expensive your marketing task may be.

If you run a local history archive and have audiences of low-income students, middle-income mothers of toddlers, and affluent docents and volunteers, logical new target audiences include the following:

- Family members and classmates of the students using the libraries
- Mothers and toddlers from a wider geographic area surrounding the libraries
- Docents and volunteers who assist other local cultural institutions
- Friends and acquaintances of the docents

Your marketing plan is then tailored to reach these groups. Attempting to reach these groups may require changes both in how you present your work and in how you spread the message about that work. Consider some of the ideas in this list to reach the following groups:

- **The students' classmates and friends.**
  - Contact local history teachers and work with them to link their lessons to archival materials in your collection. Invite them to bring their classes to see your exhibits and involve the students who are familiar with the collection as docents for the school tours.
  - Invite the students who currently use the library space to help in planning, researching, and presenting an exhibit. Honor them for their involvement at the exhibit's opening and provide them with invitations for their friends and acquaintances.

- **The students' families.**
  - Work with local teachers and your student audience to design family-friendly weekend events at the library. You can offer a variety of activities for different age groups — puppet shows, art projects, scavenger hunts, and picnic meals — based on themes in your historical materials.

How market research can open your eyes

A small nonprofit alcoholism treatment center for women was started in San Francisco in the late 1970s in response to studies that demonstrated multiple programs existed to help alcoholic men but few focused specifically on women. No local service of this type focused on helping Spanish- speaking immigrant women.

The program's mission was to provide comprehensive counseling and alcohol treatment services to low-income women, particularly those originally from Mexico or Central America.

Four years into the nonprofit's history, its programs were full and effective, and it had won prestigious contracts from the city. The center had even launched a capital campaign to create a permanent home. It appeared to be very successful.

With one exception. The women being served were mostly middle class and white. A few were African American. None came from the neighborhood where the program was based.

The board realized that the center needed to change its image and marketing strategy. Through interviews with women from the center's target population, board and staff realized the stigma associated with alcoholism was particularly strong among Mexican and Central American families and women from these cultural groups were struggling with alcoholism in private.

The center began a multifaceted campaign to change this situation, beginning with cultural sensitivity training for counselors. When the center hired new staff, an aggressive effort was made to find Chicanas and Latinas to fill positions. The group published all brochures and other informational materials in Spanish and held press conferences for the Spanish-language press. The center hired a Chicana outreach counselor to meet with community groups, churches, and schools and develop connections and a system of referrals to the agency.

Within two years, more than one-third of the women served were low-income women from Mexico and Central America. The marketing aimed at this community was well worth the investment. Fulfilling the organization's mission depended on it.

✔ **More mothers and toddlers.**

- Advertise or place articles about your organization's work in local newsletters for parents of young children.

- Post flyers about your organization's work at parks, playgrounds, local stores that sell goods for small children, and at other cultural institutions with children's events.

✔ **Docents and volunteers who also help other organizations.**

- Advertise or place articles in your local volunteer center's newsletter.

- Exchange mailing lists of docents and volunteers with other local cultural organizations, and then use the new lists to extend invitations to a special get-acquainted-with-us event.

> ✔ **Friends and acquaintances of your current docents.**

> • Hold a volunteer recognition party and provide each of your volunteers with ten or more invitations for friends and acquaintances.

The cost of implementing new programs and spreading the word about them can add up quickly. Consider what resources you have available (including your time) before committing to big changes in your organization.

Using Mass Media to Reach Your Audience

What if you want to reach all the people some of the time? (Sorry, you can't reach all the people all of the time.) That's when you're likely to move to the mass media — newspapers, magazines, radio, television, and the Web. Although some nonprofits pay for advertising to spread the word, most organizations rely on free publicity.

Planning for effective publicity

Before contacting the media, first decide what story you want to tell and who you want to reach with that story. What is distinctive and important about your organization's work? Why is it newsworthy? Be honest: Analyze your idea as if you're a news editor who has to choose among many different stories from many sources. How does yours stand up in the competition?

Marketing on a shoestring

Effective marketing doesn't have to be expensive. It can be based on multiple grassroots efforts that are small in scale and very specifically targeted. *Guerilla marketing* is the term for marketing that's cheap, creative, and effective.

The guerilla approach may use stickers affixed to parking meters, cards tacked on the bulletin boards at local health food stores, fliers mailed along with supermarket coupons, bookmarks

stacked by checkout counters, and e-mail discussion groups.

These efforts work if they are based on knowing the habits of the people you want to reach. Using them, you can reach some of the people all of the time. Jay Conrad Levinson's Web site (www.gmarketing.com) is a good place to begin learning more about guerilla marketing.

The art of shaping a news story

A few years ago we were involved as grant-makers in supporting the creation of a mural on the exterior of a community center next to a small urban park. One of San Francisco's best-regarded mural artists led the project. She spent a great deal of time talking to the park's neighbors and people who used the building about images to use in her mural. Those people she talked to kept mentioning a young couple who had been killed in the park in a random, accidental shooting several years earlier. Although it wasn't her original subject idea, she included the couple's portraits in the painting surrounded by images representing peace and renewal.

The story of the mural's unveiling was presented to the media as a public memorial event for the neighbors and families of the young couple. Front page, color images of the piece appeared in both the morning and evening papers the next day, and five television stations covered the event that evening. An acclaimed artist completing another mural wouldn't have been a story, but a neighborhood mourning two lost teenagers was hot news.

We hope your nonprofit is never thrown into telling the story of a tragedy, but we give this example to show that not all good work is news. Tragedy is news. Drama is news. Breakthroughs are news. Surprises are news.

Developing a media list

A media list is a compilation of names, addresses, e-mail addresses, and phone numbers of contacts at local (and maybe national) newspapers, radio and television stations, magazines, and Web sites. You also want the list to include wire service contacts in your area, such as Associated Press and Reuters.

A media list is a valuable tool that you refine and expand over time. Some metropolitan areas have press clubs and service organizations from which you can buy membership lists, providing a basis for your list. If no such service is available, you can begin building your media list at the public library, using *Broadcasting Yearbook, Editor and Publishers Yearbook, BPI Media Services,* and other reference books. In a pinch, you can use the classified pages of the telephone book.

For all the nuances of media list development and management, we recommend that you take a look at *Public Relations Kit For Dummies* by Eric Yaverbaum with Bob Bly, published by Wiley. In general, your objective is to build two working lists, one that you use with practically every press release you send out and the other for specific opportunities for publicity. The latter group may include the following:

- ✔ Social and entertainment editors to whom you send news of your annual benefit gala

- ✔ Social and business editors to whom you announce new members and officers of your board

- ✔ Opinion page editors for letters to the editor

- ✔ Sunday magazine supplement editors for in-depth profiles of leaders in your field of work

- ✔ Features columnists for amusing anecdotes or unusual news

- ✔ Internet chat room hosts to whom you give your organization's perspective and who you use to test public response to news and ideas

Starting to work with media

Here's our advice for getting started with the mass media:

- ✔ Pay attention to the areas of interest of different media outlets, writers, and reporters and match your story to these interests.

- ✔ Analyze your program or event as if you were a news editor. Is there a human-interest angle? What's newsworthy?

- ✔ Write (or record or film) a basic document and vary it to address the different media interests that you appeal to, making use of your multiple story angles.

- ✔ Persist in following-up on every item you send to the press, but don't become annoying.

- ✔ Keep the press fully informed about any changes in your story. Printing incorrect information makes them look bad and may hurt your chances of future coverage.

- ✔ Prepare for a visit to your program or orchestrate other forms of direct interaction.

- ✔ Take no graciously when media decide not to use your story. You need to be able to go back to these people in the future.

Different media outlets require different amounts of lead time. In an ideal situation, you want to begin your efforts to reach the media four or five months in advance of that hoped-for coverage. The first two months are spent creating press releases and public service announcements and shooting and developing photographs. Then you start distributing the materials:

- ✔ Most monthly magazines need to receive your press release and photographs at least three months in advance of publication (even earlier if they're published quarterly or bimonthly).

✔ At the same time that you're mailing to magazines, you want to send advance notice to your most important daily and weekly outlets.

✔ We recommend sending public service announcements (see the section on PSAs later in this chapter) two to three months prior to the time when you hope they'll be used. Although most stations have set aside time for broadcasting nonprofits' announcements, they need time to rotate through the many announcement materials they receive.

✔ Press releases to daily or weekly papers should be sent four to six weeks in advance of the event you want covered. You also may send follow-up releases approximately ten days prior to the event. You certainly want to make follow-up phone calls.

✔ Releases inviting members of the press to a press conference or to witness a special event or announcement may be sent close to the event (three to ten days in advance). Generally such announcements are conveyed with a sense of urgency.

Reaching your media contacts

Each section of a newspaper and each part of a TV or radio program is made up of materials from multiple sources that are competing for time and space. You improve the odds of receiving attention in the media by providing clear, accurate, and provocative materials in time for consideration and possible use by reporters and broadcasters.

We recommend the following steps when you submit material to the media:

1. **Call to identify the most appropriate contact person at the newspaper, radio station, or TV station, and ask about the format that each wants you to use in your submission.**

   The better you get to know your contacts, the less frequently you have to take this step.

2. **Submit clear, accurate written materials, labeled photographs, or recorded audiotapes, videotapes, or compact discs, as is most appropriate.**

3. **Call to see whether your materials have been received.**

   Take this opportunity to ask whether more information or a different format is needed.

4. **If requested, submit additional information and call to confirm its receipt and clarity.**

5. **If you don't receive a clear response (either "Yes, we'll cover it" or "Sorry, I don't see the story here") to your initial release, update it, resubmit it, and call again.**

6. **If a member of the press comes to cover an event you've announced, have a press packet ready.**

   A press packet is usually a press release with background information and photographs. The packet briefs the reporter about your event and makes it easy for him or her to combine notes and materials from the event with your organization's official overview of the story.

   Introduce yourself and be available to answer questions or to introduce the reporter to key spokespeople, but don't be a pest: Let a reporter find his or her own story.

7. **If your situation changes and the press release is no longer accurate, immediately call in the change and, if necessary, revise and resubmit your original release.**

A sample press release (CD1103), press alert (CD1104), calendar release (CD1105), photo caption (CD1106), photo permission form (CD1107), and public service announcement (CD1108) are on the CD. They can help you understand the approaches and formats to use.

Getting listed in the calendar

Getting your organization's events listed in newspaper calendars and broadcast on TV and radio can be critically important to attracting a crowd. Readers, viewers, and listeners use these calendars to help decide how they are going to spend their time on, say, a Thursday night. If your event is listed clearly and accurately, you're in the running.

Larger newspapers and many other media outlets assign the preparation of calendar sections to specific editors. When you put together your media contact list, make sure you identify the calendar editors. And to improve your access to this important source of publicity, contact the calendar specialists in advance and ask for instructions about how they prefer calendar listings to be formatted and how much in advance of the event they want to receive your information.

Preparing public service announcements

Many radio and television stations allot a portion of their airtime to broadcasting public service announcements (PSAs) on behalf of nonprofit causes. Although these stations rarely give away their best viewing and listening hours to this free service, sometimes they do tack PSAs onto the end of a newscast or special program during prime time. But even an announcement played during the morning's wee hours can reach many people.

Public service announcements are brief. Most are 15, 30, or 60 seconds long. You may submit them as written text to be read by the stations' announcers, or you may submit them recorded or filmed on audiotape, CD, or on video-tape for direct broadcast. Many stations are more willing to use PSAs that are already recorded or filmed, but this isn't true all the time. If you submit a pre-recorded PSA, also include a print version of the text. Some stations string several announcements together in a general public announcement broad-cast, and it's easier for them to work from text.

If you choose to submit a fully completed PSA, make sure that it's of broadcast quality with excellent sound and/or images. If you're the narrator, spit out your gum! If you mumble or if the videotape is blurry, stations can't use it.

The challenge to writing public service announcements is to convey a lot of information in a short time and to be very clear. Write your message and test it against the clock. If you're rushing to finish it in time, it's probably too long. Ask someone else to read it back to you and time that person. You don't want to be the only one who can finish it in 15 seconds.

Table 11-1 summarizes an appropriate format for presenting a public service announcement to a media outlet.

Table 11-1	Presenting a Public Service Announcement
Placement	*Content*
Top left of page	"For immediate release to public service directors for use between [identify dates during which the release is timely]." Also clearly indicate the length of the release (15, 30, or 60 seconds).
Top right of page	"For further information contact:" followed by the name, phone number, and e-mail address of a person who can answer questions about the announcement.
Centered	Brief headline that both orients the reader to the subject of your story and that can become part of the reading of the release.
Below headline	The announcement in large print (sometimes all caps), double-spaced. Make sure that your release can be read within the length of time that you specify and that it flows well. If it includes names or words with unfamiliar pronun-ciations, spell them phonetically in parentheses next to the challenging words.

Chapter 12

Creating a Home for Your Nonprofit — and Insuring It

In This Chapter

▶ Selecting the right location

▶ Protecting your enterprise with the right insurance

S ome nonprofits can travel light. The service they provide can be managed out of a spare bedroom or small commercial office. Others need specialized, technically sophisticated facilities.

Some nonprofits fit easily into a wide variety of locations. Others can fulfill their missions only if they're located in specific neighborhoods or geographic regions.

Some nonprofits pay nothing for their space: A church, a school, or a public agency gives them shelter. Some save money by buying or leasing property with other nonprofits. Still others pay top dollar for highly visible homes that are an important part of their identities.

Lots of options, lots of decisions. This chapter explores the ins and outs of finding a suitable home base for a nonprofit organization, and of protecting the entire enterprise — furniture, fixtures, real estate, staff, volunteers, and board — against the risks of everyday life.

Finding a Place to Do Your Work

If your organization is grappling with a move to a new (or to its first) building, you're facing important decisions about how, when, and where to go. This effort is likely to have three phases:

✔ Planning for your needs

✔ Identifying possible locations

✔ Analyzing the feasibility of the locations you find

How much space and of what kind?

Before you go out to seek a location, make a list of your organization's specific needs. If you've ever shopped for an apartment or house, you know that some features are critically important and some are desired but not essential. Breaking down your space needs by function and then including a list of general requirements helps.

To help you anticipate and specify all your organization's facility needs, check out the list of questions to ask yourself in CD1201 and the list of required spaces worksheet in CD1202.

Location, location, location

Many nonprofit organizations have learned the hard way that having a beautiful new facility doesn't necessarily mean that their students, patients, or audiences will go there. We suggest that an organization conduct a simple marketing test of a location they're considering. This "test" may take the form of a written survey, interviews, or an open house/walk-through at the proposed site followed by a discussion with current constituents. Also, talk to nearby residents, merchants, and the local police; and spend time observing the site at different times of day.

Many organizations move to larger facilities when they want their programs to grow, and they discover the hard way that offering more seats, classes, or therapy sessions doesn't necessarily mean that they'll be used. Do you have clear evidence of growing demand for your services and that your organization's current physical space is inhibiting its growth? When you conduct your marketing test, you need to know whether more people will go to your new location: Reach out to both potential clients and your current followers.

Your ideal location may change over time as the neighborhood changes. Even if your organization has been based in one place for a long time, before signing a new lease, explore whether its location is still meeting its needs.

Owning, leasing, or finding something free

Stability, convenience, and cost — in addition to location — are key factors to consider in selecting your organization's home. In this section, we discuss the implications of ownership, leasing, and receiving donated space and invite you to weigh the pros and cons.

In considering your real estate choices, also consider your context. Is the real estate market changing? Are interest rates rising or falling? How well are tenants' rights protected by law? Is the building that you lease or enjoy for free likely to be sold?

The pros and cons of owning

Because of the tax benefits of private home ownership, many people automatically assume that owning its own building is best for a nonprofit organization. Although a nonprofit's building can be a valuable asset, remember that a nonprofit is already exempt from paying most business taxes, so any interest it may pay on a mortgage or building loan isn't a deductible expense — it's just an expense.

Two possible advantages of building ownership are

- ✔ **Ownership stabilizes costs.** If your organization is based in a real estate market where prices are rising, purchasing a building may help to prevent steep rent increases or an untimely eviction.

- ✔ **Ownership improves the public image of your organization.** Organizations owning their own buildings appear in the public eye to be more permanent institutions. This perception may help them raise money.

Major disadvantages of building ownership for nonprofits can be that it increases the staff's workload and requires a continuing investment. If the organization buys a building that's larger than its needs, it may become a landlord to others and must be prepared to advertise the property, negotiate leases, and manage maintenance and repairs. Whether or not it has tenants, it becomes fully responsible for the building's care.

If your nonprofit organization buys its own building, set aside a cash reserve for building maintenance. Otherwise, if a boiler explodes or the roof leaks, you may need to suspend operations for an extended period of time.

Considering renting

When you rent a home for your nonprofit organization, you're taking on costs that you need to cover month after month. Often these costs increase from year to year. Rent may not be the only such expense. A few things you want to understand fully before signing a lease:

- ✔ What costs are covered? Is your nonprofit responsible for all or some of the utilities?

- ✔ How long is the lease and does it include options for you to renew it at a similar rate?

✔ If property or other taxes increase while you're a tenant, do you pay for the increase or does the landlord?

✔ Which repairs are the landlord's responsibility and which ones are yours?

✔ Who's responsible for routine building maintenance?

✔ What will the landlord permit you to change about the building?

We recommend budgeting for your monthly building costs and your one-time move-in costs, and creating a facility contingency fund to cover minor repairs or occasional expenses (from tree trimming to clogged plumbing).

Deciding whether to take a freebie if it's offered

Taking a free ride through the donation of public or private space to your nonprofit sounds wonderful, doesn't it? Indeed, it lowers your operating costs and allows you to use more of your resources for programs. But you must be willing to look a gift horse in the mouth. A free building is worthwhile only if it's in the right location and the right size. Doing effective work is very difficult in an inappropriate space. Ask yourself, if the building wasn't free, would you have chosen it for your nonprofit?

Two possible disadvantages to accepting free space are

✔ **Inappropriate connections:** Making use of free space belonging to another public or private entity identifies your organization with the building's history and other uses.

✔ **Loss of control:** If someone provides something free to you, you're put in a weak bargaining position. You may not have a lease, ensuring your use of the space for a prescribed period of time. You may not feel that you can complain if building maintenance is sloppy or repairs are postponed.

Estimating costs

Organizations with what seem to be straightforward plans for moving into new facilities often can overlook the true costs of making such a move. Some spaces may need to be altered to suit your organization's needs. Even when you fit right into your new offices, you encounter one-time charges such as signs, cleaning deposits, phone and Internet hook-up, and fees or deposits for starting up your utilities.

We organized those costs into four general categories:

✔ **Moving**

- Moving van rental or moving service

- Boxes and shipping containers

- Thank you party or recognition gifts for volunteers

✔ **Setting up services**

- Transfer of utilities (garbage, water, and power)
- Transfer of services (phone, cable, and computer lines)

✔ **Making alterations**

- Constructing new workspaces, service spaces, and shelving
- Moving electrical outlets and adding phone and computer lines
- Buying furniture, computers, and fixtures

✔ **Announcing your change**

- Public notices about your move (postcards, newsletters, press releases, Web site revisions, and e-mail announcements)
- Revision of basic printed materials (reprinting brochures, stationery, and other publications)
- Signs on your new location
- Open house or party for constituents

The most important *things* for you to move are your constituents. You want to make a thoughtful, sustained effort to invite them into your new facility.

Taking on a capital project

What if no existing building suits your organization's needs? You may just need to move some walls and expand the bathrooms; or you may be in for a major effort to substantially renovate a space or construct a new building. If you're one of these brave and hardy types, you want to read this part of the chapter along with Chapter 18, which addresses planning and raising money for building projects in greater detail.

Even a small organization with the right board and campaign leadership can manage a successful capital campaign if its expectations are reasonable. So can organizations whose projects are happening at the right place and at the right time — such as those organizations qualifying for redevelopment agency funds or for low-interest bank loans for community development. To determine whether your organization can manage a capital campaign, you should ask yourself some questions, including the following:

✔ **What will the project cost?** Although you can't design an accurate budget until you've approved architectural drawings and contractor bids, an architect or contractor who's friendly to your organization should be willing to look at the space and offer rough cost estimates.

✔ Are your board members in a position to contribute to a capital campaign above and beyond their usual annual gifts to your organization?

> ✔ Do public or foundation resources in your region support capital projects? Would they be likely contributors? (Include in this inquiry low-interest loans for nonprofits.)
>
> ✔ Do you have staff knowledge and time to contribute to this effort?

Various items that we've included on the CD should help you think through a possible capital project carefully. CD1203, "Planned Change and Facilities"; CD1204, "Change, Facilities, and Program Choices"; and CD1205, "Organization Capacity Worksheet," will help you assess your organization's readiness. CD1206 points out common justifications nonprofits use to barge ahead, even if doing so is foolish. CD1207, "Your Project's Relative Size," illustrates the impact a capital project is likely to have on your organization.

You can find leads to community loan and development funds for nonprofits on two helpful Web sites: www.communitycapital.org and (focused more on investors than those seeking help, but still rich with information) www.socialinvest.org.

Having examined these preliminary questions, organizations that are considering capital campaigns often go through a process called a "feasibility study" — research most often led by a consultant who interviews people who support the organization and other generous donors in their communities whose grants and gifts are essential to its success. Through these interviews, the consultant estimates how much the organization is likely to raise with a capital campaign. You find more about this practice in Chapter 18.

The costs of renovating a building are likely to increase (at a rate of some 10 percent per year), and major donors may pledge contributions but wait a year or longer before sending a check. For those reasons, borrowing money to complete construction (if reasonable interest rates are available) can help contain costs while you're conducting a capital campaign and starting construction. In some areas, local government, foundations, community economic development corporations, or banks may consider awarding low-interest loans as an important form of philanthropy.

As new technology changes the needs of working spaces, and building code requirements become more stringent, renovation of existing buildings may be very costly. Sometimes building a brand-new facility to suit your nonprofit's needs may be your cheaper and more efficient choice.

Insuring Against What Can Go Wrong

Many people who start nonprofits hope to improve conditions in the world, and they conduct their work with modest resources. They're not naïve, but they may have little time to dwell on the things that possibly can go wrong.

(Okay, okay, we're making a generalization. The nonprofit arena has its share of serious worriers too.)

But things can go wrong. That's why nonprofits need insurance like everyone else. For the eternal optimists and worriers alike, we highly recommend practicing risk management and finding a good insurance broker who can help you make appropriate choices of insurance and find the most reasonable rates.

Managing your risks

Risk management means identifying and analyzing the risks your organization faces in carrying out its daily business. If you're a smart manager, you eliminate as many of these risks as possible (within reason). You're financially rewarded for pursuing this course: The more risks you can eliminate, the lower your insurance premiums are.

Here's a simple example to illustrate risk management: The sidewalk in front of the entrance to your office is beginning to crack in two places. The concrete is uneven and may cause someone to trip and fall. Repairing the sidewalk is better than risking the chances of injury to a visitor.

Adding smoke alarms, sprinkler systems, and emergency lighting are other ways to practice risk management. Those safety features are wise investments and will probably lower your property insurance. Although no one can think of everything that may go wrong, try to eliminate as many risks as possible. Insurance agents and brokers can be helpful in this exercise. You can find more information about risk management at the Nonprofit Risk Management Center (www.nonprofitrisk.org).

You must be honest on insurance applications, fully stating your agency's risks. If falsehoods are uncovered, your coverage doesn't protect you.

Determining your insurance needs

A nonprofit's insurance needs vary according to the following:

- ✔ Whether it has employees
- ✔ Whether it makes use of volunteers
- ✔ Whether it has direct contact with clients, students, patients, or audiences and the nature of that direct contact
- ✔ Whether it offers services within its own (or a rented) piece of property

Providing health insurance

Beyond the employee benefits required by law, you'll want to provide health coverage for your employees if at all possible so that they can afford medical attention if they're sick or injured. Offering this benefit also helps you recruit better-qualified employees.

In most cases, an organization can secure group health insurance for its employees at a more reasonable cost than what employees would have to pay if they bought it on their own. Generally, health insurance becomes more affordable as your organization grows and the group for which you're buying it becomes larger. For small organizations and those just beginning to consider providing health insurance for employees, here are some ways to get started:

✔ **Begin with insurance that covers only major, expensive medical problems.** Usually such insurance is less costly because major crises occur less frequently. You can add insurance for more routine medical attention later, just as you can add dental and vision care.

✔ **Begin with a higher deductible amount.** Most insurance doesn't begin to cover costs until the employee has paid a certain amount upfront, the amount that is referred to as the *deductible*. Sometimes you can secure comprehensive health coverage for your employees if the deductible amount is relatively high — say, $1,000 rather than $200. Then, as you can afford it, you can improve their coverage by getting insurance with a lower deductible.

✔ **Try to join with a group.** Some nonprofit service organizations offer their members the benefit of joining a group health insurance plan. In selecting your insurance options, don't forget to contact your local United Way office, your statewide association of nonprofit organizations (find yours at www.ncna.org/states/htm), or service organizations specializing in the type of work your nonprofit provides. They may provide group insurance plans you can join.

If you're a new entity and using a fiscal sponsor, that sponsor may provide access to health and other types of insurance as a service to sponsored projects.

Insuring against workplace injuries

If an employee is injured in the course of performing duties for your nonprofit, workers' compensation insurance covers the cost of medical treatment and — in some cases — the cost of retraining the employee for a different profession. The cost of your workers' compensation insurance is calculated according to your number of employees, the number of hours they spend on the job, and the nature of the work they do. Rates for office clerks are considerably lower than rates for lion tamers and trapeze artists.

In most states, workers' compensation insurance isn't an option like health insurance is. It's required by law. As a nonprofit manager, therefore, you don't make a choice about whether to buy it, but simply attend to doing it correctly. As you plan, don't forget to consider the following:

- **Do you use docents or other consistent volunteers?** We highly recommend including them in your workers' compensation insurance coverage. We've witnessed two instances in which volunteers were seriously hurt in the course of assisting nonprofit organizations but weren't covered by workers' compensation insurance. The results were nearly catastrophic for the agencies.

- **If your organization's staff size or the nature of the work your employees do changes during the course of the year, contact your workers' compensation insurance carrier and change your coverage accordingly.** Don't forget to make this change in coverage if you make temporary changes in the nature of your employees' work. For example, do you conduct an annual fundraising event for which employees are working on ladders, stringing lights and garlands? If you plan ahead to change the definition of the type of work they perform, you can be confident that they're covered.

Workers' compensation insurance is a specialized field of law. If you encounter a legal problem about your coverage, seek assistance from an attorney with expertise in this field.

Some nonprofit organizations require volunteers to sign waivers that release the nonprofits from responsibility for insuring them. However, waivers may not stand up in a court of law.

Purchasing liability insurance

Someone carelessly stretches an electrical cord across a hallway, and a client trips and falls. A shingle falls from the roof and hits a visitor on the head. Liability insurance is based on the oops and ouches of daily life and human error. No matter how minor it may seem, if you make a mistake while performing your organization's duties and someone is injured as a result, you can be sued.

By purchasing liability insurance, you have access to a source of revenue for settling a lawsuit if someone sues you for this kind of mistake. Your insurance company also may provide legal defense, if it's needed. Most businesses purchase liability insurance as a matter of course. You may get by without it for a time, but you may be required to get it if you meet any of the following conditions:

- You accept a contract or grant from a government source.

- You rent offices or other facilities.

- You seek a city or county permit to use public property.

- You seek an operating or construction permit.

You need to purchase specialized kinds of liability insurance if your organization has significant direct client contact that involves a potential risk. Health clinics and therapy programs need such insurance to protect them if a client is hurt or handled inappropriately. So do programs offering activities with possible physical dangers, such as rock climbing, sail boating, or horseback riding.

If your organization occasionally produces events or conducts work in locations other than its central office or building, double-check to make sure that you're covered for these off-site events. You may want to purchase a rider to your regular liability insurance policy to cover such situations.

Protecting directors and officers from lawsuits

Although corporate laws vary by state and nation, in most contexts, the personal assets of directors and officers of nonprofit organizations are protected from legal proceedings against those nonprofits if the directors are providing reasonable oversight of the organizations. Nevertheless, just to make sure, you can purchase directors and officers' liability insurance.

What is "reasonable" oversight? Board members usually are protected if they attend meetings, ask questions, and keep well informed about the organization — in other words, if they're doing a reasonably good job being board members. If they're not doing their jobs, they may be considered personally negligent and become vulnerable.

Board members' personal assets can be in jeopardy if the nonprofit organization isn't paying its federal employee taxes. However, even in this dire situation, if the nonprofit has contacted the Internal Revenue Service and worked out a payment plan, board members are unlikely to be affected.

So why would you want to pay for directors and officers' insurance? The biggest advantage is that it covers the cost of your organization's legal defense against lawsuits. It also may be reassuring to board members and potential board members. Some people refuse to serve on a board if the organization doesn't have directors and officers' insurance. Here are some examples of situations in which it's highly recommended:

- ✔ Your organization has to lay off or fire employees. The most common type of lawsuit brought against nonprofit organizations is for "wrongful discharge."

- ✔ Your organization's work is controversial, making the organization a potential target for lawsuits.

- ✔ Your organization is a hospital, health clinic, or another kind of entity that — because of the intense, professional service it provides — is more liable to malpractice and other kinds of liability lawsuits.

✔ Your organization has weathered a severe financial crisis. In attracting new board members, you want to firmly reassure them that this financial crisis won't come back to haunt them personally.

✔ Your organization has grown and thrived. It has a large endowment and cash reserves, increasing the likelihood of being a target for lawsuits.

✔ You have the good fortune to have wealthy and influential board members. Although their assets should be protected if they're attentive board members, they're natural targets for nuisance lawsuits.

Protecting property and vehicles

If you own a home and your own car, you undoubtedly value those possessions enough to insure them in case of damage, loss, or theft. You need to protect your nonprofit's building and vehicles in the same way. Suppose that the big bad wolf comes by and huffs and puffs and blows your nonprofit down. Say that a tornado swoops past, taking with it more than you and your little dog Toto. You need property insurance, including — if you're lucky enough to find it — coverage against malicious animals and tornados.

The cost of your property insurance varies according to the size and value of your property and how the buildings are constructed. In many places, insuring a house of straw is more expensive than insuring a house of bricks. A terrible irony is that the disaster that you're most likely to face is the one for which your insurance will be most expensive. Sometimes you simply can't get insurance for your likeliest disaster.

Ideally, you want your property insurance to cover your organization for damage repairs — both to the building and its holdings — and provide business interruption insurance covering your losses of income if you're forced by a disaster to be closed for a period of time. In some instances, you won't be able to find property insurance that includes coverage for a likely disaster and you'll have to purchase a separate policy for protection from that potential crisis or do without that protection. Day-to-day drips and clogs, creaks, and rips are both more likely to happen and more affordable to cover with property insurance. And the higher the deductible, the lower the cost of your insurance.

Most property insurance policies cover the contents of a facility in addition to the building itself. Your policy may place a limit on the amount it pays toward replacing those contents if something goes wrong. Make sure that the coverage is adequate to cover the replacement cost of your organization's furniture, fixtures, and equipment.

If your organization owns its building and has tenants, you need a particularly comprehensive and flexible property insurance policy. Insist that your tenants have their own insurance: You can include this condition in the terms of their leases.

Your organization may own or dream of owning a company car, van, bus, truck, or other vehicle. So, of course, vehicle insurance is necessary. If you can't limit the use of this vehicle to one or two drivers, such insurance may be prohibitively expensive.

Maybe your organization doesn't own a building or vehicle. You still need insurance that protects your property. Buy theft insurance to protect your equipment and furniture, and renters' insurance to cover the cost of repairing accidental damage to the property caused by you or others at your organization.

Getting even deeper into insurance

Health, property, and liability insurance are the primary types of insurance that an organization needs to consider, but they're by no means the only types. Here are a few more:

- **Employee dishonesty insurance or fidelity bonds:** Insurance of this type protects the organization against employee theft or embezzlement.

- **Umbrella insurance:** This policy covers some types of extraordinary losses. For example, if you have a general liability policy that pays for losses up to $500,000, you may want to get an umbrella policy that kicks in if a settlement is higher than $500,000. Umbrella policies also set an upper limit on coverage but tend to be less expensive than basic liability policies.

- **Long-term disability insurance:** Although the cost may be prohibitive for small organizations, offering long-term disability insurance is an excellent employee benefit.

Part III
Successful Fundraising

The 5th Wave   By Rich Tennant

My Park-It
OFF STREET PARKING LOT
INITIATIVE

"...and I can guarantee you that 99% of your
contribution will go directly into My Park-It.
Hello? Hello?"

In this part . . .

We lead you into the realm of grants and annual fund drives, galas and golf tournaments, revealing the mindset of people who receive your requests for funds, including charitable foundations, private corporations, individuals, and the government. And we help you to understand the language of fundraising. In the event a fund drive or building project is part of your plans, we give special attention to capital campaigns.

Chapter 13

Crafting a Fundraising Plan

*I*f an organization is going to provide a public service, it needs money. Plain and simple. It may be run by volunteers and need just a little money, or it may need lots of money to pay for employees, office space, and formal research. If it's a brand-spanking-new organization, it needs start-up money, or what's called seed funding.

Any nonprofit — whatever its purpose — grows out of someone's idea, someone's passion (maybe yours!) to make the world better. Raising money is inviting others to share in that belief, in that passion.

Different kinds of causes appeal to different people or institutions. Your organization may get most of its money from the government, grantmaking foundations, businesses, or individuals. Successful fundraising is based on a plan, and a good plan is based on understanding an organization's likeliest sources of funding. A good plan is also balanced. No organization should put all its eggs in one basket or imagine its entire omelet coming from one chicken.

In this chapter, we show you how to create a plan for gathering your funding eggs from a number of nests. If your organization is new, we give some ideas for where to begin.

Recognizing Who Raises Funds

Federal tax codes designate more than a dozen different kinds of nonprofit organizations (which we discuss in Chapter 2). This book focuses on those authorized under section 501(c)(3) of that tax code and qualifying as public charities. Such nonprofits are exempt from paying some kinds of taxes, and their donors may take tax deductions for their contributions to them. Because many individual donors, foundations, and corporate foundations are motivated, in part, by wanting that tax deduction, this chapter and the fundraising chapters that follow are written about 501(c)(3) nonprofit organizations with public charity status.

Churches and very small organizations (those with an annual revenue of less than $5,000) that are performing a public service can receive contributions that are tax-deductible to their donors even though they may not have applied for and received 501(c)(3) status from the IRS.

Most states require charities to file registration forms before engaging in fundraising solicitations. Thirty-five states and the District of Columbia accept the Unified Registration Statement (www.multistatefiling.org) — others have their own forms. Only a handful of states don't regulate charitable fundraising. See CD0402 to link to the state offices that regulate nonprofits.

Naming Your Sources of Funds

Before plunging ahead, we need to introduce some of the terms that we use in this chapter to describe the different kinds of contributions an organization may seek or different ways of raising money. Some important terms include the following:

- ✔ **Grants.** Grants are formal contributions made to an organization by foundations, corporations, or government agencies, often to help the nonprofit address defined goals or manage specific programs. Some grants (called *project* or *program grants*) are for trying out new ideas or enhancing existing programs. Others (called *general operating grants*) support the overall work of an organization.

- ✔ **Corporate contributions.** Some corporations create their own foundations (which award grants) and some award contributions directly through what are called corporate giving programs — most often out of their public affairs, community relations, or marketing departments. Many corporations give *in-kind gifts,* which are contributions of goods and services instead of or in addition to cash contributions.

- ✔ **Individual contributions.** Along with government support, gifts to organizations from private individuals represent the largest portion of money given to nonprofit organizations. They may support specific activities or the nonprofit's general costs. You may seek these contributions through the mail, over the phone, through your Web site, in face-to-face visits, or at special events. Common types of individual contributions include

  - **Annual gifts.** A contribution written once a year to a charity is, appropriately enough, called an *annual gift.* The consistency of such gifts makes them of great value to the recipient.

- **Major gifts.** As suggested in the name, a *major gift* is a large amount of money. *Large* is a deliberately vague word here: For some organizations it may be $100, and for others it may be $50,000.

- **Memberships.** Similar in some ways to an annual gift, a *membership* is a contribution made once per year. The difference is that you often make a membership in exchange for some benefit or service from the nonprofit, such as a discount on tickets or a free tote bag. Some nonprofits are structured so that their members play a role in their governance and that's a different, more formal relationship than calling a contributor a member. (See Chapter 4 for a discussion of the implications of having members in your corporation.)

If a donor contributes $75 or more to your organization in exchange for a gift or service, your nonprofit must inform that donor in writing about the value of the gift or service she received and the portion of her contribution that she may claim as a federal income tax deduction. Additionally, your nonprofit must substantiate in writing to a donor any gift of $250 or more.

- **Planned giving/bequests.** These gifts are contributions that donors make to nonprofit organizations through their wills or other legal documents specifying what happens to their money and property after they die. Generally, the donor works with a trust officer at a bank or law firm to design his or her planned giving. Large organizations often have staff who specialize in providing technical assistance in this area to donors.

- **Special Events.** From marathons to chicken dinners to celebrity concerts, fundraising events generate income that supports organizations. Contributors can deduct from their taxes the portion of their event tickets that's above and beyond the cost of producing the event. Individuals, corporations, and small businesses are the likeliest supporters of special events. We talk about special events at greater length in Chapter 15.

- **Endowment.** If a donor designates a gift to a nonprofit as being for the endowment, the nonprofit must invest the money so that earnings from the investment are, in the future, used to support the work of the nonprofit. Some foundations make endowment grants. Individuals (sometimes through bequests) also make endowment gifts. The nonprofit's board sets a policy for how much the organization can use each year from the money it earns on its endowment investments.

Analyzing Your Potential

Different approaches to raising funds work best for different kinds of organizations. You have to be both ambitious about your goals and realistic about what's likely to work for you when you make a fundraising plan. As you try to figure out how much money you can glean from each possible funding source, keep in mind the following questions:

- ✔ **How far do your services reach?** Do lots of people understand, care about, and benefit from your organization's cause? Do you focus on a small geographic area or work at a national or international scale? The answer to this question tells you whether your nonprofit should be casting its net close to home or all over the country or world.

- ✔ **Are you one of a kind?** If you're unique, you may have a harder time explaining to potential donors who you are and what you do. But you may have an advantage when you appeal to foundations that like *model programs* — distinctive efforts that may be replicated in other places.

- ✔ **How popular is your cause?** One year everyone is talking about healthcare, another year public education, and still another year it's pollution or disaster relief. Regardless of what's happening in the world, the focus of your organization's work will go through times of gaining and losing media attention and broad-based donor support.

- ✔ **Does your cause elicit strong feelings?** Even if it's not a cause that's backed by large numbers of people, a hot topic that a small number of people believe in strongly often can attract major gifts. Similarly, if an organization focuses on something that's potentially controversial — like abortion, use of pesticides, or incarceration of juveniles — it may find that corporations and businesses are uncomfortable with having their names associated with the cause.

Research is important for all types of fundraising, but it's particularly important if your cause elicits strong feelings and potential controversy. You want to focus in on the right people, right corporations, or right foundations that share those strong feelings.

- ✔ **How well known and highly regarded are your leaders?** Most of us feel better about supporting an organization if we believe in its leaders. If an agency is conducting medical research and the doctors with whom it's working are well regarded, widely published, and nationally known, it may be in a strong position to secure government grants or contracts. Your organization's leaders are equally important in private fundraising.

- ✔ **How well known is your organization?** If your organization is a theater group, do critics frequently review its performances? If it's dedicated to helping young mothers, do news stories often feature its services? Or is it the type of agency that works quietly behind the scenes? If it's the behind-the-scenes type, it may be wise to focus on funding sources — the government, foundations, or corporations — that know your organization's field well and understand the quality of its work and the key role that it plays.

A behind-the-scenes organization doesn't do as well with trying to raise money from large numbers of individual donors: Educating donors about what the organization is and what it does is just too expensive. Individual donors may be attracted to it if board members or community leaders whom they trust approach them individually.

✔ **Who do you know?** Your nonprofit's contacts are important to its ability to raise money, especially when seeking funds from individuals. Knowing somebody who may write a big check to an organization is great, but knowing a lot of people who may write small checks is just as good.

✔ **What can you give back to a donor?** Maybe your organization produces sumptuous musical concerts and can offer contributors the best seats in the house, print their names in the programs, and give them special access. Maybe your organization is based in an attractive building where a corporate donor's banner can be displayed.

Individuals have a wide variety of preferences when it comes to receiving personal recognition for gifts. Some want to give anonymously. Others want to have buildings named after them (sometimes referred to as *the edifice complex*). Corporations (particularly when they give directly out of their marketing budgets) often want their gifts to be visible to the public.

✔ **Do you have the money you need to cover fundraising costs?** Special events and *direct mail* — fundraising letters sent to large numbers of people — are expensive forms of fundraising. Grant writing takes time, but its cost is relatively low.

✔ **Do you have expertise?** Do staff, board members, or volunteers have experience with raising money? If not, is your organization able to hire expert help? Trained experts may be particularly important in the area of planned giving (seeking bequests) because they know about the legal issues and estate taxes. Working with an expert also may be a good idea if you're undertaking direct-mail fundraising, telemarketing, and special events. Professional grant writers may help you identify foundations you haven't considered in the past or strengthen your proposals.

Check on whether your state or county requires registration for participating in charitable solicitation. If you hire an outside consultant to fundraise, both your organization and that consultant may need to register. To find the rules for your state, see CD0402 for links to state agencies that regulate nonprofits.

If a nonprofit's staff is undergoing training in a new area of fundraising, a board member should try to take the class also. This step not only ensures that the knowledge stays with the organization if the staff members leave but also builds a greater understanding of development and commitment to it within the board.

> ✔ **How does this year's fundraising climate compare to last year's?** Apart from the value and importance of your wonderful organization, donors give money according to their abilities, and those abilities change with the times. Corporate mergers, changing foundation guidelines, natural disasters, and downturns in the economy all can affect how much money your organization can raise. Do you have good reason to believe that your donors are able or willing to give as much or more to you in the coming year as they gave in the past?

Drafting a Fundraising Strategy

Making a fundraising plan is a lot easier when you have a guide to follow. We recommend a process that follows two stages. In the first stage you create a fundraising strategy that defines reasonable goals. In the second stage, you identify the specific activities to address those goals, set a schedule, decide who will do the work, and make sure that you have the tools you need to succeed. This section takes you through the three steps necessary for creating the fundraising strategy.

Create a list of prospects

If your organization is brand new, brainstorm with your founding board members names of people and organizations they know who may support your cause. If your organization has been around for a while, begin by listing its previous contributors. Annotate your list by identifying which supporters are likely to support it again. Then stretch your thinking to consider new prospects — people who know you or who support other causes that are related to yours.

After you begin this effort of generating names and ideas, you begin to notice prospects all around you. A good sleuth is ever vigilant, collecting names from newspaper stories, track meet programs, public television credits, donor walls in buildings, and related organizations' annual reports. You want to make sleuthing a regular habit!

This kind of brainstorming is a good approach to identifying possible individual donors. You can use better, more focused ways (see Chapter 16) to identify foundation and government sources, but don't restrict your thinking at this stage. Go ahead and name prospects in some (maybe all!) of the following categories:

✔ Government grants or contracts

✔ Foundation grants

    ✔ Corporate contributions

    ✔ Individual contributions (gathered from special events, personal visits, mailings, and other approaches)

Refine your prospect list

Professional fundraisers will tell you that the three keys to raising money are research, research, and research. After you identify specific foundations, corporations, and government agencies on your list, you want to check on their current guidelines and giving priorities. Approximately 5,400 foundations have Web sites that can help you; you can find many more of them in The Foundation Center's directories. You can search for federal government agencies and programs on the Catalog of Federal Domestic Assistance Web site (www.cfda.gov). See Chapter 16 for more information about conducting foundation research: As you conduct your search, you're likely to uncover other prospects you didn't think of when brainstorming.

Go back through your list of individual donor prospects with board members, volunteers, and trusted associates. Note who knows whom. Try to discover as much as you can about them from media sources and people who know them. Based on their apparent interest in your organization's cause, whether someone you know can contact them personally, and their records for giving to other causes, mark which of your prospects seem to be highly likely, somewhat likely, and not very likely to support your efforts.

Fill in the numbers

Identifying names of possible donors is just the beginning of the puzzle. You also need to estimate the amounts your donor prospects may give. For this estimate, you have to continue to be a sleuth: You may find clues by tracking down the approximate amounts of their contributions to other organizations. In researching your foundation prospects, if they give grants of $10,000 or more, you can find grants lists in *The Foundation Grants Index* and see what they have given to similar projects. You can find grants lists for foundations that award amounts smaller than $10,000 by downloading their 990 tax reports from www.guidestar.org.

Estimating these figures requires research in each of your categories for types of donors. They're also based on overall goals that you set. These goals probably include sustaining many of the contributors your organization has had in the past, convincing some donors to increase their gifts, and expanding the number of contributors and types of sources.

Securing funds to save sea creatures

For years, a prominent North American organization has had the mission of rescuing injured marine mammals. Well-regarded scientists manage the organization, and it's received international awards for its contributions to animal welfare and the environment. Recent news stories have drawn public attention to the effect of pollution in the oceans and recreational boating that endanger animals. The organization maintains several facilities where animals can recover before being released back into the ocean, and school groups visit these sites. Staff members do most of the organization's fundraising. It's put aside some money to work with consultants.

The fundraising plan for this organization may include

✔ Government grants for protection of coastal watershed areas, preservation of endangered species, and research.

✔ National foundation grants for publication of research that may assist similar centers in other parts of the United States.

✔ Grants from local foundations and corporations to go toward aid internships for teenagers who are thinking about careers in marine biology, school field trips, a summer institute for local teachers who want new ideas about how to teach biology and ecology to their classes, and building new tanks and facilities to care for rescued animals.

✔ Personal visits to high-profile individual donors conducted by the well-known scientists leading its staff.

✔ Personalized fundraising letters to families who have visited its facilities.

✔ Fundraising letters addressed to individuals and including photographs of rescued animals and dramatic stories about how they were saved. These letters may be mailed to people who live along the coastal area that the organization serves, to those people who give to other animal rescue causes, or to people who subscribe to science and wildlife magazines. The paid consultants probably will design this campaign, test sample letters, and choose the most appropriate mailing lists.

If your organization is new, estimating how much you'll receive in donations is challenging, and we recommend that you be conservative. Often we look at the prospect list we've created and set goals for the contributions we intend to secure from our highly likely (maybe 50 percent), somewhat likely (maybe 20 percent), and not very likely (maybe 5 percent) lists. Setting these numbers gets easier in subsequent years, but donors change their behaviors all the time, so never assume consistency.

Getting Down to Business: Moving from Strategy to Action Plan

Taking your planning effort this far is very useful, but a good fundraising plan fills in the practical details that move it from being a list of goals and contacts to being a roadmap for your organization's direction. The next three steps bring in those details.

1. **Assign tasks, gather tools, and make a calendar.**

   For each of the revenue areas in your plan (government, foundations, corporations, or individuals), indicate who's going to work on raising the money, how many prospective sources you need to meet your goal, and tools you need to meet your goals (such as fundraising letters, brochures, or membership cards). Then outline a general timeframe for how long it will take.

   Before taking action based on your plan, take a second look at it. Is the plan piling much too much work onto one person? Are all the major deadlines falling in February? Perhaps you should reschedule and reassign work to adjust and balance these pressures.

2. **Figure out the cost of achieving each fundraising goal.**

   Many forget that it costs money to raise money. It's a good idea to estimate costs and create a fundraising cash flow outline that shows when you need up-front money and when you can expect to secure income from your efforts. Look back at your goals and identify the list of tools you need to meet them. Maybe you need to print fundraising brochures, photocopy newspaper clippings for a grant proposal, or buy the fixings to make pancake batter.

3. **Put the fruits of your labor together in one document, and you have your funding plan!**

   Your finished plan likely will be made up of the following elements:

   - Sources sought and fundraising goals (For example: foundation grants, $75,000, and special event revenues, $2,200.)

   - Prospects identified (both current and prospective contributors), along with amounts they may be expected to give

   - The number of prospects you need to achieve your goals in each category

   - List of who's responsible for making particular contacts or contributing other services to raising the funds

   - Estimated costs of pursuing the contributions in each category

   - Timeline and cash flow projection

Many agencies create an optimum fundraising plan and a bare-bones fundraising plan — one based on their hopes and one based on what they must secure to survive. During the course of the year, they rebalance and adjust their plans.

The CD accompanying this book includes two sample fundraising plans (CD1301 and CD1302) and two sample fundraising budgets (CD1303 and CD1304), one set for a small school music organization and another for a slightly larger neighborhood park improvement organization.

Budgeting for Fundraising

We've said before that raising money costs money. And no organization receives every grant or gift that it seeks. It needs to be sure up front that it can afford its potential fundraising costs and that the costs are appropriate in relationship to the possible return for the nonprofit. Fundraising costs should be a modest part of an organization's budget, but when that organization is starting up or when it's launching a major new fundraising effort, the fundraising costs will rise. Recruiting a new donor almost always costs more than securing a second gift from a past supporter.

From the beginning, the nonprofit will want a system allowing it to keep timely records on all its donors. This system may be a handwritten card file or a complex database. It's important, for instance, that nonprofits remember when they receive grants, how much money they receive, when reports are due, and what kind of reporting is required.

Nonprofits also need to keep information up to date about individual donors: who in the organization knows or knew them, how and why they gave their gifts, and whether any special recognition or invitations were promised to them when they gave. Because nonprofits hope to talk to or keep in touch with these people over time, recording their spouse and children's names, their interests, their business affiliations, and any other pertinent personal information is important.

So the first investment in fundraising may be to acquire a record keeping system. You may also have to budget for the time it takes to keep the system up to date. Current information about fundraising and accounting software usually can be found on the TechSoup Web site (www.techsoup.org). One good, inexpensive option is eBase (www.eBase.org), a free program that runs on FileMaker Pro. You don't need FileMaker unless you want to customize eBase. Specialized fundraising software is terrific, but it can be quite costly. We recommend investing in it when your fundraising depends on large numbers of grants, corporate gifts, and contributions, and when your annual operating budget is $1 million or more.

Some other fundraising activities and their costs include

> ✔ **Grants and contracts:** Most of the cost of securing grants and contracts are labor costs for planning and writing the grant proposal. Some

proposals may require videotapes, audiotapes, or slides of past work, which cost additional money. If you need numerous copies, that too is an expense, as is shipping the proposal. Sometimes you may want to travel to meet in person with the agency awarding the money and if that foundation is far from your location, that's another expense to consider. Also, as more foundations are creating electronic application systems, you may need to invest in upgrading your computer systems to be compatible with theirs.

Nonprofits need to pay attention to a grantmaker's requirements for reporting the results of a project and make sure that they can afford to do the report. Some grants require collection and analysis of extensive data. Some require audited financial statements.

✓ **Individual contributions:** Costs related to securing individual contributions stem from time spent by staff or volunteers compiling lists of possible donors, conducting research about those donors, and developing a script for soliciting a gift. Direct mail is another common technique for reaching individual donors and a relatively costly form of fundraising. Expenses may include a consultant to write the mailed materials and select appropriate lists, and certainly include printing and postage. Some organizations hire companies to handle telephone solicitation campaigns. Be cautious if you take this step: Some of these companies charge a very high percentage of the money raised in exchange for providing this service while others are reputable and valued by the nonprofits they serve. Another expense that may serve your organization is adding capacity to its Web site so that donors can make gifts electronically.

✓ **Special events:** Producing special events can be one of the most expensive ways to raise funds. Spending 50 or 60 percent of the income from an event to pay for costs is common. Printing, advertising, food, and entertainment all cost money. Also, special events are labor intensive. An agency wants to have an experienced volunteer group or staff for special events.

✓ **Planned giving:** If a nonprofit isn't familiar with tax laws regarding wills and estates, it will want to employ or hire on contract (or attract as a board member) a planned giving expert. Bringing this person on board can be expensive in the short term but doing so can yield important long-term support for the agency.

Planned giving works best for organizations that have been around for a long time and show good prospects for continuity. Universities, museums, and churches come to mind. Small, new groups have a hard time attracting bequests.

Why an endowment isn't a silver bullet

We can't tell you how often we've been part of a conversation about raising money for a small, new nonprofit organization when someone has said, "We need an endowment! We shouldn't have to be uncertain about our finances and raise all this money every year."

As practical and solid as this idea seems to be, not every organization can, will, or even should have an endowment. An endowment comes with the idea and the responsibility for your organization to be perpetual. It suggests that whatever cause you're addressing, the problem isn't going to go away — the disease isn't going to be eradicated, the trees are never going to be planted. Some kinds of institutions *are* intended to be around "forever" — museums with collections of antiquities, major colleges and universities, hospitals, land trusts. Donors make endowment gifts both because they care about the organization's work and because they expect its work to be lasting.

Aside from the question of your organization's perpetuity, endowments raise practical concerns for nonprofits.

✔ **Contributions awarded to endowments are "restricted funds" (see Chapter 10) that can't** be used for other purposes. An organization can't treat its endowment like a personal savings account. Spending a percentage of the money earned from an endowment on an annual basis is fine, but dipping into the funds that have been invested isn't okay.

✔ **An endowment that truly covers the annual operating costs of an organization would generally be twenty times the size of that organization's annual budget.** That's a lot of money to raise! The effort that goes into raising your endowment requires an upfront investment of time that won't provide the resources you need for a number of years. Making that effort may draw attention (and donors) away from the important operating funds that your organization needs in the current year to do its work.

✔ **Endowments may not be the stable resources that organizations imagine them to be.** If the stock market drops or other investments fail, an organization is likely to lose money from its endowment and may have less money than it needs for its operating budget.

Planting the Seeds for a New Organization

One tried-and-true rule of fundraising is that people give money to people they know. They also give money to causes they care about, but making a contribution is an expression of trust. That means that the likeliest contributors to a new nonprofit organization are people and agencies that know and admire its founders and their work.

Hitting up people you know

We know of people who have launched their organizations with major grants from a government agency or a large, national foundation, but many more of them start close to home with gifts from their founders, their founding board members, and from the people who know them. They then build out from that inner circle of relationships, gradually creating networks of associations with the friends, family members, and business associates of their initial contributors.

We asked some people who founded organizations how and when they got their first sources of income. One invited 20 people to her house and, after a convincing pitch and some good wine, got most of them to write checks. Another started a youth mentoring program out of his dorm room when he was a college student: He talked his campus into paying him a work study stipend to begin his project and charged his volunteer mentors modest membership fees to cover basic costs. Another noticed a city department's neglect of small city parks after budget cutbacks and, by knocking on local politicians' doors, secured a city grant to involve volunteers in small park clean-up.

Many organizations start up with contributions from individuals in part because individuals often make up their minds more quickly than businesses or foundations.

Branching out with special events

Although special events are one of the more expensive ways of raising money, you can see real advantages to including them in the fundraising plan for a new organization. Events create a way to inform multiple people about your organization at the same time: They begin to spread the word about your good work. And events don't have to be elaborate. A gathering of a dozen people can be a good start.

Approaching foundations

In approaching foundations, you may think that you're at a disadvantage because your project doesn't have a track record, but some foundations specifically like to support start-up projects and organizations. You find more information about conducting foundation research in Chapter 16. If your agency is new, check the "types of support" listings to see whether the foundation awards *seed funding* — that's specific encouragement to new activities. If it also makes grants in your field of interest and geographic area, it may be a good prospect for helping you launch your organization.

Considering government grants

Government grants and contracts may provide significant underpinnings for a new effort, but they come with these three distinct disadvantages for new nonprofit organizations:

- ✔ **In general they take longer to secure.** The review and approval process may be slow, and many government agencies have one annual deadline. If you miss that deadline, you may have to wait many months to apply.

- ✔ **They often require grantees to comply with rules and regulations regarding permits, board policies, hiring practices, and financial reporting.** Although their rules may be good rules, when you're just starting out, your organization may still be working out its systems and policies.

- ✔ **They sometimes require their funded organizations to spend money up-front and then submit invoices to them to be reimbursed for an agreed-upon amount of money.** If you have few sources of income, you may not have available funds for this up-front spending.

Chapter 14

Raising Money from Individuals

. . . .

In This Chapter

▶ Figuring out donors' reasons for giving

▶ Writing a case statement

▶ Tracking down possible donors

▶ Asking for major gift contributions

▶ Soliciting donations via direct mail

▶ Securing funds through telemarketing

▶ Raising funds on the Web

. . . .

Everyone has had some experience with asking for money. Maybe you sold cookies for a scout troop when you were a child. Maybe you sold ads for the high school newspaper. Maybe you once had to call Mom and Dad when you were stranded at a bus station in Toledo and couldn't get home for Thanksgiving.

These moments can be awkward, but asking for money for yourself and asking for money for an organization or cause you believe in are very different. Organizational fundraising can feel good because it helps you to do something important for a cause you care deeply about. The hard part is finding the right words to say, the means for conveying those words, and the audience who's receptive to those words.

Responding to the right cause, the right message, and the right person, individual donors give to many kinds of organizations. In fact, they represent the largest portion of contributions in the United States. This chapter shows you how to flex your own fundraising muscles and convince individual donors to give to your organization.

Knowing Why People Give and Asking Accordingly

The key rule of fundraising is "If you don't ask, you won't get." Taking the step of asking is critical, but so is knowing how to ask. According to marketing experts who study motivations for doing just about everything, people contribute to nonprofit organizations because they want to

- Feel generous
- Change the world
- Exercise compassion
- Have a sense of belonging to a group
- Feel a sense of well-being, of safety
- Be recognized

Does it surprise you that belief in the work of a particular nonprofit agency isn't on the list? By understanding these "hidden" donor motivations, you can phrase your request in the most effective way. Appeals to new donors often ask them to "join," "to become part of" a movement or cause in order to touch upon the desire for belonging. Appeals also call upon donors' compassion and idealism, and commonly link the needs of particular constituents served by a nonprofit to the well-being and security of an entire community. That's making the most of asking.

When you find yourself hesitating to ask someone for a contribution, keep in mind that you're not begging, you're offering them an opportunity to be part of something worthwhile. Giving your organization a gift can make them feel good.

Stating Your Case

A *case statement* is a tool often used when asking for a contribution. It's a short, compelling argument for supporting the nonprofit that can be presented as a brochure, a one-page information sheet, or a glossy folder filled with information sheets, photographs, budgets, or charts. It should be professional, factual, and short enough that readers will read it all the way through.

A good case statement can be used in many ways in fundraising:

✔ After talking about the agency with a potential donor, you leave behind a copy of your case statement for her to consider.

✔ If you need to phone a potential donor, you keep the case statement close at hand as a reminder of the key points to make about the agency.

✔ If you send a fundraising letter, you can borrow wording from the case statement to write that letter or include a copy of the case statement with the letter.

Instructions for writing a case statement resemble a recipe for stew or soup. A few basic ingredients make any version of this dish delicious, and the cook can spice it up with whatever other quality ingredients he has at hand.

1. **Make notes about the following subjects. Be selective; allot no more than 100 words to any of these items.**

   • The history of the organization

   • The services it offers

   • The organization's key accomplishments

   • Affidavits, reviews, or quotes from enthusiasts who have benefited from the organization's work

2. **Toss in no more than 50 words on each of these topics:**

   • The organization's philosophy or approach to providing service

   • If appropriate, how the organization relates to or works with other organizations — locally, nationally, or internationally

3. **Stir in whatever else you have on hand. The herbs you select may include**

   • Compelling photographs of the organization's work.

   • Charts or maps illustrating growth — for example, increasing numbers of clients the organization serves or the increasing geographic area it serves.

   • An overview of the organization's budget and finances, particularly if the budget is balanced and the finances are healthy. For example, maybe the nonprofit has achieved steady growth or has had a balanced budget for 14 consecutive years.

   • Anything else that shines a light on the agency: publications completed, awards received, testimony given, and so on.

4. **State what giving opportunities your nonprofit offers. In your case statement, the giving options must be clear and not too complicated.**

Sometimes opportunities are linked to the cost of providing services, such as the following:

- The cost of immunizing one child against a deadly disease

- The cost of replacing one chair in a symphony hall

- The cost of rescuing and rehabilitating one injured wild burro

- The cost of college tuition for one year for one student

- The cost of planting one tree in a reforestation area

Sometimes opportunities are linked to premiums or gifts the donor receives in return. For example:

- For a gift of up to $50, the donor receives a coffee mug as a token of thanks. A larger gift is acknowledged with a tote bag.

- For a gift of several hundred dollars, the donor's name appears on a brass plate on the chair the gift has paid to refurbish.

- For a gift of $1,000, the donor receives quarterly progress reports from the scientist whose research the gift is supporting.

- For a gift of several thousand dollars, the donor's name is etched on a tile in the lobby of the new building that the gift has helped to fund.

- For a gift of several million dollars, the lobby is named after the donor.

For a contribution of $75 or more, you must acknowledge the gift in writing and specify the amount that represents the value of any gift or service the contributor received because of that donation. Even if you aren't giving gifts or services to the donor, contributions of $250 or more must be acknowledged in writing.

Sometimes the donor's gift to the nonprofit is identified in a public document — a newsletter or performance program — as a Supporter, Patron, Guarantor, or Chief Mucky Muck depending on the size of his contribution. Some organizations create clever donor category names, such as a poetry organization whose contribution levels begin with a haiku, build to an ode, and top off with an epic. Still others invite donors to contribute in ways that pass on a gift or recognition to others, such as planting a tree in honor of a loved one.

In choosing how to recognize your donors, you want to consider the cost of that recognition, the nature of the activity supported, and how donor recognition advances (or doesn't suit) your organization's purpose and mission.

A simple, printed list of names is dignified and inexpensive. Although donor gifts cost money, having your organization's name printed on T-shirts, key chains, and tote bags that your donors wear and distribute throughout the community may be an effective way of promoting your work. If you spend too much, you can annoy donors or leave them wondering how much you really need their contribution.

In writing your own case statement, you need not follow the exact order in which we list the elements here. Lead with the strongest points and leave out the less compelling items. Choose a strong writer to draft the piece and then test it on others — both within and outside your agency — to see if it tells a clear, impressive story.

When your case statement is written and you're ready, produce it for distribution and make sure to match its look to your nonprofit and its intended audience. If your nonprofit is a modest, grassroots organization, your case statement should be simple and direct — maybe printed on newsprint. If it's an environmental organization, you want to produce the case statement on 100 percent post consumer waste or forest-free paper. If it's an internationally known opera company, your case statement should look dramatic and elegant.

You'll find a sample case statement for the Bay Area Discovery Museum's successful "My Place by the Bay" campaign on CD1401.

Identifying Possible Donors

Your doorbell rings, and you open the door to greet an adorable child you've never met before. The child is selling candy bars to raise funds for band instruments at school. You played in a band when you were young, so you buy a candy bar, wishing the little fundraiser success.

A few minutes later, the doorbell rings again, and you open the door to greet a second adorable child. You know this child because he lives next door. You remember when his mother brought him home as a newborn, and you watched him ride his first bicycle down the sidewalk. He's selling the same candy bars to benefit the soccer team at his school: They need equipment and uniforms. You buy *five* candy bars.

Rich or poor, most of us have strong personal feelings about money, and making gifts to charitable organizations reflects our values. Even more important when we make charitable giving decisions is our comfort in contributing our money to people we know, either directly or indirectly. Mapping the personal connections of each member of your organization is a key first step in identifying possible donors.

Drawing circles of connections

Figure 14-1 represents a common brainstorming exercise that nonprofit organizations use to identify possible individual donors. This exercise is most effective if both staff and board members participate. Follow these steps:

1. **Identify the people who are closest to the organization — those within the "inner circle."**

   This inner circle includes staff and board members and may also include active volunteers or clients who frequently use the organization's services.

2. **Identify those people who have the second closest relationship to the organization.**

   This second circle may include family and close friends of those people in the inner circle, former staff and board members, neighbors of the organization and its inner circle, and clients and volunteers who sometimes use its services.

3. **Take one more step backward and identify the people who make up the third circle.**

   They may include grandparents or cousins of those people in the inner circle, old friends whom they haven't seen recently, friends of former staff and board members, and former or infrequent users of the organization's services.

4. **Identify the friends, relatives, and other associates of those who make up circles #2 and #3.**

5. **Search for your cause-related friends and associates.**

   Look for people who may not know anyone involved in your organization, but who demonstrate an interest in the subject, the purpose it represents (as indicated by their memberships, their magazine subscriptions, or their contributions to similar organizations). Read local newspapers and watch for people who take an interest in your cause because they have personal experience with the problem your agency addresses. For example, maybe their child was born with the congenital disease that your nonprofit is studying, or maybe they come from a beautiful, forested part of the state and care about the preservation of old-growth trees.

You can continue enlarging your circle of connections, but with every step you take, the bond between the organization and the potential donors weakens. As that occurs, the cost of raising money from the people who inhabit those circles increases. Eventually, the cost of securing gifts from an outer circle becomes higher than the likely amount of income to be gained, and it's time to stop and reconsider the names closer to the inner circle.

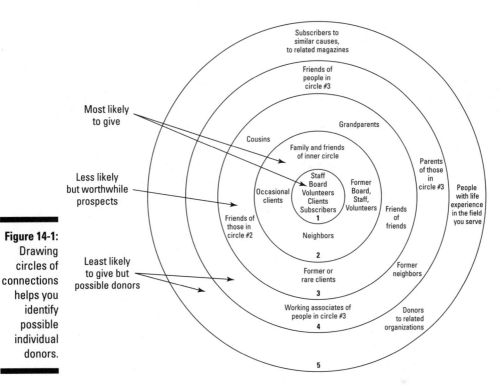

Figure 14-1:
Drawing
circles of
connections
helps you
identify
possible
individual
donors.

How do you know when it's time to stop and back up? Most organizations try to keep the cost of their overall fundraising at or lower than 20 percent of their organization's budget. However, when you're starting out, particularly with some kinds of fundraising strategies, such as direct mail or special events, your percentages may be higher in the first few years. These approaches generally begin to bring in significant contributions as they're repeated and donors renew their gifts. If you're still just "breaking even" in year three, it's time to back up and refocus your approach.

Stay alert to the identities and connections of possible donors. You and your volunteers become sleuths, constantly following clues, keeping track of people you meet at social gatherings or business meetings, clipping newspaper articles, and following the business and social pages and the obituaries. You want to identify not only the people who may be interested in your cause, but also their families, business associates, and social contacts.

Getting a list of contacts from your board of directors

Every year, or before you start work on a special event or letter-writing campaign, ask each of your organization's board members to provide the names of ten or more people they know. This exercise is useful for developing a solicitation list.

Most people can sit down and list ten friends and associates off the top of their heads. However, when asked to produce a list in that way, it's unlikely that they will exhaust all their connections and relationships. If you hand board members starter lists of people they may know and then ask them to edit and add to that list, you're likely to get many more names.

To develop this "starter list," think about your board members and their probable networks and connections. Say, for instance, that your nonprofit is lucky enough to have a local business leader on its board of directors. Scouring the Web and local business pages to note this leader's affiliations can bring up a variety of connections, such as

- Business partners or coworkers
- Leaders of banks, investment houses, or law firms that handle the company's money
- The accounting firm that prepares the company's annual financial reports
- Heads of printing companies that produce the company's brochures and annual reports
- Advertising, marketing, or design firms that do the company's public relations and advertising
- Members of social, athletic, and business clubs to which the board members belong
- College or university alumni affiliations
- Members of other boards on which your board members serve
- Close neighbors

If your board member is quite prominent, your staff may also want to check *Who's Who;* but remember that everyone, no matter how modestly he or she lives, has a web of professional and personal connections.

A worthy next step in developing your organization's network of connections is to address personalized letters from your board members to the people on their lists of ten, asking each of those ten people to contribute and also to provide names of ten others who may be interested in learning more about your cause. When writing for their help, make it easy for your contacts to respond: Provide a form for them to fill out and a self-addressed, stamped envelope or postcard to convey their responses. You may also save postage by sending your query by e-mail.

See CD1402 for a sample letter from a board member asking associates for a list of ten possible donors.

After you have your list of contacts, you can use it as the basis for a face-to-face individual donor campaign, for mailings, and for event invitations. As you talk to your board members and their friends about their connections, find out as much as you can about how you can best approach these people. Personal preferences vary. Some people prefer to be anonymous donors while others want to be applauded by a room full of society leaders when they give.

The cause for which you're seeking money matters, your timing matters, and your organization's reputation matters, but the most important element in raising money from an individual is to have someone he knows and trusts ask for the contribution. This fact is particularly true when it comes to major gift fundraising, where individuals ask other individuals (usually face-to-face) to make significant contributions, and special events fundraising (because most people are more comfortable socializing with people they know).

Growing a Major Gift

Face-to-face visits are the best way to secure larger contributions, what fundraising professionals call *major gifts* (see Chapter 13 for more information on major gifts). Rarely does one knock on a door, deliver a short speech, and depart with a check for a large amount. Generally several contacts must take place before a major donor is ready to make a commitment. This process often is called "cultivation," and the idea of planting the idea, tending a relationship, and harvesting the result when it's fully grown, is an apt one. It takes time. In this section, we break down key steps and tips for growing a major gift.

Before you talk yourself into making a phone call or sending a letter rather than sitting down to talk to a donor face-to-face, remember that it's harder for donors to say no to someone sitting before them.

Deciding who should ask

If possible, the board or staff person who knows the potential donor should make the visit. If that's not possible, the visiting team should be made up of two people who represent different aspects of the organization — maybe a client who has benefited from its services and the executive director. Be careful not to overwhelm a potential donor with a huge swat team. Two or three people are plenty.

Ideally, when asking a potential donor to contribute to your organization, the request should be peer-to-peer. If the potential donor is a prominent member of the community, for example, a board member or top ranking staff should make the request.

Preparing to make a call

Gulp. It's time to ask someone for money. In preparing for this moment, you need to remember that you're not asking for something for yourself. You're inviting the potential donor to belong, to be a part of something worthwhile. This invitation doesn't mean, however, that you want to skip over the reason or purpose for the gift. You need to step back for a moment and remember why it's so important. How did you become involved? What lives (or lands, or seas) have you seen changed by the organization's work? Sally forth armed with your case statement, which will remind you of the key points you want to mention.

Breaking the ice

Open the conversation with easy material. What did you find out about this person while conducting research, and how do you know her? Maybe your kids attend the same school or you're both baseball fans. Try to use something low-key to open the conversation instead of forcing yourself on your "victim" with a heavy sales pitch. The key is creating rapport.

Brief small talk can ease the conversation's start, but don't waste a potential donor's time. Let her know how you became involved in the organization, and then briefly give an overview of its attributes and current situation. Team members should take up different pieces of the conversation, remembering to let the potential donor talk, too, and paying close attention to the signals she sends. Keeping the meeting comfortable for the prospect is critical.

Adopting the right attitude

When soliciting gifts, be firm and positive, but not pushy. Pay attention to how the potential donor is acting or responding and step back if he doesn't seem to be feeling well or if his business has taken a difficult turn.

Just as you can see signs of when not to press the case, you may also notice signs of readiness when it's going well. The potential donor may bring someone else along to an event at the nonprofit. He may begin to tell others good things about the agency (some of which its board may not know)! He may display pride in the organization as if he's a part of it.

Asking someone to contribute to an organization is easier if you've already made a gift yourself. Even if you're a staff member and can't make a large contribution, you'll feel more confident about asking if you have contributed, and the potential donor will admire that you're willing to put your money where your mouth is. In general, it's a good idea for the people in the agency's "inner circle" of staff and board members to contribute first, before you ask outside individuals to give.

Timing the request: An inexact science

Many people don't believe in asking for a specific contribution at the first meeting. They believe in setting the stage — letting the person know that a campaign or special program is coming up and that the organization will be seeking his help in the future. At a second visit they try to get this potential donor to see a program in action or to meet other board members at an informal gathering. The goal is building a relationship, inviting the potential donor to feel as if he wants to belong with the people leading your agency.

For some major gift campaigns, the fundraisers use a feasibility study. In such a study, someone from outside the organization interviews board members and potential major donors, seeking their impressions of the organization and a suggestion of the size contribution they might make. This process both helps the organization to set realistic goals and warns the "research subjects" that the agency plans to come knocking at their doors.

As with any cultivation, the timing of the harvest is critical. When the time is right, it's like recognizing a piece of fruit that's ready to be picked. Make a date for a follow-up visit. Plan a setting where the conversation can be congenial but focused. Don't rush (a common failing), but don't leave without asking. If the answer is disappointing, ask if you can keep in touch. Sometimes contributors come around at a later time.

Deciding what to ask for

Before asking a potential donor for a contribution, find out everything you can about the person's gifts to similar causes. (To do so, you can scour donor lists and ask board members who know this person.) This information helps you to ask for an appropriate amount.

Many people believe that you should ask for an amount that's somewhat higher than what you expect to get, because making a request for a generous gift is flattering to the donor. However, you don't want to ask for so much money that the potential donor feels that whatever he gives is a disappointment. Donors commonly say something like, "I can't do $200,000, but I will consider $75,000 if that would be a help." (Add or subtract zeros as appropriate.) In most cases, once the donor suggests a level, you don't want to haggle: You may become annoying and cause him to back out of contributing. Using the personal associations angle sometimes works — "We were hoping you might become one of our $200,000 donors, along with Joe Schmoe and Sally Smiley."

Minding your manners

One of the most important parts of your major gift campaign is thanking your contributors. Do it very soon after the pledge is made or the gift is received. We recommend an immediate phone call and a handwritten note. Many organizations follow-up with some form of "donor recognition," such as publication of the donors' names in an annual report or a special "behind-the-scenes" party in their honor. If you acknowledge a donor thoughtfully and graciously, you're strengthening your future relationship with that contributor and can make her feel as if she's part of your organization. That's good manners and smart fundraising.

Raising Money by Mail

We hope that, after reading this section of the book, you never again refer to the solicitation letters you receive from charities as "junk mail." These letters may not be as welcome as personal letters, but they grow out of a sophisticated and fascinating area of fundraising. Your organization may be much too small to make investing in a major direct mail campaign worthwhile, but it can take valuable tips from the "big guys" and develop small-scale letter writing efforts that yield good results.

If you think you want to try large-scale direct mail fundraising, we strongly recommend that you hire a direct mail consultant or firm to handle your campaign. Direct mail fundraising can be a very expensive investment and you want the best, most up-to-date professional advice available.

Successfully raising money through the mail depends upon gradual development of a loyal cadre of "mail responding" donors, or what's commonly called a *house list* or *house file.* This list is a precious resource you develop after an investment of time, effort, and postage stamps. After you have it, you can send mail to the generous folks on that list and expect a high rate of return.

For example, 10 percent or more of the donors on your house list can be expected to make repeat gifts. Those donors who do make repeat contributions are likely to stick with your organization for three years, making three or four contributions in that time and increasing the size of their contributions. Adding to this value, you'll uncover prospects for major gifts and planned gifts (contributions from bequests) among these donors.

Before your house list of supporters develops into a significant and loyal resource, a direct mail campaign on your organization's behalf may only break even on the cost of the initial — or acquisition — letter writing campaign. You may even recover only half of your cost. Don't despair! You have to start with casting a wide net, and a large mailing is relatively expensive.

In time, perhaps three to four years, the people on your donor list drift away. However, by continually testing and expanding your mailings, you can replace them with new contributors.

Looking at the direct mail process

How does an organization undertake a direct mail effort with professional help? Here's a broad sketch of the steps you take:

1. **Analyze the cause.**

   Can it succeed as a direct-mail subject? Working with a consultant, you may ask the following questions:

   - Does the nonprofit have a good reputation and name recognition?
   - Is the cause it represents one that appeals to a wide variety of people?
   - Can it effectively distinguish itself from other organizations that do related work?
   - Does it have resources to invest in direct mail?

2. **Develop a written piece.**

   The written "piece" includes a letter, envelope, reply card, and reply envelope. It may also include premiums (free stuff) and other enclosures. Some premiums we've received include pennies, pencils, stickers, seeds, and address labels. They're meant to urge recipients to open the envelope. Surveys and contests are meant to encourage readers to spend more time with the piece and what it offers. Everything about the piece, including the format, design, and benefits for donors, should reinforce a clear message.

3. **Collect lists of appropriate people to receive the piece.**

   The direct mail consultant likely works with a specialized company called a list broker to identify appropriate lists for the nonprofit's mailing. List brokers have more than 20,000 lists to choose from!

4. **Test the piece.**

   Your consultant mails the piece to a small sample of people and measures their response. "Small" in the world of direct mail may seem like a lot: Organizations mailing to millions of prospective donors often test their letters on 30,000–50,000 names. A good response is when 1 percent or more of the recipients contribute, but even a smaller return can be informative and encouraging.

5. **Send the acquisitions mailing.**

   After refining the letter sent to the test group, and focusing on the kinds of lists that seemed to work best, the organization sends the full-blown mailing to hundreds of thousands of names.

6. **Keep testing versions of the piece on different lists.**

   Even though the letter is in circulation, the organization continues to test and refine its efforts. It may come up with variations on its letter for different kinds of mailing lists.

7. **Follow a mailing schedule.**

   A direct mail effort is a process, not a one-time or annual event. Organizations usually send the letter for new donors several times per year. In the meantime, as donors respond, they send follow-up appeals to them as often as every six to eight weeks. Donors should hear from the organizations in other ways, too, perhaps through newsletters or event invitations. Mailing, just like visits to donors, is a process of cultivation.

8. **As donors respond, take care to treat them well.**

   Keeping detailed donor records on efficient, well-designed computer systems is critical. (Big agencies often use professional service bureaus outside their offices to handle these databases and process the contributions.) Databases should note donors' giving patterns, who they know, which lists they came from, and anything else they can. Using these (and other) categories is called segmenting your responses. In the future, the different subcategories or segments of the list may get different follow-up letters.

   Guard your list. Don't neglect it. And send thank you letters as soon as possible to acknowledge contributions.

Good treatment of your donors includes allowing them to let you know if they don't want their addresses shared with other organizations. You can include a check box on your reply card where they can let you know if they don't want their information to be traded or sold.

Assembling the mailer

Your letter isn't just a letter; it includes a mailing envelope, a reply envelope and card, and sometimes a brochure, a copy of a newspaper clipping, or a short, handwritten note in addition to the longer letter. All these pieces should relate to one another and convey a clear, compelling message.

The envelope should be inviting to open. Did you use a first class stamp? Rubber stamp or handwrite a special message? Handwrite the address?

What if direct mail isn't for you?

Direct mail isn't the right tool for many causes and organizations. If your organization is newly established, locally-focused, technically complicated, or without the resources to invest in mailing hundreds of thousands of letters, it still can use the mail effectively to raise money and can learn from some of the techniques employed in direct mail. Many organizations of all sizes and types use the mail to invite people to become members, who receive a discount or benefit of some sort in return for their gifts, or to contribute to an annual fund. These efforts may begin with a mailing of 100 letters with ambitions of receiving 40 or more checks.

The letter should give readers enough information that they feel involved in the cause. Most of the letter should be dedicated to describing the problem that the organization is trying to solve. After that, it discusses how things can be turned around for the better and the organization's specific method or program for doing so. It closes with a vision for how things will look if the plan succeeds. You want readers to understand that your nonprofit has an urgent, yet reasonable and reachable, goal. You also want the reader to believe by the end of the letter that she's joining a winner. The letter usually includes a combination of short and long paragraphs and often a key point is underlined or printed in bold for emphasis.

The reply envelope and card should be easy to use, and the reply card should offer a variety of gift levels (appropriate to the probable giving levels of the donors you're approaching). Your nonprofit can get a permit from the post office to offer postage-paid envelopes, which make it easier for donors to respond.

Most direct mail letters include a P.S. after the signature. Research demonstrates that most people read the P.S. first, before they read the salutation or opening line of the letter. Use your P.S. to convey to your reader how her gift can make a difference.

If you're conducting a smaller, focused campaign, try out your letter at first on your organization's internal lists of board contacts, clients, and donors. Then you can build your internal list by consistently collecting names and addresses at events you present, co-presenting programs with other organizations (and collecting information from their contacts who attend), and trading lists.

Building mailing lists

Earlier in this chapter we discuss identifying your organization's circle of connections, beginning with its board, staff, and loyal clients and building outward through their networks of friends and associates. This process also works well for developing a mailing list, especially if you make use of the relationships — going to the effort of personalizing the fundraising letters the people on this list receive or having board members make follow-up phone calls.

Direct mail experts know that some people are more "mail responsive" than others. They read magazines, order products from magazines, and open their direct mail. When your organization is ready to build out from its inner circle, how can you find these people? Other organizations serving similar populations may be willing to trade lists of clients, members, and donors if you promise to use the lists for only one mailing. (Of course, the people from their lists who respond to your letter are added to your small-scale house file.) Board members may be able to secure lists of contacts from the professional organizations, clubs, and other boards to which they belong. Every time your organization puts on a benefit or public program, it can gather names and addresses from the people who attend. Co-producing conferences, volunteer work days, and other programs can be a good way to expand your constituent base, learn from colleagues, and gather new names for your list.

Just as important as attracting names to your list is taking care of those names. You want to develop a good database system for recording information about new donors in order to thank them, keep in touch with them, and ask for their support again in the future. Remember that it's acceptable to send more than one letter and to ask for their help more than once each year. And remember to keep testing, testing, testing — making your letters better, trying new envelopes, mailing to new lists, and so on. You'll find that database programs to manage your donor information come in various degrees of complexity and prices and are usually called fundraising or membership management software.

On the CD accompanying this book, you'll find a sample donor information record that you can adapt to your needs. See CD1403.

Good fundraisers recognize the importance of treating donors well. The Association of Fundraising Professionals has developed a thoughtful Donor Bill of Rights that offers standards to follow (www.afpnet.org/ethics/ethics_and_donors).

Telemarketing: Dialing for Dollars

In the mid-1980s, direct mail was a wildly successful means of fundraising for many organizations. In the late 1980s, it declined. Households were receiving too much direct mail, making recipients less inclined to read it, and the costs of printing and postage rose. That's when the dinner hour began to be interrupted by incessant telemarketing calls.

You may have to register

Many states and some local jurisdictions require organizations that solicit charitable contributions to file registration forms before soliciting. This registration is meant to protect the public from being solicited on behalf of illegitimate causes. The regulations differ from state to state. Typically, the rules don't apply unless the nonprofit raises more than a minimum annual amount. Check with your state's attorney general's office to be sure that your nonprofit is in compliance with all laws. It's especially important to check local laws when thinking about raising money through bingo games and raffles. Laws regulating these activities often differ from county to county and city to city.

Like direct mail, telemarketing is based on a directed message. Telemarketers preselect the recipients for their potential interest in the topic of the call based on their behavior with other types of telephone marketing.

The advantages of telemarketing are

- ✔ It's hard to ignore. A human voice engages you in a conversation, and you must respond. It's not like a letter that you can throw into the recycling bin without the author noticing.

- ✔ It can be less costly than a mail campaign. If you use trained volunteers to make the calls, you can manage a campaign at a very reasonable cost.

- ✔ As with direct mail, you can use the elements that shape a large-scale, professional telemarketing project for a modest campaign.

The disadvantages? No one gets to have a quiet dinner any longer. For the callers conducting the campaigns, more and more potential donors use answering machines or services to screen calls. Cellphone numbers are relatively hard to collect for calling purposes. Plus, some commercial telemarketing firms take a very high percentage (as high as 75 percent!) of any funds raised, making it a poor return on investment for donors who want to keep fundraising costs low.

 Citizen complaints about intrusive telemarketing have led to the creation of the National Do Not Call Registry, which makes it illegal for businesses to make telemarketing calls to people who register. At present, telemarketing for nonprofit organizations is exempt from these rules, but their exemption is being questioned. Check the status of these regulations before embarking on a telemarketing campaign. The U.S. public policy page on the Association of Fundraising Professionals Web site is a good place to check (www.afpnet.org).

The key steps to beginning telemarketing are writing a script, training volunteers, organizing follow-up calls, and — of course — thanking, cultivating, and upgrading donors over time.

Writing a script

Every call should open with a clear, direct, personal greeting: "Hello, Mr. I'm-Getting-the-Person's-Name-Right, I'm Ms. Call-a-Lot and I wanted to talk to you about the Scenic Overlook Preservation Fund Committee's work."

Having connected with the call recipient, the caller then tries to link that person's interests and behavior to the reason for the call:

- ✔ If she's a past donor, begin with a hearty thank you.

- ✔ If she's been involved in a related cause or effort, mention how important that work is.

- ✔ If she lives near the scenic overlook, mention how beautiful it is and the community's concern for the fragile surrounding environment.

You may notice a tricky moment in the call when you want the potential donor to relax and listen so that you can tell your story and not be interrupted. To increase the caller's chances of keeping call recipients on the line, the script should be

- ✔ Engaging and information-packed (to hold the listener's attention)

- ✔ Upbeat about the possibility of improvement or change

- ✔ Deeply concerned about the current situation

- ✔ Specific about the time frame in which things need to change

- ✔ Specific about the amount of money the caller hopes the listener can contribute

On the CD accompanying this book, we've included a set of telemarketing "dos" and "don'ts" and a sample telemarketing script. See CD1404.

Getting the callers ready

Telemarketing can be an excellent board or volunteer group effort. If someone involved with your organization works in an office that has multiple telephone lines, see whether you can borrow the office for an evening. Early evening (6:00–8:30 p.m.) on weeknights is generally considered the best time to call, but — as you've probably noticed from the sounds of your own telephone — telemarketers now frequently call during the day and on weekends as well.

Gather your volunteer team an hour before beginning. Feed them a good meal and give them a pep talk. Building camaraderie among the callers can relax anyone who's nervous. Setting a group goal for the evening and mapping it on a big chart can build morale.

Inform the callers that they must deliver the message in a crisp, clear, and friendly voice. They shouldn't rush, but they also shouldn't leave holes in the conversation that the call recipient can close before the caller can ask for a contribution. They should ask for a specific contribution and confirm the amount.

Provide your callers with information about each household they're calling, including a recommended gift request. You base your request on the potential donor's past contributions to your or other organizations. Sometimes you're just guessing. That's okay if your callers are also good listeners and deftly adjust the amount they're requesting in response to what they hear. If, after a gift is pledged, you feel that you asked for too little money, don't despair. You can ask the donor to upgrade his gift next time.

Collecting the pledge

If a pledge is made, the caller should thank the new donor and try to get him to promise to return the contribution within a certain time (or to give credit card information over the phone so that the gift can be charged then and there).

Confirm the spelling of the name and address before saying goodbye to the new donor. At the end of the evening, everyone present should write brief, personalized thank you notes and send them with pledge forms (indicating the specific amount of the promised contribution) and return envelopes to the people they reached who promised to make contributions.

Every telemarketing campaign suffers from a percentage of unrealized promises, and callers want to keep that percentage as low as possible. You may ask a small number of your volunteers to reconvene for a short follow-up calling session two months after the initial campaign to jar loose any contributions that haven't yet been received.

Web Site and E-Mail Campaigns

Just as your Web site and electronic communications system are tools for serving your constituents and marketing your work, they can be tools for raising money. The world of e-commerce and e-marketing is developing and changing rapidly: More and more people buy books, skis, and airline tickets on the Web, manage their banking on the Web, and spend hours each day on the Internet.

Why haven't we all dumped those expensive postage stamps and phone banks and moved our fundraising to the electronic arena? Although the number of people who make online contributions is increasing, money raised on the Internet is still a drop in the bucket compared to more traditional ways of giving. Large national and international nonprofits receive nearly all the funds raised online. Online fundraising faces two challenges:

✔ Many people find it relatively impersonal and that makes it difficult for organizations to cultivate relationships with donors.

✔ Giving is based on trust and not everyone trusts that her money is going where it's supposed to go when contributed online.

However, online fundraising has worked well in a few contexts. It's been a very effective tool for disaster and emergency relief campaigns, where donors want to respond quickly. People also respond well to online fundraising by organizations they already know well, like their college alumni associations.

Although you don't use telephones or letters in Internet transactions, e-philanthropy isn't free. The investment in staff time and online services can be significant.

Using e-mail to build and maintain relationships

Fundraising is about building relationships with people. Individual donors want to feel that they're appreciated, so it's in a nonprofit's best interest to thank donors regularly and keep them informed about what the organization is doing. It can't hurt to get to know the people who give money to your non-profit, either. Here's where the Internet can be of help.

The most frequently used feature of the Internet is e-mail. It's easy to use, you don't need the latest hotrod computer to use it, and it's cheap and fast. If you're keeping in touch with your mother through e-mail, you can keep in touch with your donors, too.

Your organization doesn't need a Web site to begin using e-mail to build and maintain good relationships with your supporters. Adding an e-mail address to your printed correspondence and newsletters is a good start. And, if you want to give people an opportunity to discuss issues important to your organization, you can start a mailing list (or *listserv*) for free at a number of Web sites.

Don't add people to your mailing list unless they ask to subscribe, and always make it easy to unsubscribe from the list. Nothing kills a good relationship faster than unwanted e-mail.

Here are some other tips for using e-mail effectively:

✔ Answer your e-mail promptly, within 24 hours if possible.

✔ E-mail correspondence can be less formal than typed-on-paper business letters, but it shouldn't be overly familiar.

✔ Answer questions succinctly — don't ramble on and on.

In fact, it's a good idea to have a short paragraph description about the organization already written and waiting to be cut and pasted. It can be added to and edited as needed. Figure 14-2 shows how a nonprofit uses e-mail to answer a question but then adds a bit more about the organization — and an offer to provide more still.

How does e-mail tie into fundraising? Consider it prospect development. If you're e-mailing a new correspondent, ask whether he wants to be added to your mailing list. If the correspondent says yes, count one more new prospect. If he says no, keep the name and e-mail address in your To Be Pursued file. In two months, send an e-mail asking whether he has any more questions about the project or organization. If the person responds, go back to Step 1 and begin again. If you don't hear from the correspondent again, put the person in a Maybe Someday file, and maybe someday when you have time, you can try again.

Finding prospects with e-mail address lists

E-mail address lists, like mailing address lists, can be purchased, traded, or borrowed. A nonprofit may be willing to lend or trade its list with another nonprofit with a similar mission.

When using a borrowed list, it's important to respect the privacy of the list names. Don't pass it along to others without permission.

Be extremely cautious when purchasing a list. E-mail addresses change as often as, if not more so than, street addresses. Finding a list of names who have expressed interest in specific causes also may be difficult.

You're on your way to accumulating the names and e-mail addresses of people who have expressed interest in what you're doing and even have asked to be kept informed of future developments. You can invite these people to special events, ask them for contributions, make available planned giving opportunities that benefit them and your cause, and maybe even ask them to volunteer one day a week. You have prospects.

Bethseda Zoological Society

Dear Mr. Jones,

Thank you for your interest in the Bethseda Zoological Society.

Yes, we do operate the small children's zoo at Heathway Park. We are happy that your daughter enjoyed her visit this past Sunday.

BZS was founded in 1983 with the mission of providing information about the animal kingdom to residents of Bethseda County. We are supported by individual contributions, foundation grants and admissions to our small zoo. Besides the children's zoo, we work with elementary school teachers to provide curriculum materials and in-class presentations about wildlife in Bethseda County.

If you would like more information about BZS, please send us your mailing address, and we will mail you our annual report and a schedule of upcoming events. You can also visit our website at http://bza.org.

We also have an email newsletter that is sent once each month. If you would like to be added to the subscriber list, send email with the word "subscribe" in the subject line.

Thank you again for your question.

Sincerely,

Henry Peters

Executive Director

Bethseda Zoological Society

hp@bza.org

http://bza.org

Figure 14-2:
Using e-mail
to build a
relationship.

Making your Web site a cultivation tool

A Web site can never replicate a face-to-face encounter with another person, but in designing your site to appeal to possible donors, you can remember that challenge and attend to making it engaging and appealing. Strategies may include

✔ Short profiles of clients served and of donors

✔ Behind the scenes tours of the organization's activities (Our local zoo kept a Web camera on newborn lion cubs so that the public could see them before they were on display in an exhibit.)

✔ Links to information and resources about the field in which your agency works

✔ Involvement techniques such as e-mail campaigns to political leaders or electronic petitions

✔ Bulletin boards and chat rooms on subjects related to your work

Like a fundraising letter, the longer a Web site keeps visitors involved, the likelier it is to build their trust and interest.

Most Web sites include a "contact us" page. Make sure that this option is user-friendly and that someone on your staff is responsible for replying to queries quickly and courteously. Include opportunities for readers of the Web site to sign up for an electronic newsletter or other services and to leave a mailing address and/or telephone number.

You may build the most amazing Web site on the planet, but if Web readers aren't finding it, it's not fulfilling its role for your organization. One critical question is how to attract the notice of search engines. Some agencies sit back and wait for a Web spider to find their pages, some submit their pages to search engines one-by-one, which can be time consuming; and some hire a service to submit their information to the leading search engines. See Search Engine Watch (`www.SearchEngineWatch.com`) for tips on getting your site noticed by search engines.

Collecting money online

A key first step to raising money through the Internet is to add a "donate now" button to your organization's Web site. To take advantage of already developed software and services, many organizations contract with a "donate now" service. The number of options available can be daunting. We recommend that you read the online discussions on TechSoup, a nonprofit Web site addressing organizations' technology needs, before you sign up for a service. (See `www.techsoup.org`.)

As you shop for the right service for your organization, consider the breadth of the services you're purchasing. Will the agency design your Web site for you? Will it thank your donors? Will it manage a donor database for your online contributions?

Also, look carefully at how and for what an agency charges fees. Most online contribution services charge a setup fee, a monthly fee, and a per contribution fee. Sometimes you can avoid the monthly fees, but when you do, often you pay a higher fee for each contribution you receive. Some less expensive nonprofit technology services charge lower fees but send you your contributions in a lump sum so that you only receive the money, not the donor records. On the other hand, some services charge for keeping the donor records or for allowing you to upload them onto your computers.

If you want to skirt the issue or cost of installing a "donate now" service, you can use the "contact us" function on your Web site to collect e-mail addresses for future cultivation.

If your organization is sending fundraising appeal letters by e-mail, you should know that the Federal CAN-SPAM law makes it unlawful to send unsolicited commercial e-mails unless the e-mails contain a "clear and conspicuous identification that the message is an advertisement or solicitation" (this information doesn't necessarily have to appear in the e-mail subject line); an ability to opt-out electronically from future emails; and a valid postal address of the sender. While this law may change, at present charities must comply with these regulations.

Your organization can choose among these techniques for raising funds from individuals, but we highly recommend that most agencies include individual giving as a focused part of their fundraising plans. National statistics illustrate that individuals represent a larger portion of giving than do foundations or corporations, and most individuals allow you to use the funds contributed for whatever your greatest needs may be. That kind of flexibility adds considerable value to a contribution, even to a contribution of $20.

Chapter 15

Making the Most of Special Events

*F*rom glamorous dances under the stars to pancake breakfasts at the local firehouse, most nonprofits include social gatherings as part of the fundraising mix. Special events don't just raise money. They're often credited with raising friends as well as funds. New donors — who don't know the organization — may come forward because the event itself sounds fun and interesting, because of who invites them, or because someone they admire is being honored. Special events can be a wonderful catalyst for attracting businesses that like to be recognized when they make contributions, or for attracting people who like to socialize and be seen.

At their best, special events raise substantial amounts of money, draw attention to an organization's good work, and attract new volunteers. If fundraising is about cultivation, a special event can be a greenhouse for nurturing growth. You hope to create a special event that becomes an occasion that people look forward to, an annual tradition. Still, a special event can be one of the most expensive ways to raise money. Expenses may eat up half or even more of the gross event income. And the staff time needed may be substantial.

Bottom line? Special events need careful planning. Putting together a special event draws upon all your nonprofit management skills and can drain staff and board time and energy away from other important activities. In this chapter, we show you how to plan a successful special event — and steer clear of obstacles.

Thinking through the Whole Event

If you think that a special event is in your future, we recommend sitting down with staff and board members and raising questions like these:

- ✔ What would our organization's followers enjoy doing and how much can they afford to pay to do it?

- ✔ Who does our organization know who could provide event elements — donated goods, celebrity auctioneers, entertainment, or printing services?

- ✔ Who do we know who could be honored at the event or serve on an event committee? The event leadership and volunteer committee are critically important to attracting donors to the occasion.

- ✔ When can we focus attention on a special event? The last six weeks before an event are generally the most labor intensive. Look for a relatively clear six-week block of time in which you don't have grant writing or other commitments.

- ✔ When can we hold an event without competing with our other fundraising drives? (If you have an annual fund drive in October, why not plan your special event in the spring?)

We offer some additional advice regarding these questions in the following sections.

Deciding on your event according to your budget

Special events can be produced on a bare-bones budget, for princely prices, or for any amount in between. As with most kinds of investments, event planners expect a higher return in exchange for a higher investment. But don't exceed your means. In this section, we outline some ideas for tailoring an event to your organization's budget.

In deciding on an event, we recommend avoiding anything that can make your guests uncomfortable or deter them from coming, such as:

- ✔ Events that limit your guests' ability to come and go as they wish — like a soiree on a boat in the middle of lake.

- ✔ Events at which your intended audience finds the attire, time, or place awkward.

- ✔ Events that are designed to reach an audience that's completely unknown to your organization or its supporters. Do you like to go to a party where you don't know anybody?

After you've sketched out an idea for an event, go to your staff and board members and ask them directly: Would you attend this event? For this price? At this time of year? If your core followers and supporters aren't enthusiastic, the event isn't going to raise money. If they've had a central role in the event planning, you're on your way to success.

Low-budget special events

Most nonprofit organizations have a wealth of talent simply waiting for a showcase. Some of the suggestions in the list that follows aren't going to work for your organization, but they can get you thinking about similar events that would be perfect for your nonprofit:

- **Sign up neighborhood children for a summer read-a-thon that benefits the library or an after-school literacy program.** By sending forms home to parents in advance, secure their permission and help with collecting pledges. Write to your community newspapers inviting them to help you spread the word as event sponsors.

- **Offer a bake sale with a distinctive theme celebrating a cultural group or holiday.** Organize your volunteers around three primary activities: setting up and pricing, selling, and taking down the sale. Plan in advance what to do with items that don't sell.

- **Hold a cocktail party in a board member's home focused on a theme that's related to your organization's work or honoring a special guest.** Although single cocktail parties for 15 people may not raise much money, don't rule this idea out. If every one of your board members signs up to host such a party over the course of a year, the cumulative amount raised may pleasantly surprise you.

Mid-budget special events

If the treasury is a bit fatter and you can afford a few more features in your special event, you may want to do something like one of these ideas:

- **Identify an up-and-coming performer or community musical group and ask for a donation of a performance in exchange for the promotion that your event will bring to him, her, or them.** The club or theater rental is likely to be your highest cost. If you choose an unusual site that's donated to you, make sure it can accommodate your performer's needs — acoustics, electrical outlets, and the like.

- **Sponsor a day-long cleanup of a coastal area, park, or preserve.** Volunteers can be sponsored by having their friends sign up to pledge a certain gift amount to the organization for each pound or garbage bag of trash that they remove. Offer prizes for the most unusual refuse items found and the largest numbers of sponsorship sign-ups.

✔ **Buy out an interesting new restaurant or a beloved community favorite for a night (usually a Monday or Tuesday when it otherwise would be closed) for your guests only.** Work with the restaurant to discount the cost charged to your organization (but not to your guests!) by offering a more limited menu than usual (three to four choices) and by promoting the restaurant through your public relations for the event.

High-priced special events

If money is no object — at the front end, at least — these events may be of interest. All require lots of upfront cash:

✔ **Hire a major speaker or entertainer from a lecture bureau or through a theatrical agent and use that person as the focus of a dinner party or private concert.** Also honor one or more business and community leaders at the event. Form an event committee and have these people invite their friends and contacts and people who may want to come for the sake of the honorees.

✔ **Present a costume ball featuring a live band.** Decorate elegantly. Make sure your crowd likes to dance and that the repertoire of your musicians suits the dances that the crowd knows! Because your board plays a key role in inviting the guests, ask their advice about their friends' tastes in music and dancing.

✔ **Organize an opportunity for amateur athletes to pay to play a sport alongside professionals or other kinds of celebrities.** Celebrity golf tournaments are popular. The idea can be applied to bowling, softball, pool . . . you name it. Create teams pairing professionals with amateurs or liberally handicap the amateurs so that everyone has a fair chance of winning. Provide trophies or other forms of recognition for many kinds of "achievements" — longest drive, bowling ball most often in the gutter, best break. Often these events end with celebratory dinners.

Budgeting for an event

The bottom line is very simple: Your total earnings from a special event must exceed your total cost — by a lot, you hope. But how do you get a handle on revenue and expenses? In this section, we offer some thoughts.

If you're staging an event for the first time, it's particularly important *early in the process* to ask your core supporters — board, volunteers, and event leadership — how much they intend to give. Because these people are the most likely to give generously, knowing their intentions helps you forecast the overall results.

Another way to estimate the fundraising potential of an event is to check with organizations that produce similar events. If they have presented a program year after year and yours is a first-time outing, ask them where their income levels began. Try to objectively weigh your event's assets against theirs. Are your boards equally well connected? Is your special guest equally well known?

The CD accompanying this book includes three sample special event budgets — CD1501 for a tribute dinner, CD1502 for a concert or performance, and CD1503 for a benefit auction.

Figuring the income side

Try to design your event so that it creates income in more than one way. A rummage sale may also include a raffle and the sale of some baked goods. An auction may include ticket sales to the event and advertising in a printed program along with the income generated from the auction itself. Standard event income categories include:

- Individual ticket sales
- Table or group sales
- Benefactor, patron, and sponsor donations (for which donors receive special recognition in return for contributing higher amounts than a basic table or seat costs)
- Sponsorships of event participants (for instance, pledging to contribute a particular amount per mile run by a friend)
- Food and/or beverage sales at the event
- Sales of goods and/or services
- Advertising sales (in printed programs, on banners, and so on)
- Purchasing a chance (raffle tickets, door prizes, and so on)

Capturing expenses — expected and unexpected

Unless a wonderful sponsor has offered to cover all your costs, your event will cost money to produce. The general categories can include the following:

- Building/facility/location (space rental, site use permits, security guards, portable toilets, tents, clean up costs)
- Advertising and promotion (posters, invitations, publicist costs, postage, Web site development)
- Production (lighting and sound equipment, technical labor, stage managers, auctioneers)

- ✔ Travel and per diem (for guest speakers, performers, or special guests)

- ✔ Insurance (for example, liability should someone be hurt due to your organization's negligence, or shipping insurance to protect donated goods)

- ✔ Food and beverages (including permits for sale or serving of alcohol, if necessary)

- ✔ Décor (flowers, rented tables and chairs, linens, fireworks, banners)

- ✔ Miscellaneous (prizes, awards, talent treatment, nametags, signs, T-shirts)

- ✔ Office expenses (letter writing, mailing list management, detail coordination)

- ✔ All other staff expenses

In spite of your careful planning, certain expenses can appear unexpectedly and cause you to exceed your budget. If you plan to serve food at your event, keep these tips in mind so that you can avoid surprise charges:

- ✔ Confirm whether all service and preparation charges are included in the catering budget.

- ✔ If you need to add additional meals at the last minute, find out whether your caterer charges extra.

- ✔ Similarly, if meals that you ordered aren't eaten, you probably still need to pay for them: Check on your caterer's policy.

- ✔ If some of the wine that you've purchased isn't consumed, find out whether the wine store is willing to buy it back from you.

- ✔ If wine has been donated to your event, serving it may not be completely free. Find out whether your caterer charges *corkage* fees for opening and serving it.

Non-food related expenses can sneak up on you too. Be sure to do the following:

- ✔ Confirm whether you're expected to pay for the shipping costs for the items that are donated to your event.

- ✔ Ask whether printing costs include tax and delivery fees.

Soliciting in-kind gifts for your event

When you think about what your event will cost and how you can pay for it, think about the business contacts that your board, staff, and outside supporters have. Often, a business's contribution of *in-kind* (noncash) materials is more generous than any cash contribution to your event. You may need to be flexible about timing and willing to drop things off or pick things up, but don't overlook in-kind gifts. Examples of in-kind gifts include the following:

✔ Businesses in your community that have in-house printing equipment may be able to print your invitations and posters, saving you thousands of dollars.

✔ A florist may contribute a roomful of valuable centerpieces in exchange for special recognition in the dinner program.

✔ A sculptor may contribute a small work you can give your honoree as a distinctive award.

✔ A donor may let you use her beautiful residence as your event site.

You may not want or need all the in-kind gifts that are offered to you. In cases such as these, do look the gift horse in the mouth! Don't accept an in-kind contribution if it's not up to the standards that you need for your event. Also, consider the implications of accepting the gift. For instance, if your agency helps young people recover from drug or alcohol addiction, don't accept a sponsorship from an alcoholic beverage company. If you're afraid of offending the donor or hurting a relationship, you can ask to use the gift in another context and — unless it's inappropriate — acknowledge the donor publicly for his generosity at your event.

Your donors will want to claim tax deductions for their in-kind contributions. They need to be able to substantiate the value of the gifts they give. If they make a contribution of noncash property worth more than $5,000, generally that item must be appraised before a value is assigned to it. For more information, see the IRS Web site at www.irs.gov.

Building your event committee

Strong volunteer leadership is the backbone of special events fundraising. Some of the most important work you and your board will do as event organizers is to recruit a chair or co-chairs for an event committee. Choose people who are smart, well-connected, and who bring different contacts to their committee work — perhaps one community volunteer, one business executive, and one local athletic hero. Many organizations include a board member on the event committee, but they also use the event as an opportunity to recruit beyond their boards, recruiting new, short-term volunteers.

Your co-chairs' job is to build a network of support for the event. Usually they invite other well-connected people to join them as members of an event committee. Perhaps your board will recruit three co-chairs and those co-chairs will recruit 25 event committee members. Your committee members and co-chairs together then will send personalized letters and invitations, and will make phone calls urging people to support and attend the event. If each of them brings 20 people, you'll have quite a crowd!

You'll find two related sample letters on the CD. CD1504 is written by an event co-chair and addressed to someone who's being invited to join an event committee member, and CD1505 is written from a committee member to a potential donor.

Setting a date and location

Check around town to find out whether you're planning to hold your event on the same date as a program by another nonprofit agency. Be as thorough as possible in this date checking. Competing for the same audience on the same date — or even dates that are close to each other — hurts both organizations' results. Also, in general, avoid dates that are too close to holidays, as people want to be with their families.

While the idea may not seem very innovative, good hotels generally are excellent sites for special events. They often have several banquet rooms, and catering, podiums, sound systems, and parking valets are all available at the site.

Some of the best special events we've attended have been inside the nonprofit organizations that they supported or in sites thematically linked to the cause being supported — such as an historic building, a maritime museum, a public park, or an art gallery. Outdoor locations, such as vineyards, formal gardens, and mountaintops can be beautiful but require backup plans for variable weather, and climbing rocky pathways or crossing uneven lawns may make your event inaccessible to some of your hoped-for supporters.

Another creative angle on choosing a location is to match it to an event theme. We've put on a great Halloween party in a former mortuary.

If you're running short on ideas, ask your friends and colleagues about interesting places they've attended events, or hold a brainstorming session with your board.

Starting the Countdown Six Months Out

Although events vary greatly in size and complexity, and although we've pulled off adequately successful events in two or three weeks, we recommend working against a six-month schedule. This section outlines a scheduling checklist for a tribute dinner. It can easily be modified to fit other types of events.

✔ **First three months.**

❑ Develop the plan and pick the event's key leadership.

❑ Recruit co-chairs or hosts.

❑ Secure entertainment and a location.

❑ Select a theme and a caterer.

The first three-month period is, not surprisingly, the slowest part of event planning. You can wait for several weeks to hear back from an invited celebrity, and you may need several more weeks to find a replacement if you get turned down.

✔ **Last three months.**

❑ Recruit an event committee or a core group of volunteers.

❑ Visit the site at which the event will be held, checking out all the regulations and recommendations for its use.

❑ Solicit in-kind contributions of materials you need for the event.

❑ If your event is appropriate for a public relations drive, you should be sending out initial press releases and preparing public service announcements (PSAs) at this point too. (See Chapter 11 for PSAs and other parts of a marketing-PR program.)

As you come inside the two-month zone, you pass some additional check-points:

✔ **Two months before the event.**

❑ Call all potential committee members and develop your invitation design. All the text on the invitation should be ready for final design and printing by six weeks before the event.

❑ Include a printed list of the final event committee members or core volunteers.

❑ Select your menu and start working on décor ideas.

✔ **Four weeks before the event**.

❑ Mail the invitations.

❑ Mail a second batch of press releases.

❑ Make phone calls to the press and to invitees to confirm coverage and travel plans.

❑ Design the printed program to be passed out at the event.

❑ Assist honorees with their speeches (if necessary).

❑ Gather the elements — baskets, banners, confetti — needed for décor.

✔ **Last week before the event.**

❑ Confirm the number of guests that you expect. A few days before the party occurs, call *everyone* who has made a reservation and confirm whether they're coming. A few people will have had to change plans, increasing or decreasing the number of guests you expect. You don't want to pay for uneaten meals or to run out of food. In ordering food from your caterer, assume that under normal circumstances, 5 percent of your guests won't attend. If the event is free, 10 percent of them won't attend.

❑ Plan the seating at the event (if necessary).

❑ Prepare place cards and table cards.

❑ Decorate the site.

We've included additional event timelines on the CD. See CD1506 for a tribute dinner or luncheon timeline, CD1507 for a benefit concert timeline, and CD1508 for a benefit auction timeline. We also provide a sample copy for an invitation to an event in CD1509.

You may think that nobody can rain on your parade, but you want to have emergency backup plans anyway. What if your performer is ill, a blizzard shuts down roadways, or your permits aren't approved on time? You need to quickly move, replace, reschedule, or cancel your program. The faster you can communicate any changes, the better your constituents feel about sticking with you and your cause.

Issuing a memorable invitation

Make your invitation something your potential guests will open and remember. Addressing the envelope by hand and using stamps rather than printed postage makes it look more personal, and an intriguing phrase or logo on the outside may lead to its being opened.

What do recipients see first when they open your invitation? Most invitations are made up of an outer folded piece, a reply card, and a reply envelope. Want some more attention? What if a pinch of confetti or glitter falls out of the envelope? Or a small black cat, spider, or bat falls out of your Halloween invitation?

In spite of our recommending these bells and whistles, we are firm believers in clarity. Make sure that the reader of your invitation can easily see who's extending the invitation, what the event is, where and when it's being held, how much it costs, and how to respond to the invitation. If people have to search for these basics, the invitation will land in the recycling bin. And remember that people look forward to your event more if other people they know are going to be there. Make sure the names of the people on your event committees are clearly and prominently presented.

Print the address to which your guest should respond somewhere on the reply card, even though it's also printed on the reply envelope. Sometimes the pieces of an invitation become separated. You want your guests to readily know where to send their reply (and money!).

Media Coverage: Letting the Public Know

If the mantra of fundraising is "If you don't ask, you won't get," the mantra for special events fundraising is "Nobody will come if they don't know about it."

The advantage of having your event covered in the media is that you reach a large number of people for a relatively modest cost. We emphasize the word *relatively*. Press relations work isn't free.

If your event has a newsworthy angle, send press releases to the media in the hopes of their writing about it or broadcasting the news. (You can find information about writing press releases in Chapter 11.)

Finding a news angle

Think about all the angles you can exploit for publicity. Try to look at it from the point of view of every section of a newspaper or newscast. Modify your basic press release to suit the content of appropriate newspaper and magazine section editors, producers of radio feature shows, and TV newsrooms. Follow-up your mailed release with a phone call. A few possibilities include

- ✔ **Entertainment section coverage of performers.** You may be able to arrange interviews between your special guests and the local entertainment press that can run on radio, television, or in the newspaper prior to your event.

- ✔ **Business section coverage of your event chair or honoree.** Many papers run a column of activities of local business and corporate leaders.

- ✔ **Feature stories about the community improvements that your agency has helped to bring about.**

- ✔ **Food section coverage of your picnic lunch or outdoor benefit concert.**

- ✔ **Health advice connected to your event.** If your organization is sponsoring a 10K run, what's the current advice about dietary preparation for long distance running? Any medium can be appropriate, but what about a feature in a runners' magazine?

- ✔ **Society page coverage of your honorees, event committee members, or other guests at your event.**

- ✔ **Radio broadcast of your honoree or guest speaker's speech.**

- ✔ **Fashion page or television coverage of attire worn to your gala.**

> ✔ **Coverage in a small newspaper.** Many communities have newspapers that are focused on particular neighborhoods, suburbs, or cultural groups. Are any of your honorees, performers, or special guests from those communities?

Printing posters that announce your event or sending personal invitations by mail is more expensive than sending out press releases. But these methods have the advantage of being direct. You can mail invitations to the right individuals and post your posters in high visibility spots in the right neighborhoods.

Getting a mention on radio or TV

The mass media need great gobs of news, announcements, and other content every day. You can get some media exposure if you, for example:

✔ Prepare a prerecorded public service announcement (PSA) for broadcast by radio stations. (See Chapter 11 for guidelines on PSAs.)

✔ Donate free tickets to your event to radio stations to use as prizes of various kinds. If a station picks up on the idea, you get a free mention — maybe a number of free mentions.

✔ Invite live weather or traffic reporters to cover conditions from your location. It can be a novel way to draw attention to your event.

Chapter 16

Finding the Grant Givers

In This Chapter

▶ Discovering private grant sources

▶ Looking at public funding

Great mystique has been woven around the writing of grant proposals. Consulting careers have been made based on that mystique. Don't be fooled by the smoke and mirrors! Securing a grant is a competitive effort, but small organizations with volunteer grant writers can succeed if they have good plans and sound organizations.

A classic rule for effective writing of any kind is to know your audience and keep that audience in mind. Grant writing is no different. In shaping a proposal, the grant writer considers the known and likely traits of the people or organizations she is addressing.

This chapter shows you how to find sources of grants and figure out your approach to a grant giver. (Chapter 17 covers writing a grant request.)

Planning a Grant Request to a Foundation

Grant sources can be grouped into two broad categories: private and public. Private sources are generally foundations and corporations, and public sources are based within some level of the government — city, county, state, or national. We write about public sources later in this chapter, but here we provide the scoop on foundations and corporations.

When you look at the entire nonprofit sector, government support and gifts from individuals provide the largest portion of contributions. Because they play a smaller role, many foundations see their job as being a source of flexible support for innovation or program improvement. When your nonprofit has a new idea, wants to expand to a new location, or wants to compare and evaluate different methods, foundations often are a good source of support. It's tricky to generalize. Some foundations do provide flexible dollars that can be used for a nonprofit's rent and light bulbs. Some only want to build buildings or provide new computer systems. Grant seeking can resemble putting together pieces of the puzzle that represent an organization's total needs.

Foundation research generally has two phases: Developing a broad list of prospects, and then refining that list until you find the likeliest sources. We discuss both of these phases in this section.

Your time as a grant writer is better spent when you use some of it to study the priorities and behaviors of the foundations you're approaching. *Shotgunning*, or sending the same proposal to a large number of foundations, is a waste of effort. *Targeting*, or focusing your attention on your most likely sources and writing to address their preferences, is much more effective.

Assembling a broad list of prospects

Over the past 50 years, information about funding sources has become increasingly available to the public. One milestone in this movement was the creation of the nonprofit *Foundation Center* in 1956. Originally intended to collect information so that foundations could learn about one another, the Foundation Center quickly became a key source of information for grant seekers.

The Foundation Center manages five libraries across the United States and a number of official cooperating collections within other libraries and nonprofits. (See Appendix A for more information.) It also publishes several directories in print, on CD-ROMs, and through a subscription service on the Web at www.fdncenter.org.

The Foundation Center directories are dense with information, but each of them contains a helpful introduction and annotated sample listing to help you identify where you can find answers to your questions. Here are a few points to help you as you cast your net using these tools:

✔ The Foundation Center organizes its information in two ways: brief profiles of foundations and indexes of actual grants of $10,000 or more. As you conduct your research, look at both kinds of information. The grants index only represents larger foundations: roughly the largest 1,000 in the country.

✔ Although you can find separate CD-ROMs for foundation profiles and for grants awarded, we recommend the Foundation Center's FC-Search, a CD-ROM that contains both foundation profiles and actual grants. You also can subscribe to FC-Search online.

✔ The information contained on the CD-ROMs and online sources is exactly the same as that contained in the books. Use the tools that best serve your research style.

✔ The most detailed indexes are in *The Foundation Grants Index* (book) or in the "Grants" part of the FC-Search CD-ROM. These indexes are good places to start.

✔ Although the United States has some 80,000 foundations, many of them are very small. As you begin your research, focus on the largest 20,000 by working with the indexes for those foundations listed in *The Foundation Directory* or *The Foundation Directory, Volume 2*. Listings in these two books represent 90 percent of the foundation dollars awarded each year. (Full contents for these books are on FC-Search.)

✔ Don't forget that corporations also award grants. The National Directory of Corporate Giving profiles corporate foundations and giving programs.

If you can't find a nearby Foundation Center branch library or cooperating collection, community foundations, larger public libraries, and college and university libraries often have copies of these materials. The books and CD-ROMs can be expensive for individuals to purchase. If you can't find them in a nearby library collection, we recommend that you purchase a short-term subscription, through the Foundation Center's Web site (www.fdncenter.org), to its online services.

For a step-by-step guide to the foundation research process, see CD1601. To help identify the tools that will help you most, check out CD1602, the Foundation Center's Helpful Hints.

So what are you looking for when you're using these search tools? You want to search for the names of foundations that meet three basic criteria:

✔ **Geography.** Does this foundation award grants in the area where your nonprofit is based?

✔ **Subject.** Does this foundation award grants in your organization's field?

✔ **Type of support.** Does this foundation award the kind of grant that you want?

If the answers are yes, good work! You have found an entry for your broad list of prospects.

For each entry on your broad list, jot down notes and questions on a *foundation prospect evaluation sheet* (you can find a sample evaluation sheet on the CD; check out CD1603). Through cross-checking and deeper study — as we explain later in this section — you narrow your broad list to the five or six best potential sources.

Asking for a grant by name

Grant givers refer to their various kinds of grants by name. Grant seekers should use the same vocabulary. Here are the categories of the most common kinds of grants:

- ✔ **Capital.** For property and building purchases and/or renovations, and for endowments

- ✔ **Endowment.** Money the agency can invest to secure a stable source of operating funds

- ✔ **Equipment.** Money for computers, vehicles, and other expensive items

- ✔ **General operating.** For day-to-day operations

- ✔ **Program related investment.** A loan paid from the foundation's endowment to a non-profit organization at a very favorable interest rate

- ✔ **Project grants.** For short-term support of specific activities

- ✔ **Seed funding.** Money for starting a new activity or organization

- ✔ **Technical assistance.** Money for professional advice from experts or for staff and volunteer education

Digging deeper to narrow your prospects

It's time to take your broad list of prospects in hand and find out more about each of them. See what you find out from the following sources:

- ✔ If one of your prospects is among the 1,000 largest foundations in the United States, turn to *The Foundation 1000,* a book that provides helpful, detailed information. A similarly detailed guide for corporate sources is *Corporate Foundation Profiles.*

- ✔ Larger foundations publish guidelines, annual reports, newsletters, and grants lists. Annual reports can be particularly helpful; they often include essays or introductory letters that provide insight into a foundation's philosophy and current directions. You can find these publications in libraries or call the foundations and ask them to send them to you.

- ✔ Gradually more and more foundations are developing Web sites (some in lieu of published annual reports).

- ✔ Foundations are required to make their three most recent 990 tax reports available to the public. Many of them do so by listing them electronically. Both the Foundation Center's Web site (www.fdncenter.org) and Guide Star (www.guidestar.org) can link you to 990s, and some state agencies provide online access to 990s. You also may request a photocopy of a foundation's 990 either in writing or in person.

A foundation's 990 tax report may be the only place you can see a complete list of grants, but PDF files for the nation's largest foundations are enormous: We recommend against downloading a 990 for one of the larger foundations. It's a less daunting tool when you're looking at smaller entities.

✔ If a foundation listing includes a contact person and phone number, and if it doesn't say you shouldn't call, after you've done your basic research, you can phone and double-check your understanding of the foundation's focus and deadlines, and ask any unanswered questions you may have.

If you're rock climbing and save the life of someone wealthy who asks what he can do for you, you can find out whether the person serves on a foundation board by checking the "Trustee, officer, and donors" index to *The Guide to U.S. Foundations: Their Trustees, Officers and Donors.* Each foundation description is brief but the index of trustees is exhaustive, and if you find promising information, you can learn more by reading the foundation's 990.

The Foundation Center's books aren't your only options. Some regions publish their own guides and some universities have developed excellent databases. We identify some other choices in Appendix A.

Knowing who you're dealing with: Different kinds of foundations

Foundations are formed and governed in different ways. These differences may affect the way you address them as a grant seeker. Four basic kinds of foundations are independent foundations, company-sponsored foundations, community foundations, and operating foundations. In this section, we describe ways you can recognize and understand which is which.

Independent foundations large and small

Most foundations in the United States are classified as *independent* — also called "private" foundations. Some of the country's largest foundations — such as the Bill and Melinda Gates Foundation, the Ford Foundation, and the Lilly Endowment — are independent foundations, but many medium-sized and small grantmaking foundations also fall in this category. When conducting your research, note whether they have paid staff members who can answer your questions. While they vary widely, key characteristics these foundations share include the following:

✔ They're started with funds donated by individuals, families, or a small group of people.

✔ Their purposes and modes of grantmaking are set by their boards of trustees, who may be family members (in which case they're called "family foundations"), or their appointed representatives.

✔ Many of these foundations award grants in the places where they were formed, but they may also award grants in multiple locations.

✔ They must file a 990 with the IRS each year.

Company-sponsored foundations and corporate giving

Corporations and businesses may support nonprofits by creating company-sponsored foundations, or they may award money directly from their company budgets. Some do both!

Whether they manage their giving through a foundation or directly from company coffers, the staff members who coordinate grantmaking also may play other roles within the corporation — such as public affairs director or human resources manager. You may notice that many — both company-sponsored foundations and direct corporate giving programs — give away goods and services or provide technical assistance, and many of them support educational causes.

Common characteristics of company-sponsored foundations include the following:

✔ They are started with funds that come from a business or corporation.

✔ Some of them maintain assets that they invest and award grants from the money they earn on those investments. Many of them add to their grantmaking budgets when their business is having a profitable year. For this reason, their grantmaking budgets can fluctuate dramatically.

✔ Often they are governed by a board made up of company executives.

✔ Sometimes they award support to organizations where their employees volunteer or contribute, or that their employees recommend to them.

✔ Most of them award grants in the communities where their employees live and work, and they see their grant giving as part of their role as "good citizens."

✔ Some of them are cautious about supporting causes that could alienate their employees or stockholders.

✔ They must file a 990 with the IRS each year.

Corporations and businesses' "direct giving" programs share characteristics with company-sponsored foundations, but have a slightly different profile:

✔ All funds available for grants come directly from company budgets and depend upon the business's available resources. In lean years they may not support charitable causes.

✔ They don't receive tax benefits for making contributions; in fact, the IRS limits the percentage of their earnings they can contribute.

✔ Like company-sponsored foundations, they tend to award grants in the communities where their employees live and work.

✔ Many corporate giving programs want to receive public recognition for their gifts.

✔ It can be harder to gather information about these programs because they don't need to specify their support of charities in their financial statements.

✔ They don't file 990 tax forms.

Many corporate giving programs match contributions their employees make to nonprofit organizations. When seeking information about your individual donors, ask whether they work for a company that would match their gift to your cause.

In your neck of the woods: Community foundations

The first community foundation, The Cleveland Foundation, was created in 1914. Today more than 600 such foundations exist worldwide. Community foundations have a different, advantageous tax status from other kinds of foundations. The Internal Revenue Service classifies them as "public charities." Other characteristics that they share with one another include the following:

✔ They are started with funds contributed by many sources — trusts and contributions of all sizes from members of the communities they represent. Those communities may be as large as a state (Hawaii and Maine have community foundations) or may be a county or city (Sonoma, California, or Chicago, Illinois).

✔ Community foundations aim their grantmaking at specific locations.

✔ Community foundations are governed by boards of directors made up of people who represent the communities they serve.

✔ To keep their desirable "public charity" tax status, they must raise money as well as give it away. For that reason, even a very small community foundation has paid staff members.

✔ Donors to community foundations may contribute to their general grantmaking programs or may create "donor advised funds" within their community foundations and play a role in recommending how to award grants derived from their contributions. The number of donor advised funds in the United States is growing rapidly.

When reviewing a grants list for a community foundation, if you see a grant that doesn't seem to fit within the foundation's published guidelines, it may have been awarded by a donor from an advised fund.

The category of "grantmaking public charity" is broader than community foundations, although community foundations are the most common kind. Some public charities focus on addressing specific topics or population groups rather than defined geographic areas. They, too, must raise money as well as give it away. One example is The Global Fund for Women.

Operating foundations — locked doors for grant seekers

Operating foundations don't award grants. They're formed to provide an ongoing source of support for a specific nonprofit institution — often a hospital or museum. When you come across an operating foundation, skip right over it!

Going for a Government Grant

Before you start daydreaming about massive state or federal funding, it pays to compare the pros and cons of private foundation funding to public funding. Table 16-1 sorts things out for you.

Table 16-1	Comparing Private to Public Grant Sources
Private Sources	**Public Sources**
The purpose of the grant-giving entity is set by donors and trustees.	The purpose of the grant-giving agency is set by legislation.
Most funders award grants to 501(c)(3) nonprofit organizations; some award fellowships and awards to individuals.	Most funders award grants, contracts, and loans to nonprofit and for-profit entities, to individuals, and to other government entities.
Most grants are awarded for one year, and, in general, grants are smaller than those awarded by public sources.	Many multiyear grants are awarded for large amounts of money.
The application process requires a limited number of contacts with individuals within the funding agency.	The application process is bureaucratic and may require applicants to work with staff at multiple levels of government.
Grants are sometimes awarded in response to simple two-page letters with backup materials.	Many proposals are lengthy (as long as 40–100 pages).

Private Sources	Public Sources
Agency files are private; applicants may not have access to reviewer comments or successful grants submitted by other agencies. Review panels and board meetings may be closed to the public.	Agency records must be public. Applicants may visit many review panels, reviewer comments must be provided, and successful proposals submitted by other agencies may be requested.
Foundation priorities may change quickly according to trustees' interests.	Agency priorities may change abruptly when new legislation is passed or budgets are revised.
Developing personal contacts with trustees or with foundation staff may enhance the applicant's chances of securing a grant.	Developing personal contacts with senate and congressional aides for state or national representatives may enhance your application's chances.
After accepting a grant, in most cases the agency is required to file a brief final narrative and financial report.	After accepting a grant, agencies may be required to follow specified contracting and hiring practices and bookkeeping and auditing procedures. They may have to prove other compliance with federal regulations. Grants can be relatively costly to manage.

If you decide you're up to the task of seeking government grants, read on.

Federal grants

To pursue government funds, you want to study a different set of research guides than those that help you with foundations and corporations.

Although you can look in more than one place, the federal publication that's most likely to help you is the _Catalog of Federal Domestic Assistance._ The bad news about the _Catalog_ is that it's written in ponderous language and has so much information that it can be overwhelming. The good news is that it opens with a very helpful introduction to guide new readers, and it's available for free and easily searchable on the Web (www.cfda.gov).

You read it here: Searching the _Catalog of Federal Domestic Assistance_ on the Web can be fun. You can find federal programs for everything from eradicating blight in trout to rebuilding homes after hurricanes. Think of two or three topics of interest, dial up the Web site, and search for what's available. It's amazing!

When you get to the point where you need to select the best potential sources of federal grants, use the *Catalog* to check the:

✔ **Applicant eligibility index.** Listing six different types of applicants — not all of whom are 501(c)(3) nonprofit organizations.

✔ **Functional area index.** Listing more than 20 major subjects — like agriculture and environmental quality — and subcategories.

✔ **Type of funding.** Federal agencies provide 15 types of funding, and some of them don't resemble the kinds of support provided by foundations. Distinctive categories include the following:

- **Formula grants** are allocated to states and other geographic areas according to distribution formulas (commonly an area's population or size). Individual nonprofits can't apply for them directly.

- **Non-grant financial aid** consists of direct payments of things like college loans and retirement and pension plans.

- **Direct payments with unrestricted use** are benefits paid to veterans and other defined population groups.

- **Loans and guaranteed insurance** often are issued to cover losses sustained under specific conditions (such as when an area is declared a "federal disaster area").

- **Sale, exchange, and donations** transfer or sell federal property and goods.

- **Provision of Specialized Services, Advisory Services, and Training** provide federal employees to give advice or conduct trainings.

- **Dissemination of Technical Information** publishes and distributes technical or specialized data that your organization may have gathered through a research project.

A great thing about the *Catalog* Web site is that it invites you to conduct your search in multiple ways. Say it's your first time visiting `cfda.gov` and you want to be sure that you aren't about to miss an important deadline. You can search by deadline to find out what's coming up soon. Maybe you run a program benefiting children in foster care: You can search the catalog by beneficiary. If you know the name of a program you want to investigate, you can search by program title.

The *Catalog of Federal Domestic Assistance* tells which agencies and offices manage the funds for different opportunities. After identifying federal programs of interest, experienced grant seekers always, always, always call, write, or e-mail those offices to confirm the information that's in the *Catalog*. Even though this information is updated frequently, it also goes out of date quickly.

Lean on your legislators

Because members of the U.S. Congress are very interested in seeing federal money going to the people and places they serve, some make sure that their staff members keep up-to-date about available resources and help their constituents with applications. The staff members may review and assist with a proposal, write letters of support for a project, or place key phone calls in support of a project.

Also, these government offices receive frequent publications about new programs and — once they know of an agency's work — may refer other opportunities to the agency. The staff members with whom you work are very busy, and you can't expect to sit back and let them do research for you, but they can be important allies.

Sometimes we've grown excited reading about programs profiled in detail in the *Catalog* that were created by legislation — but when we get to the "allocations" we find they have no money in their budgets! Always check to see whether a program is budgeted.

Another key resource is the *Federal Register,* which readers can find through the Government Printing Office — www.gpoaccess.gov/fr/index.html. It's printed each business day by the United States government and is readily available on the Web. Reading the *Register* allows you to stay up-to-date on the latest federal grant giving happenings.

We've listed more sources of information about federal grants and contracts and suggested further steps to take in your research: See CD1604, the Federal Government Program Research Checklist.

One great advantage of pursuing money from the government is that information of all sorts is public. If grant seekers apply and are turned down, they can ask for (and get!) the comments of the grant reviewers. Sometimes they can see copies of successful proposals or sit in on review panels to hear their proposals discussed.

Non-federal government grants

In some cases, the federal government distributes money for locally-based programs. You can find information about these programs in the *Catalog of Federal Domestic Assistance.* However, information about state and municipal grants (which state or local tax dollars generate money for) can be trickier to find because it's not always compiled in a central resource guide.

Checking the Web site for the state or local agencies related to a project (such as the Department of Education or the Office of Children and Youth) and visiting with local government officials and congressional office staffs are good steps in your research.

Finding government money sounds daunting, right? But remember that one or two major government grants may provide general operating support or may award a grant to your program for as long as five years. The time spent wading through bureaucratic offices and regulations can be very worthwhile.

Chapter 17

Writing a Grant Proposal

*E*ven though grant seeking is highly competitive, writing a good grant proposal isn't particularly mysterious or difficult. Grant proposals are a lot like basic business plans or even simple scientific proofs: First you identify a problem and make it compelling, then you set goals for improving the situation, and last you propose a possible solution and a way to test the results.

In the course of laying out the plan, you also want to assert the special strengths of your organization and a sensible financial plan for the project, both in the near term and later.

Some proposals are quite long and elaborate. Some are just a few pages. Some are submitted on paper, and others are submitted online. Your research into funding sources (which we describe in Chapter 16) will uncover preferences of different foundations and government programs, so you can figure out the best mode of presentation, appropriate level of detail, and best method for submitting your proposal. You'll encounter many variations, but this chapter shows you the basics of how to write the grant.

The Windup: Tasks to Complete before the Proposal

Generally a grant writer develops a proposal in one of two ways. Either a funding source announces a specific initiative for which it's inviting proposals — called a Request for Proposals (an "RFP") or a Program

Announcement — or a nonprofit organization initiates an idea about a problem that needs to be addressed. In the first instance, the grant writer resembles a job seeker who's convincing a prospective employer (in this case the foundation or government agency) that she (or rather the nonprofit she represents) is the best one for the job. In the second circumstance, the grant writer first has to convince a funding agency that a certain job needs to be done and then sell the agency on the idea that her nonprofit is worthy to do it.

Government sources usually issue requests for proposals, and foundations usually issue program announcements.

Any grant writer, whether responding to or initiating contact with a funding source, is working to convince her reader of a clear connection between the funder's mission and the organization's work.

Asking for permission to ask

Many funding sources want to screen proposal ideas before they receive extensive, detailed documents. This screening process allows them to encourage only truly promising proposals, saving both themselves and grant seekers the time and effort that goes into reviewing and writing a longer proposal.

When a grant writer encounters a request for a *letter of inquiry,* she should boil down the essence of the proposal — all eight areas covered in the following section — into a readable, compelling letter. The letter doesn't ask for a grant directly, but it asks for permission to submit more detailed information. Most letters of inquiry are two pages in length (they range from one to four pages). Follow the foundation's stated preferences.

CD1701 offers a sample letter of inquiry, and CD1702 illustrates a typical foundation application form that you may be asked to fill out if the foundation wants to learn more after reading your letter of inquiry.

Passing the screening questionnaire

Some funding agencies screen potential applicants by asking them to respond to questionnaires. These days you can find a growing number of those questionnaires on funders' Web sites. Questions may determine specific eligibility — such as whether the nonprofit organization provides services in a particular county — while others ask for substantive answers to questions. As with a letter of inquiry, this questionnaire may seem like a barrier to applying but is intended as a tool to keep unlikely applicants from wasting their time and efforts.

A grant seeker shouldn't pass off the letter of inquiry or a questionnaire as an inconsequential hurdle: First impressions can be lasting impressions.

The Pitch: Writing Your Proposal

Deep down, every good proposal is based on a well-considered plan, and designing the plan is a creative, even fun, part of the task. The differences from source to source are in how to pitch that plan and the order in which its parts are assembled. But the parts are fairly standard:

- ✔ **Cover letter and summary:** Provide a brief overview of the entire project and its costs, linking the project to the interests of the funding source

- ✔ **Introduction or background:** Discusses the applicant's strengths and qualifications

- ✔ **Problem statement or needs assessment:** Describes the situation that the proposed project will try to improve or eradicate

- ✔ **Goals, objectives, and outcomes:** Outline a vision for success in both broad and pragmatic terms

- ✔ **Methods:** Describe the project activities, who will manage them, and why the proposed approach is the best

- ✔ **Evaluation:** Explains how the organization will measure whether it met its goals, objectives, and outcomes

- ✔ **Budget:** Presents the project's costs and sources of income

- ✔ **Future and additional funding:** Discusses how the balance of funds needed will be raised if a grant is awarded (but doesn't cover the entire cost) and how project costs will be covered in the future

In this section, we cover each of these parts in detail.

CD1703 and CD1704 illustrate two kinds of proposals — a general operating support grant and a project grant addressed to an agency. The project grant is addressed to a city agency that requires its applicants to use a printed form.

Setting out with the cover letter and summary

Technically, the *cover letter* isn't part of the proposal narrative. It's attached to the top of the proposal where it serves as an introduction to the document's primary points. One of its key roles is to convey how the proposal addresses the foundation's stated priorities. Often a board member signs the letter.

The letter mentions any contact the organization may have had with the funding source before submitting the proposal. For example, you may say, "When I tripped over your umbrella last Tuesday, I couldn't help but notice you were reading a book about frogs. Here at the city park aquarium, we've planned an astounding amphibian exhibition."

Although the cover letter's author always wants to lay out the basics of the request — how much money is needed and for what — she can also use it to say something about her personal connection to the cause. The letter always should close with clear, specific information about the contact person to whom the funding source should direct any questions.

Like many reports, the body of the grant proposal begins with a summary (similar to an abstract) containing a brisk overview of its key ideas. The grant writer usually begins the summary section with a one-sentence overview of the project and how much money is being requested in the proposal. Next come key ideas (one or two sentences each) from every section of the proposal. The summary closes with the prognosis for future funding for the program.

Don't use the exact same wording to describe your project idea in the cover letter and in the project summary. You don't want to bore your reader.

Introducing your agency

Some proposals contain *introductions*. Others contain *background information* sections. Choose which to use by following the preferences of your funding source or, if no preference is given, by deciding which approach allows you to best present the proposal idea. Whichever you use, this section of a proposal describes the nonprofit organization that's seeking money.

Usually this section begins with a brief history of the nonprofit, its philosophy in approaching its work, and its major accomplishments. Then the writer describes the current programs as well as the constituents served by the program. After these standard ingredients, the writer draws upon whatever other credentials recommend the organization for the work she's about to propose. Drawing attention to signs of outside validation is helpful. Here are some kinds of things the writer can mention:

- ✔ Reviews or coverage in the press

- ✔ Citations and awards presented to the agency or its leaders

- ✔ Credentials and/or experience of the nonprofit's leadership

- ✔ Other agencies that refer clients to the nonprofit

- ✔ Invitations extended to the nonprofit to provide expert advice or testimony

- ✔ Major grants received from other sources

Although the writer isn't yet describing the project idea, the items he introduces here should back up the nonprofit's qualifications to do the proposed work. For example, suppose that an after-school program for inner city teenagers offers multiple programs — athletics, arts, and youth-led volunteer work in the community. If the grant request focuses on expanding the community service work, the writer can focus this section on how that volunteer work began and evolved, where the teens have provided services, and who has praised it.

Grant writers are often tempted to write on and on (and on and on and on) (and on and on and on) about an agency's history or its philosophy. Don't drag this section down by including too many details or using too much eloquent verbiage. One — or at the most, two — paragraphs on these subjects are plenty.

Shaping the problem

A grant writer begins to shape the argument behind the proposal plan in the *problem statement* or a *statement of need.* Generally a writer prepares a problem statement when proposing a new relationship with the constituents who would be served by the project. A statement of need talks about the challenging situations of people (or animals or environments) that the nonprofit already serves. A well-described problem (or need) captures the reader's attention.

How do you know whether you need to write a problem statement or a needs assessment? Here's an example. If someone notices (and writes about) a high crime and drug use rate among teenagers in a particular neighborhood, the situation of those teens can be described in a problem statement. If a writer from an organization already managing a program that serves teenagers in that neighborhood notices that they're not signing up for sports offerings because they're too hungry after school to focus attention on physical activity, a needs assessment may discuss their nutritional needs.

You shouldn't describe your "problem" as a lack of money but as a situation in the lives of the constituents, whether they're spruce trees, retired adults, or former race horses.

A common mistake made in a problem statement (or needs assessment) is suggesting the problem's solution. Wait! Hold off! The rest of the proposal is boring if you propose the solution here. At the most, the writer may want to plant the beginnings of an idea, lead up to the edge, and suggest a direction that may be fruitful.

Setting goals, objectives, and outcomes

The grant writer has described a problem in ways that engage the reader's concerns. The next tactic is to introduce what the nonprofit can achieve if it takes on the proposed project. The writer hasn't yet described the project, but this section jumps ahead to the vision for results. Why? First you hope to pique the reader's interest and concern (in the problem statement), and then you show him the possibility of a better future (in goals, objectives, and outcomes), and next you tell him how to achieve that vision (in the methods section).

Goals, objectives, and outcomes are related but different terms. You find out about them in Chapter 9, which discusses planning. The following points give a brief overview of these terms:

- ✔ *Goals* are broad, general results. They may be somewhat lofty.

- ✔ *Objectives* should be measurable results. How much do you want to accomplish in what time frame, involving how many people (or trees or salamanders)?

- ✔ *Outcomes* are the trickiest to state. An outcome is the answer to the question, "So what?" So what if you provide antismoking classes to middle school students, reaching every child in four school districts? Well, the outcome may be that a lower percentage than average of those specific students begins smoking in high school. Or in college. Or ever.

  The writer wants the outcomes to be significant, measurable, and specific, but he also has to be careful not to overstate how much the project can claim or measure. What if the antismoking classes are one of a series of health classes and others also bear an antismoking message? How long do such classes hold sway over teenagers' behaviors? Over adult behaviors?

If a grant says a nonprofit intends to achieve a long-term outcome, the agency had better be prepared to conduct the research necessary to find out whether the outcome was achieved.

Presenting (ta-da!) your project idea

At last it's time to explain the project idea. Who will do what to whom over what period of time? If you're writing your proposal for a research project, generally this section is called the procedures. For most other types of projects, it's called *methods* or *methodology*.

Although this section contains the idea that inspired the organization to seek funding, the writing can be dull. The content is similar to writing a list of instructions. To avoid the dullness trap, think about constructing an argument from beginning to end. A good methods section opens with an overview of the approach and then leads the reader through the project's development step by step. It includes enough detail so that the reader can see the project clearly but not so much that he sinks into the daily grind. Other techniques to preserve vitality include the use of timelines, charts, and graphs — visual presentations of the information to break up and complement the descriptive text.

Most projects require a few months of preparation before they can be launched. Factor in time for hiring and training staff, purchasing and installing equipment, identifying research subjects, and performing other necessary preliminary steps.

Because this section contains all the project details, you may accidentally overlook or forget important information. Two topics that often are overlooked are as follows:

- ✔ If you need to hire new staff to do the project work, be sure to discuss the hiring process, job descriptions, and qualifications. See Chapter 8 for ideas on hiring paid staff.

- ✔ Just because you create something great doesn't mean that anyone will show up to take advantage of it. The proposal must explain how an organization plans to spread the word about this new project and entice the target population into becoming involved. See Chapter 11 for tips on marketing your program to the public.

The proposal must do more than explain what the organization will do. It also must explain why the organization is taking that approach — the rationale. The reason may be that nobody has ever done it this way before. The reason may be that the organization has tested the approach and knows that it works. The reason may be that another organization in another part of the country has tested the approach and the project proposes to try it in a new setting.

In an effort to raise as much money as possible to secure a grant, an organization may change its programs to match a particular foundation's interests. The organization's board and management should carefully assess new project ideas to make sure they address the organization's mission. When the grant seeker feels like Cinderella's sister cutting off her toes to cram her foot in the shoe, she should stop and reassess whether receiving the grant is in the organization's best interest.

Explaining how results will be measured

If the grant writer has carefully shaped the goals, objectives, and outcomes section of the proposal, the desired project results are clear. The *evaluation* section, then, explains how the organization will measure whether it met those goals, objectives, and outcomes.

This section says who will conduct the evaluation and why that person or organization is right for the job; what information already is known about the situation or population served; what instrument(s) will be used to measure the project's results; and how the finished report will be used.

Different kinds of evaluation are appropriate at different stages of a project. In a project's first year, the most important question may be, "How can we make it run better?" A nonprofit with a brand-new effort may want to spend the first year analyzing its internal efficiency, balance of responsibilities, and general productivity before beginning an intense measuring of outcomes.

Some organizations evaluate all their projects with project staff. Who's better suited to understand the details and nuances of the work? Who else can grasp the purpose and objectives of the project so quickly?

Of course, the opposing view is that you get biased results by asking staff members, whose livelihood may depend upon continuation of the project activity. Yet, outside consultants may be much more expensive, and they, too, are employed by the nonprofit agency. They, too, may have some bias about the report's results.

Evaluation of nonprofit activities has evolved over the past several decades. Here are some common questions addressed in evaluations:

- Were project funds spent according to the proposal plan? Did the grant recipients do what they said they were going to do?

- What is the project's cost per unit (or person)? How do its costs compare to the costs of other approaches to the same problem?

- How many units of service (hours of counseling, copies of publications, and so on) is the project producing?

- How satisfied are consumers of the agency's services with the quality of those services?

- How does this agency's work compare to industry standards for an effective work of this type?

- What changes have been made in the lives of the constituents' served?

A nonprofit often can discover a lot about the effectiveness of its work by evaluating information it already gathers. For example, individual public schools may be required to submit an annual plan to a school superintendent's office to qualify for special forms of funding. A researcher interested in understanding how many schools in a district were trying a particular approach to school reform probably could find out by reviewing the plans that are on file in the school district offices.

Other kinds of data a nonprofit may have on file include names and addresses of people participating in public programs, intake and exit interviews with staff and clients, or questions submitted by e-mail in response to a Web site.

If the agency plans to gather data from new sources (such as through surveys, interviews, and focus groups), the proposal should explain what those sources are, who will design the instruments to be used, who will gather the information and input the data, and who will analyze the results. If you've already designed your survey, it may be another useful appendix item.

On the CD, you'll find a sample final report at CD1705 and notes on the budget that accompanies that report at CD1706. This illustrates how an arts organization reported on the results of its project and tells what happened after sample grant proposal CD1704 was funded and the project completed.

Talking about the budget

Because a proposal is a request for money, at this point your proposal should present information about project costs and what other funding is available.

If the organization offers only one service for which the nonprofit is seeking money, the organization's budget is the same as the *project budget*. If the project is one of many things the nonprofit does, it's presented as a smaller piece of the overall budget.

Chapter 10 discusses how to compute the indirect costs that all programs within an organization share. Different foundations have different attitudes about covering the indirect costs associated with projects. Check with the foundation to which you're applying to see whether it limits how much can be charged to indirect costs or management expenses.

The project budget should be clear, reasonable, and well considered. The grant writer should keep a worksheet of budget assumptions with the grant file in case anyone asks months later how she computed the numbers it contains. Foundations don't want to believe that an organization is inflating the budget, nor do they want to think that the applicant is trying to low-ball them (making their proposal seem competitive by requesting less than they really need). Either approach — budgeting too high or too low in relationship to the cost of a project — can lead to wasting resources.

Unless the foundation is willing to consider a proposal for 100 percent of the project costs, the proposal budget should include both income and expenses. Some foundations ask for the information in a particular format. For those foundations that don't require a special format on the budget, here are some general standards that apply to the presentation:

✔ Income should head the budget, followed by expenses.

✔ If the organization has multiple income sources, contributed sources should be listed apart from earned sources. Within contributed sources, a writer usually lists government grants and contracts first, followed by foundation grants, corporate gifts, and contributions from individuals.

✔ All expenses related to personnel costs — salaries, benefits, and consulting fees — come first in the expense half of the budget. Usually personnel costs are subtotaled.

✔ Non-personnel costs follow and also are subtotaled.

✔ Some kinds of project budgets allow for contingency funds of a certain percentage of the project's projected costs. These funds are usually listed last among expenses.

✔ Budget footnotes can explain anything that may be difficult for a reader to understand.

The budget is like a spine for the rest of the proposal. It should support every aspect of the plan. Costs of every activity in the methods and evaluation sections must be considered.

Some project budgets seem simple and straightforward. An agency wants to purchase a piece of equipment. It researches the cost and writes it down as the one and only budget item. This approach may be foolhardy: Other costs involved may include shipping and installation, training of staff, and maintenance and supplies.

At some foundations, all project budgets and financial reports are analyzed by staff with expertise in that area. They may be separated from the rest of the proposal for this reading. Therefore, a budget needs to be clear even if it's read on its own — apart from the narrative part of the proposal.

You can find sample foundation budget forms on the CD (CD1707). You also can find a sample project budget for a tutoring program within a youth agency at CD1004.

For more detailed information about creating budgets, including budgets for specific programs or projects, see Chapter 10.

Explaining where the rest of the money comes from

In Chapter 13, we introduce the age-old concept of not putting all your eggs in one basket. Between many foundations' reluctance to pay for 100 percent of a project's costs and their preference for offering short-term project support, if you start a new project, you want to know how you can cover the balance of the costs in the present and all the costs when initial project support runs out.

Foundations reviewing grant proposals want to know the same information. What resources, other than the grant that the foundation is considering, are available to the project? And how can the agency sustain the project in the future?

Willingness to cover the full cost of a project varies from foundation to foundation and agency to agency. Some like to "own" a project and have their names strongly associated with it; therefore, they may be willing to cover full costs. Some like to be one of several supporters so that the nonprofit isn't entirely dependent upon them. That way, the project can continue even if they can't continue to support it in a future year.

An *additional funding plan* should be clear and reasonable. Because a nonprofit can't assume it will receive every grant for which it applies, a foundation understands if a nonprofit has applied for more grant funding than the full cost of the program. If a nonprofit lists another foundation as a possible source of income for a project, it doesn't necessarily have to have received that grant, but the prospect should be plausible. The size of the grant should be appropriate to others awarded by the agency, and the focus of the foundation should be aligned with the project request.

Foundation staff members talk with colleagues at other foundations. Never lie about having submitted a proposal or having received a grant from another foundation. That lie can undermine your request (and future requests, too)!

Guidelines for future funding are similar to those for additional funding. The plan should be reasonable and well considered. Generally, foundations hope to see agencies growing less dependent on grants over time and are happy to see proposals projecting future increases in earned revenues or individual contributions.

Here are some possible sources for future funding:

- ✔ A government contract to sustain a valuable service after it's been developed and tested
- ✔ The sale of publications, recordings, or services based on the project
- ✔ A membership drive
- ✔ A major donor campaign

Some proposals don't need to address these concerns. They begin and end in a short period of time. For example, a proposal to publish a report based on an agency's work may continue to bear modest marketing costs in the future, but after the agency edits, designs, and prints the report, future funding is a minor concern. For others, future funding is very important. For example, you wouldn't want to start a recreation center for low-income youths and have to close it after a few years. The lack of program continuity can have a negative effect on the clients.

Having the last word

Not all proposals include a *conclusion*. Some writers feel that a conclusion is repetitive and unnecessary. On the other hand, if the proposal ends with a discussion of future and additional funding, that part of the proposal may seem remote from the passion that fueled the project in the first place.

We recommend taking a bow: A brief concluding section may bring the reader back to the key points of the proposal, leaving a compelling finale as the last thing the reader remembers.

P.S.: The appendix

A proposal always needs an appendix. Four key items are routinely included in the appendix (and often identified by foundations as required enclosures):

- ✔ Proof of nonprofit status from the IRS
- ✔ List of the board of directors (and of any advisory boards)
- ✔ Current year's organization budget
- ✔ Prior year's financial statement

Other common appendix items include the following:

- ✔ A list of major grants received in recent years
- ✔ An organizational chart outlining staff and board roles
- ✔ A timeline of the organization's history
- ✔ Copies of newspaper clippings about the agency
- ✔ Job descriptions and/or resumes of key staff
- ✔ Samples of evaluations or reports
- ✔ A copy of a long-range plan (or its executive summary if the plan is lengthy)
- ✔ Agency brochures and program announcements
- ✔ Letters of support

On the CD accompanying this book, we include a checklist for finishing and submitting your proposal (CD1708).

Throwing Special Pitches for Special Situations

If you prepare a grant proposal following the format we describe in the previous sections, you'll have in hand a very useful document, suitable for submission to many foundations. Grant writing isn't a field in which one size fits all or even one approach fits all. In the next sections, we describe some common situations that call for variations on your basic proposal.

If a foundation gives explicit instructions about how to present your proposal, always follow them. You'll notice that example CD1704, the San Francisco Mime Troupe's proposal to the San Francisco Arts Commission's Cultural Equity Grants Program, is written in the form of answers to a series of questions.

Trolling for corporate funds with a two-page letter

Proposals addressed to corporations and company-sponsored foundations generally are brief. A two-page letter is an excellent approach. If an employee of the corporation is involved with your organization, say so in the first paragraph.

Here's what to do in your letter proposal:

✔ Ask for a specific contribution early in the letter. If you've had prior contact with the funder, mention it.

✔ Describe the need or problem to be addressed.

✔ Explain what your organization plans to do if the grant is awarded.

✔ Provide information about your nonprofit organization, its strengths and accomplishments.

✔ Include appropriate budget data. If the budget is more than a half page long, include it as an attachment.

✔ Discuss how the project will be sustained in the future.

✔ Make a strong, compelling closing statement.

On the CD accompanying this book, you'll find a sample letter proposal (CD1709) and a sample set of company-sponsored foundation guidelines (CD1710).

Proposing a research project

Research proposals are often longer and more elaborate than proposals for other kinds of projects. They vary from grant proposals and letters in the following ways:

✔ The problem statement or needs assessment includes a literature review of other research that has been conducted on the topic at hand. Different approaches are compared to one another (leading up to the approach the proposal will take).

✔ The introduction is more often placed at the end of the document and called "background information." This section includes detailed information about the research credentials of the principal investigator and the research team and institution. If several institutions are cooperating on the project, this section describes all partners.

✔ The methods section is called procedures, and each approach to be taken is compared to others outlined in the literature review.

Two new sections often come at the end of the methods section:

✔ *Deliverables* are "end products" of the research, such as published reports, books, or articles.

✔ *Dissemination* describes the ways that the nonprofit will share the research with others. These methods may include presenting papers at research conferences, and distributing published reports, or posting new discoveries on a Web site.

Seeking general operating support

If you're seeking funds for general operating support, your proposal needs to make an argument for the work of the entire agency rather than for a specific project. In this type of request, some of the information about current activities, often included in the introduction or background information sections, should be moved to the methods section. The grant making organization judges the application based on overall organizational strength and its role in its field. Increasingly, foundations consider the ability of an agency to cooperate or work with others an important criterion. If you're tailoring a proposal for general operating support, we recommend the following:

- Prepare an introduction that very quickly introduces the problem that the agency was created to solve, the goals it addresses, and its current programs. Give some attention to describing its leadership (board and staff), its history, and how its activities may have evolved over time.

- In the problem statement, discuss the human needs implied by the agency's organizational mission.

- When preparing the section on goals, objectives, and outcomes, address the external goals (how the nonprofit plans to serve its constituents) and internal goals (such as expanding the board of directors or changing the accounting system).

- Use the methods section to describe the agency's current programs.

- In the evaluation section, describe various means the agency uses to understand and improve its programs.

- Include the entire annual budget for the organization in lieu of a project budget.

- In the section on future and additional funding, briefly describe fundraising or earned income areas the organization is working to increase. Mention major grants being submitted for all aspects of the organization or include them as a list in the appendix.

As we mention earlier in this chapter, we've included a sample general operating support grant on the CD (CD1703).

Seed money: Proposing to form a new agency

A writer presenting a proposal for a brand-new organization that doesn't have a history, a staff, or any accomplishments faces a particular writing challenge. What is there to say?

Writers of such proposals should take heart. Some foundations specialize in "seed proposals" for new projects and new organizations, specifically inviting such proposals. A seed proposal has two key ingredients: 1) careful assessment of the problem to be addressed; and 2) special qualifications its founders bring to its creation.

Here's a quick outline of a proposal for a new endeavor:

- ✔ Background information introduces the people who are creating the organization, their vision, how they identified the idea, and steps they've taken to date to realize their ideas.

- ✔ The problem statement should be a strong, convincing presentation of what the founders have observed and learned about the needs to be addressed.

- ✔ Goals, objectives, and outcomes should be carefully stated. The goals may be lofty, but the founders need to realize they'll take baby steps before they run. Objectives and outcomes should be reasonable considering the developing state of the organization.

- ✔ Methods should be plans for the first year or two of activities. Include a discussion of how the organization will be structured and how services will be offered.

- ✔ Evaluation plans may "go easy" during the organization's initial phases. Founders may be testing basic ideas for their feasibility and efficiency for a year or two before studying an approach in depth.

- ✔ The budget is likely to be the entire organizational budget. Some seed grant funders don't mind helping to set up the organization and are willing to cover costs such as equipment purchases or deposits for renting an office.

- ✔ Future and additional funding should outline basic plans for supporting the nonprofit in the future (unless it addresses a discrete problem that may be solved within a few years).

A foundation may be willing to support a feasibility study for a new idea. Such a grant funds interviews and research into how distinctive the idea is, what the likeliest sources of support are, and how much funding the new organization may expect from such resources. Such a plan arms the seed project in applying for other start-up grants.

Chapter 18

Capital Campaigns: Finding Lasting Resources

*A*s nonprofit organizations mature, their staff and board may grow ambitious to develop resources that can stabilize them. One option they have is to raise *capital* — money to make specific, usually long-term, financial investments.

Some organizations raise capital funds for *ventures* — money they put aside for major program innovations. Some raise capital for *endowments* — money they permanently invest, with the investment returns providing a source of annual income. Still others focus their capital fundraising on buying property or building facilities.

If you're the director of a nonprofit that's taking on a capital campaign, imagine yourself as suddenly having two jobs: leading your organization and its programs and leading its capital project. Can you picture yourself in those two hats? Exhausting thought, isn't it? However, if the campaign project goes well, it can attract new donors and attention to your nonprofit. That benefit, combined with new resources to invest in your work or the home of your dreams, can make those hats worth wearing.

As varied as their purposes are, most capital campaigns share a set of fundraising activities. Not every organization is positioned to make those strategies work. Read ahead and proceed cautiously before stepping onto the capital campaign trail.

Beginning the Funding Plan

Your adult literacy program wants to share its innovative teaching materials broadly through a series of books, but setting up a publication program requires a substantial initial investment. Your nonprofit school for hearing impaired children balances its budget each year, but it depends heavily on a small number of income sources. Having annual investment returns from an endowment may allow it to provide scholarships for children who can't pay full tuition rates. You've found the building of your organization's dreams. It's just around the corner from where you currently serve clients, and it's bigger and better than your current building. Better yet, it's for sale at a reasonable price. You need money to buy it and money to make repairs. In each of these cases, you need to raise a significant amount of money that's above and beyond your normal annual fundraising. Where do you begin?

Capital fundraising requires you to analyze your organization's situation and to plan carefully and thoroughly. Not every organization is positioned to succeed at it. You want to do the following:

- ✔ **Preplan** by gathering information about technical assistance available to you, reviewing your donor records, and creating a rough campaign budget.

- ✔ **Test** the project's feasibility by meeting with a select group of potential contributors and gauging their possible interest.

- ✔ **Develop** your case by brainstorming with staff and board members.

- ✔ **Analyze** what you learn from the interviews against your initial goal and then refine your goal and plan.

An unsuccessful capital campaign can cost your organization money, hurt its reputation, and exhaust and demoralize your staff and board. If your research suggests that you won't succeed, do *not* be foolhardy and forge ahead.

Preplanning your campaign

After your organization begins thinking that it may want to raise funds for a capital project, we recommend that you seek outside assistance in the form of workshops, classes, or consulting. Convincing yourself that your capital campaign can work is easy, so testing your vision on others is important. Possible resources include the following:

- ✔ A program officer at a local foundation or staff in your city's economic development office or regional community loan fund may be able to suggest other nearby resources.

✔ The Nonprofit Finance Fund (www.nonprofitfinancefund.org) may offer programs in your area, including low-cost consultations, small grants for planning, and workshops about understanding and planning capital projects.

✔ Colleagues who conducted capital campaigns may be able to guide you to resources they used. Your board may contain members with professional experience in financial lending and investing, architecture, construction, real estate, city government, and law; all can provide valuable assistance. If your board doesn't include such professional skills, its members may know professionals who do.

You need to begin raising funds from individuals and institutions that know your organization and care deeply about its work. Assess your organization's primary sources of contributed income. How detailed and accurate are your donor records? Who's been donating money to your cause and at what level? Critically important in this scan of supporters is identifying a person or a small team of people with resources, dedication, and good connections, who would be willing to lead your campaign.

Begin identifying sources beyond your current supporters. Gather information about major capital resources in your area. For example, which individual donors' names appear on the walls of many nonprofits' buildings? Which foundations and corporations?

In identifying possible resources for your capital campaign, don't overlook loans, which often play an important role in facility projects, both as standard mortgages and in helping organizations complete projects on time. Often donors of large gifts don't write checks for the full amount of their pledges immediately and organizations borrow some of the money they need to finish construction while waiting to receive those gifts. Does your area have a community loan fund? Do any local foundations make program-related investments (low-interest loans) to nonprofits? Do any local foundations guarantee bank loans for nonprofits?

Developing a rough budget

Before you test your project to find out whether it's feasible, you need assistance figuring out what it will cost. A common mistake organizations make is forgetting that raising money costs them money. They may need to dedicate staff time, and invest in marketing materials and events. Often they also hire outside consultants or new fundraising staff to assist them.

For example, if you want revenues from an endowment to cover five $10,000 scholarships, you need to raise one million dollars. Your board may set a different policy, but most nonprofit organizations figure they can expect to earn at least 5 to 6 percent on their endowments, and spend at that rate each year without depleting the money they have put aside. If you estimate that meeting that goal will take you a year and a half, you may want to budget for

- ✔ A skilled fundraising consultant who will spend an average of ten hours per week on your project
- ✔ Printed materials describing your organization and campaign
- ✔ Funds to cover the cost of meeting with prospective donors — travel and meals
- ✔ Money to invest in recognizing and thanking donors, including a celebratory event at the culmination of the campaign

We have included a sample presentation of capital campaign costs as CD1801.

Budgeting for building projects is complex. If you identify a plot of land or existing building you want to renovate, you need to begin with rough estimates and develop a specific budget later — after you secure architectural drawings, construction permits from your city or county, and bids from contractors.

As you begin developing a budget, find out about the construction rules you need to follow. A local architect or city appraiser/inspector should be able to tell you what enhancements you're required to include or make in your building. For example, the Americans with Disabilities Act (ADA) sets an important set of requirements. Buildings for public use must offer ramps and elevators for wheelchair users; appropriately placed plumbing, railings, and equipment; and large-print signs or audible signals. You may think to budget the obvious, more visible modifications needed, but an experienced professional can point out more subtle requirements that you might overlook.

In this early planning stage, you will develop a list of major projects to be done. At this point, you may be able to get a contractor to give you a ballpark estimate of the cost.

Just because a building is currently in use doesn't mean that you can move right in and begin operating your programs there. Building codes often change over time, and whenever a building changes hands or its use changes, it then must comply with the most recent requirements.

Building codes are closely tied to the building's function. Rules for classrooms sometimes change according to the age of the children. Rooms in which large numbers of people may gather are likely to have stricter safety requirements than those rooms used by individuals as offices.

The CD includes "Capital: Hard and Soft Costs," a checklist from the Nonprofit Finance Fund (CD1802), and three sample capital project budgets — one for a modest project (CD1803) and two for larger-scale projects (CD1804 and CD1805).

Drafting a construction budget

In addition to architectural and construction costs, your project is likely to have eight major kinds of expenses:

✔ **Real estate fees:** Purchase of real estate often includes fees for inspections, closing costs, and other charges paid to banks, realtors, and other professions involved in the transaction.

✔ **Fees and permits:** Building or planning departments generally charge fees for approval of your architect's plans. Some projects require multiple permits, such as one for construction, another for specific safety features, and yet others for signs, exterior lights, or awnings.

✔ **Financing costs:** If you borrow money, your organization needs to make mortgage payments, which include interest and financing costs.

✔ **Fundraising costs:** You need to continue to cover the costs of raising funds for current programs while also raising funds for construction and moving.

✔ **Technical costs:** Rarely does your old technology neatly fit into a new building. If you've expanded, you may need more phone lines or more computers.

✔ **Furnishings and fixtures:** Placing your funky old couch in the lobby of your elegant new building just won't do. You may want to invest in new furniture and fixtures.

✔ **Moving costs:** You may remember to budget for the moving van, but that's just the beginning of the moving costs. You need to have services — phones, utilities, trash pickup, and others — transferred from your old location to your new one. And you need to let everyone know where you've moved, so you want to send change-of-address cards and newsletters. Stationery, brochures, invoices, and other printed materials need to be reprinted with your new address.

✔ **Maintenance:** If your new building is bigger and nicer, taking care of it costs more. Not only do you need to raise funds for janitorial services and light bulb replacements, but you also need to have enough money put aside to take care of unexpected repairs.

Testing feasibility

Remember that tried-and-true method for buying a used car? The one where you circle the vehicle, kicking all the tires? An organization's capital campaign starts with that kind of tire kicking, except that it's called a *feasibility study*, research testing the hypothesis that you can raise the amount of money you need. Four feasibility study test points are

✔ Tire One: How much money does this organization have the capacity to raise?

✔ Tire Two: For this particular need?

✔ Tire Three: At this location and at this time?

✔ Tire Four: Is that enough money to pay for what the campaign plans to do?

A member of the organization's staff or board may be able to conduct the feasibility study, but nonprofits often hire consultants with expertise in this arena. They interview key leaders in the organization, its current supporters, and others whose involvement in supporting the project is critical to its success.

The accuracy of the feasibility study is very important to the capital campaign. Whoever conducts it has to have enthusiasm for the project, yet be able to speak honestly about the organization's position and listen carefully to the direct and indirect messages conveyed in the interviews. Nonprofits often use a consultant for this reason: She's a step removed from the organization and, therefore, interview subjects are more likely to be frank with her.

Starting with the board

Whether or not an organization's board includes wealthy individuals, all of its members should contribute to the campaign. For one thing, the board's willingness to support the campaign is an indication of its being feasible. Also important, potential donors who are not board members are likely to ask whether you have 100 percent board participation. They're asking whether every board member has given a gift or made a pledge to the campaign.

Board members are expected to lead the way. Their contributions may not be the largest, but they should be made in the campaign's earliest phases.

Why is this step so important? A charismatic executive director may be able to stir up enthusiasm about a capital project, but to succeed, such a project usually requires broad-based support and the assistance of all levels of leadership in the organization. If every member of the board of directors hasn't given to the campaign, it suggests that only a few people really support the idea. Also, people asking other people to make contributions are in a much better position to ask if they, themselves, have given. Board members must be willing to be involved in the campaign fundraising.

In addition, the size of a donor's gift (in relation to what the donor can afford) is some indication of enthusiasm. If a penniless playwright who serves on the board gives $100 toward a capital campaign for a theater, he's making as clear a sign of enthusiasm as a wealthy banker on the board who makes a gift of $1 million. If the wealthy banker makes the $100 gift, it suggests that either the board has one malcontent (who, perhaps, should be asked to resign) or that the project is unsupportable.

Feasibility study interviews

A typical feasibility study interview opens with an overview of the proposed project, emphasizing why the nonprofit selected the project, and how it can enhance the organization's programs and better serve its constituents. Next, the interviewer describes how much money the project needs and how, in general, the organization plans to raise it. If any major donors are already involved, the interviewer mentions their levels of support. Finally, the interviewer suggests a possible donation to the potential contributor and makes note of whether that person is likely to give to the campaign and how much the contribution may be.

The interview should be a conversation among the parties in the room rather than a one-sided presentation. The more the interviewer can engage the interview subjects in discussion, the more the interviewer finds out about how outsiders view the organization and about the fundraising potential.

In these conversations, most contributors aren't making promises, but they're suggesting their probable levels of support. The study, therefore, is very important for two reasons:

- ✔ It gathers information that helps the organization to estimate whether its capital campaign goal is feasible.
- ✔ It begins the process of "cultivating" contributions to and leadership for the campaign.

On the CD accompanying this book, you can find an outline of a feasibility study interview (CD1806) and an overview of the parts of a finished study (CD1807).

To continue with the used car metaphor, a feasibility study is like finding out — after talking to your parents, spouse, or the bank — how much you can afford to pay for a car. Sometimes your parents may say that they'll give you money for a small sedan but not for that red sports car, and the same is true for a feasibility study. Board members, community leaders, and/or potential donors may tell you that they would support the venture or endowment if it was smaller, or the building if it didn't need a new foundation.

If the feasibility study suggests that you can raise more than you planned, you may consider increasing your capital campaign goal to include more scholarships or a cash reserve for building maintenance.

If the feasibility study suggests that you can't afford a "champagne" version of your plans, you may have to settle for a serviceable "house wine" edition. If your plans already were of the house wine variety, you may want to break the campaign into phases. If yours is a building project, over the first two years, you could make major safety and structural changes or renovate one of several floors. Then maybe three or four years later you could launch the second phase of a capital campaign to cover the balance of the costs.

You also may find out that you need to wait. Perhaps a few potential major donors gave recently to another campaign, and although they like your project, they were recently tapped (to borrow a maple syrup metaphor). You may be able to come back to them in a year and receive a major contribution. Or maybe potential donors voiced concerns about your organization. You don't have good records about past donors. Your board has dwindled in size. Your executive director just accepted another job. When you organize, recruit, and hire anew, your campaign can proceed.

And you may find out that undertaking the project isn't a good idea at all. Period. Time to start over and plan to address your goals in a different way.

Building the Pyramid of Gifts

You've sketched out your budget. You've set your sights on a reasonable goal. Your next most important need is to identify campaign leadership — a team or committee of volunteers who are willing to cheerlead on behalf of the campaign, make personal visits and calls, and sign letters asking for contributions. These leaders may be board members, but we recommend including some people from outside the board if appropriate enthusiasts can be identified. Not only do their efforts ease your board's workload, but their contacts also expand the pool of possible donors, and their involvement illustrates broader community support for the campaign.

A lot of conventional wisdom about capital campaigns exists, but each campaign develops its own strategies. Each organization has distinctive strengths to call upon, but most of them use the same diagram. It's called a gift table, and it looks like a pyramid (see Figure 18-1).

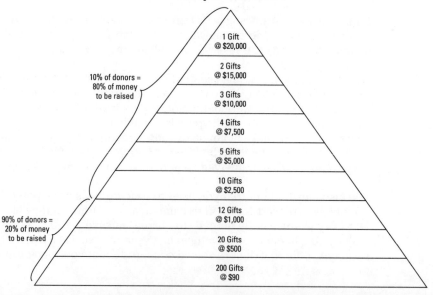

Campaign For $200,000
Sample Gift Table

10% of donors =
80% of money
to be raised

1 Gift
@ $20,000

2 Gifts
@ $15,000

3 Gifts
@ $10,000

4 Gifts
@ $7,500

5 Gifts
@ $5,000

10 Gifts
@ $2,500

90% of donors =
20% of money
to be raised

12 Gifts
@ $1,000

20 Gifts
@ $500

200 Gifts
@ $90

Figure 18-1: This sample gift table shows 80 percent of donations coming from 10 percent of donors.

Remember the old saying, "Ten percent of the people do ninety percent of the work"? A capital campaign works that way. Only a few donors are able to contribute large gifts. They go at the top of the pyramid. Smaller gifts from many other donors fill in the lower levels as the campaign moves forward and the pyramid takes shape.

Starting at the top

We know you don't start at the top when building a pyramid, but that's where you begin with a capital campaign.

We structured the sample gift table in Figure 18-1 using the following scheme:

- Ten percent or more of the money is coming from a single gift, known as the lead gift. This large donation crowns the tip of the pyramid.
- Fifteen percent of the money is coming from the next two largest gifts.
- Fifteen percent of the money is coming from the next three largest gifts.
- Overall, 80 percent of the money is coming from 10 percent of the donors. In other words, if you receive 100 contributions, ten of those people will provide 80 percent of the money that you must raise.

You're driving across town and pass the Janice Knickerbocker Symphony Hall, the Engin Uralman Medical Center, and the Jerome Kestenberg Museum of Natural History. What do Janice, Engin, and Jerome have in common? Generally, those people whose names adorn buildings made the contribution of 10 percent or more of the campaign total. They're called the "lead donors."

When you conduct your feasibility study, one thing you're trying to determine is the size of the campaign's largest gift and whether it totals 10 percent or more of the campaign total.

Your lead gift becomes one of your campaign's attractions. Some contributors may support a capital project because they like or admire the person after whom the scholarship fund or building is named even if they have little connection to the cause or organization.

In general, capital campaigns start at the top of the pyramid and work down. After the lead gift is in place, your organization begins seeking the other major gifts that make up the first one-third of the funds to be raised. (In our example in Figure 18-1, just six contributions make up 40 percent of the goal.) Individuals usually give these lead gifts that they pledge during personal visits from nonprofit staff. (See Chapter 14 for more about raising money from individuals.)

Continuing down the pyramid's structure to the widening middle, an organization usually moves beyond board members and major donors to seek grants from foundations and corporations.

Ending the quiet phase

Early on, when you're conducting the capital campaign among trustees, close friends of the nonprofit, past donors, and foundations, the campaign is in what's called the "quiet phase." When the organization has raised 75 to 80 percent of the money it needs, the fundraising style changes. The managers are growing confident that the campaign can succeed and announce it to the general public through a press conference, tour, gala party, or cornerstone-setting event.

This is the time to seek smaller donations from lots of people — neighbors, friends of friends, and grandparents. You can often raise these contributions through special events, special mailings, or even phone-a-thons to individuals and smaller foundations and businesses.

Smaller gifts from many people construct the ground-level base of the pyramid. Don't discount these gifts. They're important financially to close out the campaign and also to build a feeling of participation in all your donors.

Annual campaigns and other focused fundraising drives are structured along the gift table pattern. Whether you're raising money for your child's school, an election, or a community fair, a gift table can help to shape and focus your plans.

See CD1808 for a sample capital campaign gift table.

Using a case statement

In Chapter 14 on raising money from individuals, we outline steps in writing a case statement. A capital campaign cries out for a *case statement* — a brief, eloquently stated argument on behalf of the capital project. Sometimes these case statements are fancy brochures with profiles of scholarship recipients, drawings of a planned building, or clients of the future taking advantage of new opportunities. Sometimes they're simple typed and copied statements.

A capital campaign case statement should incorporate the following elements:

- Mission and brief history of the organization
- Major accomplishments

✔ Compelling information about constituents served

✔ Vision of how the mission can be served better as a result of the capital project

✔ Vision for the results of the capital investment

✔ The campaign's leadership and goals

✔ Naming and giving opportunities

Shaping a campaign proposal

Grant proposals for capital projects follow the general outline of a standard grant proposal (see Chapter 17), with some variations and additions. The grant writer needs to describe the organization's goals and activities and its constituents' needs, and convincingly describe how a stronger organization with stronger capital assets will better serve the organization's goals and clients. Although your proposal may focus on any kind of capital investment project, we discuss a standard building project in the following outline of a campaign grant proposal:

✔ The introduction includes general information about current facilities and leads up to a discussion of the need for a new or renovated building.

✔ The problem statement describes needs of clients or potential clients and how the organization's current building (or lack of a building) hinders their satisfaction of those needs.

✔ The goals and outcomes section discusses aspirations that the organization holds for serving its clients and its goals for the capital project (the building's dimensions and amenities).

✔ The methods section briefly touches on how you're delivering services but primarily focuses on how you're conducting the capital campaign, how construction will proceed, and the activities you're undertaking to connect current and future clients to the building. Organizations often include a discussion of the results of the feasibility study in this section as a rationale for how they set goals and how they planned the campaign.

✔ The evaluation section should focus both on whether the building project will meet its goals (such as achieving all city fire and safety code standards) and on how the improved building serves clients.

✔ The budget usually includes two major sections: hard costs (for land or building purchase or construction) and soft costs (for financing, fundraising, and promotion).

✔ The future and additional funding section should discuss how the capital campaign is progressing and where the organization anticipates raising the necessary funds to complete it. This section also should provide information about how the finished project will affect the organization's operating costs and how any additional expenses will be covered in the future.

Realizing Benefits and Risks

Although you may describe your request for capital support as a one-time need to potential supporters, many campaign donors continue to give after you finish the campaign project. They've been introduced to the agency, they've left their names in its lobby or attached to a scholarship fund, and they want to be sure that it succeeds over time. In the best situations, capital campaigns strengthen the nonprofit organization's programs both by enabling it to improve services and by broadening its donor base. A capital project can also be good for staff morale because it improves physical working conditions.

But capital campaigns also have their drawbacks:

✔ Capital campaigns may detract from organizations' basic fundraising. If you ask a donor to your programs to contribute to a building project, he may or may not contribute to the organization's ongoing programs in the same year.

✔ Capital campaigns may double, triple, or quadruple an organization's fundraising needs while they're being conducted.

✔ Campaigns that don't succeed or that drag on for a long time can damage an organization's reputation. Because buildings tend to be visible entities, the public may be more aware of an organization's slow-moving construction project than of a problem with the programs or services.

✔ Organizations often have turnover in their fundraising staffs after a capital campaign. Employees may stick around to achieve the end of the project, but a heavy workload may cause burn-out that leads to quitting soon after they finish the project.

In short, capital projects offer both opportunities and pitfalls, buy-in and burn-out, and new donor development and loss of current annual fund donors. But when completed, they often pay for concrete, lasting benefits and are worthy of celebration.

Part IV
The Part of Tens

The 5th Wave   By Rich Tennant

"I have everything ready for you to start filling out your 501(c)(3). Writing materials, a copy of the IRS tax code, a morphine drip..."

In this part . . .

Here's a place to turn for some quick reminders and encouragement. We debunk some common biases, prejudices, and misconceptions about nonprofit organizations. You'll also find tips on getting help when you run into problems. And we return to the theme of fundraising, summarizing our experience and advice into easy-to-follow tips.

Chapter 19

Ten Myths about Nonprofit Organizations

*I*n this chapter, we expose common myths about nonprofit organizations. Here are our favorites. Let the truth be told!

Nonprofits Can't Charge for Their Services

We think that this myth came about because of the word *charity*. Most people think of charity as giving money or assistance to people in need without expecting anything in return.

Some nonprofits do give free services to the poor, the homeless, and others less fortunate than themselves. Many organizations provide food and clothing programs, legal services, and advocacy for certain groups without billing those people who benefit. But many nonprofits charge fees for their services or charge for tickets to performances or museum exhibits, for instance.

Nonprofits that provide programs such as counseling or health-related services typically have sliding-scale fees. In other words, the amount you pay is based on your income and the number of people in your family. Contributions to the organization make up the difference between the actual cost of providing the service and the fee received.

Nonprofit Workers Can't Be Paid (or Can't Be Paid Very Much)

This myth brings up the image of a dedicated worker toiling away for no remuneration. You *do* find a lot of these people in nonprofit organizations — they're called volunteers. And many paid nonprofit staff members work for less than they could make in the private sector.

But some nonprofit staff members may be well compensated. Salaries vary depending on the size of the organization's budget, the type of services provided, and geographic location. Finding good salary information isn't easy, but *Nonprofit Times* does an annual survey of its readers. The publication reported that projected salaries for executive directors in 2005 will average more than $92,000. This figure is based on 209 organizations that responded to the paper's survey. Over 50 percent of the organizations had budgets between $1 and $10 million. So the belief that nonprofit workers can't be paid, or even paid fairly well, just isn't true.

Nonprofit Board Members Can't Receive Compensation

This claim is actually more or less true in practice. Very few board members receive payment for serving on nonprofit boards. But board members can be paid.

We don't recommend that nonprofits pay their board members, but good reasons for doing it sometimes exist. If an organization serves low-income clients, for example, having representation from that group on the board is a good idea. The offer of a stipend in exchange for board attendance and service may encourage more people to be actively involved.

The Better Business Bureau Wise Giving Alliance Standards for Charitable Accountability state that no more than one board member (or ten percent of the entire board) should be compensated. Of course, board members can be reimbursed for reasonable expenses associated with serving on the board, such as travel costs. And some nonprofits have a paid staff member serving on the board.

Nonprofits Can't Make a Profit

Many people think that nonprofits can't end the fiscal year with money in the bank. Not true. Nonprofits should end the year with extra money if possible.

Nonprofits can't distribute surplus funds (profits) to board members or staff, but this doesn't mean that nonprofits can't pay salary bonuses. Surplus funds can also be kept in reserve for the future, invested in a variety of ways, or used to start new programs.

Nonprofits Can't Own and Operate For-Profit Businesses

Nonprofits *can* own for-profit businesses. A good example of nonprofit success in business is Minnesota Public Radio, or, more properly, its parent organization, American Public Media Group. In 1981, Minnesota Public Radio began selling posters associated with its successful *Prairie Home Companion* radio show. This mail-order business grew into a multi-million-dollar mail-order operation that was sold to the Dayton-Hudson company for an estimated $120 million. The sale generated $90 million for Minnesota Public Radio's endowment and generated cash reserves approaching $20 million to invest in new programming and equipment, or to keep for a rainy day.

Generating income does come with a downside, though. Nonprofits that generate income from activities unrelated to their charitable purpose must pay taxes on that income. It's known as Unrelated Business Income Tax (UBIT). We cover the topic in Chapter 2.

Nonprofit Organizations Aren't Run As Efficiently As Businesses

If the Minnesota Public Radio story from the previous section doesn't convince you that this is a myth, we're not sure what will. What we want to attack with this myth, however, is the idea that nonprofit managers are less effective than managers in the private sector.

This myth is hard to dispel because you can find poorly-managed nonprofits almost as easily as you can find sand on a beach. But keep in mind that, at the end of 2004, the IRS had over 925,000 501(c)(3) organizations in its database. That doesn't include the organizations that are too small to file regular tax returns. Our point is this: Nonprofit organizations abound, and making generalizations about them is dangerous.

Skills needed to be an outstanding nonprofit manager include good salesmanship, an ability to inspire confidence and communicate complex ideas, knowledge of the programs being provided by the organization, an understanding of budgeting, and frugality. It's a daunting job description.

Consider the manager of a nonprofit organization that has a budget of, say, $350,000. Depending on the type of programs the organization offers, the manager may have two or three staff members. About half of the organization's income comes from program services, and the other half comes from individual contributions and grants from foundations and corporations. Any new equipment acquired to improve efficiency must be paid for by writing a grant or by scrimping and saving from meager surplus funds. This manager is no doubt doing six things at once — raising money, communicating with the board of directors, supervising staff, developing new programs, meeting with foundation officials, and writing a publicity brochure.

This scenario is typical for nonprofits. So although this manager may not be privy to the latest organizational management theory, he or she is juggling enough balls to make a cat dizzy. How can you say that isn't good management?

Any Organization Not Making Money Is a Nonprofit

You may have heard someone say, "My company lost money last year. I guess I work for a nonprofit." Chances are the speaker was just making a little joke, but who knows? Misconceptions about what is and what isn't a nonprofit organization are plentiful. Survey results reported in 2004 suggest that as many as one-third of those asked didn't understand the concept of "nonprofit." Clearly, they need to buy and read this book.

Several varieties of nonprofit organizations are out there, and the fundamental fact about them all is that they aren't *owned* by an individual or group of individuals. Any profit or surplus that the group accrues must be dedicated to furthering the purpose of the organization. See Chapter 2 for more about nonprofit ownership.

Nonprofit Fundraising Costs Are Too High

According to one poll, 43 percent of Americans agree that nonprofits are wasteful with their funds. But we agree with the 57 percent who don't believe that nonprofits are wasteful. At least we're in the majority.

Take fundraising as an example, because fundraising costs receive the most criticism. Let's talk about what most people call "junk mail." In the fundraising business, it's called *direct mail* (see Chapter 14) and, believe us, you wouldn't receive so much of it if it didn't work.

The simple truth about fundraising is that few people donate to charity without being asked. If nonprofits waited patiently by the mailbox for unsolicited gifts, they'd soon be out of business. Raising money costs money, for paying fundraising staff, preparing brochures and fundraising letters, and postage. These efforts aren't wasteful; they're necessary.

Most agencies that issue standards for nonprofit organizations say that fundraising and management costs together should be less than 40 percent of a nonprofit's total costs. We think that 30 to 35 percent is a better target, especially for larger, more established organizations. The larger the nonprofit, the easier it is to control management and fundraising costs.

Working for a Nonprofit Is Easy

Working for a nonprofit isn't any easier than working anywhere else. Work is work, after all. Nonprofit employees work long hours, take work home, and suffer sleepless nights just like everyone else does. Of course, nonprofit workers do have one advantage: They work for a double bottom line. Yes, the organization's books need to end up in the black rather than the red, *but* they're making progress toward accomplishing the organization's mission. Maybe this drive to accomplish meaningful goals is the reason people think that nonprofit work is easy — they see nonprofit workers doing something they believe in and enjoying it.

All Nonprofits Are Essentially the Same

People sometimes talk about the nonprofit sector as if it was one homogeneous entity.

In fact, the nonprofit sector has more variation than similarity. Kaiser Permanente, one of the largest health care operations in the world, is a non-profit organization. Compare Kaiser's operations with the church around the corner from your house or your local PTA chapter. Think about Harvard University, with an endowment of $14 billion or so (yes, we said billion), and then think about the Head Start program in your town or the group that's trying to raise money to protect wetlands from a housing development.

Chapter 20

Ten (or So) Tips for Finding Help When You Need It

You're certain to come across problems and questions for which you have no ready answer. When the inevitable occurs, don't despair. You can find help in some of the most unlikely places.

Working by yourself, or even with a small group of volunteers, can make you feel like you're the only person left in the world. Knowing you're not alone makes your job easier.

You may find that only a few of the sources of help we give in this chapter offer the kind of advice you need. But, we think you'll also discover that the best place to seek help may change depending on the challenge of the day.

Remember that you can find places to ask for assistance, and most people are willing to offer advice. We think one of the most exciting features of working for a nonprofit organization is the opportunity to learn as you go along. You'll be more successful in achieving your nonprofit mission if you approach your career as a learning experience and ask for help when you need it.

Ask Your Friends

This may be the best place to begin. Even if your friends work in the world of business or government, they often can provide good common-sense advice to help you clarify a problem. After all, starting and managing a nonprofit organization isn't rocket science — it just seems that way sometimes.

You'll find a lot of overlap between running a business and running a non-profit organization. You may have questions about your computer network, your phone system, your copier, your office lease, your health plan, and so on. The list is endless. Nonprofit experience and expertise aren't needed to provide useful advice about some questions you may have in operating your programs.

Get Help from Colleagues

Don't hesitate to ask other nonprofit managers and staff for advice, either, especially if they've been in the business longer than you have. They may have faced a similar situation. You'll find that most people are generous with their time and do their best to offer good suggestions. If they don't have a ready answer, they often can point you in the right direction to find a solution to your problem.

Another possibility is building a group of professional friends who meet together regularly to talk about work and provide advice and support to one another. It can be an informal group that meets when everyone can find the time, or you can organize the group more formally with assigned topics and a volunteer group leader to guide the discussion. In the more formal modes, these groups often are called learning circles or study groups.

Finally, you can find a mentor to go to for advice. A *mentor* is a trusted teacher or advisor. Yours should be someone who has more experience than you do and is willing to spend time with you on a semiregular basis to pass on advice and act as a sounding board for ideas.

Contact Your Funders

If your organization receives foundation funding, a program officer or other foundation staff member may be a good person to contact. Someone who has awarded your organization a grant has a stake in your success. Don't be shy about asking for help.

Some foundations have programs to help their grantees. You may be able to get consultation help for long-range planning, program development, or other areas that need attention. Sometimes foundations bring their grantees together to talk about the particular problems facing a specific field, such as community development, human services, or the arts.

Organizations receiving United Way funds shouldn't overlook contacting the local United Way to ask for help.

Look for a Consultant

You may face a situation in which paid temporary assistance is the best choice. Consultants, sometimes called contractors, can be hired for any task. Maybe your computer network needs tweaking or you need some help in reviewing your programs or completing a long-range plan. Like we said, you name the task and a consultant can be found to do it.

There are several ways to find consultants. You can look in the phone book or search the Web for nonprofit consultants who work in your area, but we think that the best way is to use word of mouth, if possible. A few calls to other nearby nonprofits may be necessary to get some leads, but that's time well spent.

Some consultants can prepare grant proposals for your organization. But although a well-written grant proposal is important, writing alone won't nail down the grant. You need to have a solid program or project, a well-thought-out argument for why it deserves funding, and a solid financial plan.

We prefer consultants who have more than one way of doing things. Not all nonprofits are alike, and what works for one may not work for another. Some consultants have either accepted a particular school of thought or have developed a favorite method. Be cautious when a consultant tells you that there's only one way to do something. See Chapter 8 for more information about hiring consultants.

Find a Nonprofit Support Organization

Some nonprofits have the mission of helping other nonprofits do their jobs better. They're known as *nonprofit support organizations* or *technical assistance providers.* These organizations get their funds from fees for their services and from grants from foundations and corporations interested in *nonprofit capacity building,* the jargon for helping a nonprofit develop infrastructure and management techniques so that it can do its job more effectively.

Nonprofit support organizations often have consultants on staff who do the same work as private consultants and consulting companies. They also may provide training workshops in a variety of topics ranging from building your board of directors to personnel matters. Most nonprofit support organizations charge a fee for both consulting and training workshops, but the fees often are based on a sliding scale keyed to the size of your annual budget.

If you live in a major metropolitan area, you likely have one or more of these organizations near you. The Alliance for Nonprofit Management (www.allianceonline.org) has a search function on its Web site that lets you find the nearest support organization in your area.

Seek Help from Professional Organizations

Check to find out whether organizations doing work similar to yours have an umbrella group by asking a colleague at a similar organization or checking on the Web. These *umbrella groups,* essentially trade associations for nonprofits, often provide technical support and training to their members. They also provide access to colleagues running similar organizations around the country. You probably need to pay an annual membership fee to join, but it's money well spent. For example, if you're running a local symphony orchestra, you could join the American Symphony Orchestra League (www.symphony.org).

The American Society of Association Executives (www.asaenet.org) provides support to nonprofit managers, mostly of large organizations. You can find state, regional, and city organizations by following the <u>Directories</u> link on their Web site.

Many U.S. states have state associations organized to help nonprofits, no matter what sort of service they provide. If one of these organizations is present in your state, your nonprofit can join and take advantage of association benefits that may include training sessions, publications, group insurance programs, and consulting services. You can find out whether your state has an association by visiting the National Council of Nonprofit Association's Web site (www.ncna.org).

Go Back to School

And you thought you'd never have to take another test. But after you get involved with a nonprofit organization, you may find that you want or need formal training. In the last decade, an explosion in graduate degree programs for nonprofit managers has occurred. Researchers at Seton Hall University have compiled a list of programs that you can see by visiting tltc.shu.edu/npo/.

As the nonprofit sector grows, more and more nonprofit managers hold either graduate degrees in some aspect of nonprofit management, or generic degrees such as MBAs or Masters of Public Administration. Sometimes colleges and universities also offer non-degree programs, often through continuing education departments, called *certificate programs.* Many programs schedule evening and weekend classes for the convenience of working students.

For training in fundraising, we recommend one book and two long-standing programs. The book is *Grant Writing For Dummies,* 2nd Edition, by Beverly A. Browning (Wiley). The programs, both of which offer workshops throughout the United States, are

- The Grantsmanship Center (www.tgci.com). The Grantsmanship Center's classes are, as you may guess from the name, focused on preparing grant proposals.
- The Fund Raising School (www.philanthropy.iupui.edu/funds.html). This school is associated with the Center on Philanthropy at Indiana University. Its classes cover everything from fundraising for small nonprofits to running capital campaigns.

These programs require registration fees and tuition. We know that finding the resources (and the time) to sign up can be challenging. You may be able to obtain scholarships to attend some of the programs, and colleges and universities have financial aid and loan programs available. Also, your organization may be able to get a small grant to pay for all or part of your tuition.

The Foundation Center (fdncenter.org) offers free or low-cost introductory workshops on grant seeking and grant writing at its libraries in New York, Atlanta, Cleveland, San Francisco, and Washington, D.C.

Much closer to home, you can dip into Chapter 16 of this book for easy reference on seeking and winning grants.

Search Online

Online resources for nonprofit organizations are becoming more abundant every day. You can find everything from IRS forms to discussion forums and listservs. We think that the amount of resources available on the Web will continue to grow and that more people will turn to the Web for information to help them run their nonprofit organizations.

All the resources listed earlier in this chapter have Web sites and many even allow you to register for courses online. But you still have to get in a car or climb on a bus to get to those classes. Some formal programs in grant writing and nonprofit management are now being taught exclusively on the Web. This program means, of course, that you can sit at home or in your office and learn at your leisure.

Using search engines

Look for online help by using a search engine. Search engines maintain a database of Web pages. You type one or more keywords into the search window, click the search button, and a list of Web pages containing the keywords you entered, ranked for possible relevance, pops up on your screen. Different search engines use different formulas for searching pages, so two search engines rarely return the same order of pages.

In using most search engine searches, you get thousands of possible pages returned. We find that usually only the first 10 or 20 or so are worth taking the time to check out. After that, you're likely to end up at the Ukrainian Water Treatment Plant home page.

One of our favorite search engines is Google (`google.com`), but many other search engines are out there. Your Internet service provider may have a search engine that you typically use.

Accessing e-mail lists and discussion forums

If you don't find what you're looking for on a Web page, you can ask someone online. Although online discussions about nonprofits will never surpass sports talk or attempts at romance, you can find people who like to talk (that is, type) about nonprofit organizations (and your particular field) and are happy to answer your questions.

An electronic discussion list is an e-mail list that is focused on a specific topic. You subscribe to the e-mail list and wait until the e-mail starts to arrive. Some people ask questions to members of the list; others respond with answers and opinions; electronic conversations are the result. Many lists maintain digests of past conversations, so catching up if you're just starting out is easy. *Web-based forums* are similar to e-mail lists in terms of the discussions, but you must go to the Web site and sign in with your login ID and password to read online conversations (called *threads*) about various nonprofit topics. Use your favorite search engine to find these resources.

Chapter 21

Ten Tips for Raising Money

*R*aising money is essential to managing a successful nonprofit organization. There's nothing easier than knowing you should be raising money — and nothing harder than asking for it. In this chapter are our ten tips for that all-important task.

Ask

One of fundraising's oldest adages is "If you don't ask, you won't get."

Developing fundraising plans, compiling lists of potential donors, and designing invitations are labor intensive. But those tasks aren't the things that slow you down. Many people pause when picking up the telephone or ringing the doorbell — when it comes to "the ask." Then, when it's a little too late for the prospective donor to make a decision, write a check, or forward a proposal to a board meeting, they make their move and stumble over their own procrastination.

We repeat, "If you don't ask (and ask at the right time), you won't get."

Hit Up People You Know

Some fundraisers believe that the entire money-raising game is in knowing people with money and power and working those contacts — charming them to bend their wills and write those checks. To be honest, if yours is a good cause, that approach isn't bad. But what if you don't know wealthy people? Does that mean you can't raise money?

No, it doesn't. Begin with people you know. Don't be afraid to ask your friends and associates. From a donor's point of view, saying no to someone you know is harder than saying no to a stranger.

Tell Your Story

The best way to write an effective fundraising letter or make a successful presentation to potential donors is to tell a story. You don't have to explain how your organization was founded and everything it's done since then (although that history may be worth a brief mention). The best stories focus on the constituents you serve and how they benefit from your efforts. They're free of jargon, and direct in manner. They're hopeful stories that paint a picture of a better future and describe what "better" looks like in clear, specific terms.

Pace the story so that it has a bit of drama (but don't stoop to melodrama or hyperbole). Include facts. Recognize and discuss the complexity of the field in which you work, but don't drone on and on about technical matters.

Tell How You're Improving Lives

In grant writing terms, this piece of advice would be worded as "clearly describe your outcomes." Providing training about nutrition to a group of 50 seniors isn't enough if those seniors don't change their eating patterns and live longer, healthier lives. Removing toxins from a lake isn't enough if its fish population and ecosystem aren't revived. Exposing 500 children to formal music lessons isn't enough if none of them can read a simple score later.

Outputs is the word used for the quantity of work that a nonprofit organization produces — the number of meals served, shelter beds offered, workshops led, miles covered, or acres planted. *Outcomes* is the word for the changes that occur as a result of those outputs. Well-defined outcomes are the hallmark of a good proposal, fundraising letter, or pitch.

Don't leave potential donors thinking, "Sounds nice, but so what?"

Make the Numbers Sparklingly Clear

Effective requests for money include information about how much is needed to achieve change or to test an idea. Make sure to present any data you cite in clear terms. In most cases, letting your reader or listener know how much making a needed change costs — the cost per child to participate in a special classroom for a year, the cost per injured sea mammal rescued, the cost per village to provide emergency food for a week — helps to make your point.

Nothing undermines a well-written proposal or case statement faster or more thoroughly than a confusing budget or a muddled financial statement. Double-check your presentation to make sure that every activity in your proposal is represented in the budget and that every item in your budget can be traced easily to the work outlined in your proposal. If some items may be confusing to your reader, include budget notes. In all cases, check your math.

Research, Research, Research

We told you to ask people you know. We're not taking back that advice, but at some point you need to move beyond your immediate circle of acquaintances. That's where doing your homework pays off.

Before you send a fundraising letter, submit a proposal, or visit with a corporate giving director, find out as much as you can about the prospective contributor. Do you have anything in common on a personal level? Maybe the foundation director you're meeting recently published an article. If you read it, you have a conversation topic to break the ice. This advice holds true even when your approach is a direct-mail appeal: You want to know as much as you can about the people whose names are on the lists you borrow or purchase.

More important, you want to find out as much as you can about your potential donor's giving behavior. Does this person give small amounts of money to a wide array of organizations or generous gifts to a few selected agencies? Does the foundation like to be the only contributor to a given project, or does it prefer to support an activity along with others? Does the corporate giving program prefer a low-key style, or does it like to have the company's involvement highlighted?

You can turn to many sources for this information. Much assistance can be found in the Foundation Center library and in its published and online resources. Other helpful directories are available from Oryx Press, Taft, and other publishers (see Appendix A for more details). For personal information about individuals, check the *Who's Who* directories, local newspapers, and college alumni associations. Follow business and social news along with obituaries to keep track of people's families, professional developments, and affiliations. When you attend events at other nonprofit organizations, pay close attention to their contributor lists. Make research a habit.

Think like a Trout (Know Your Donors)

Remember the old saying, "To catch a trout, think like a trout"? The point of conducting research is to be able to talk or write about your organization in ways that are compelling to your listener or reader. You don't want to warp your message or change your mission, but you do want to think about it (and talk or write about it) in ways that respect your audience's point of view. To do so, you need to think about your organization as if you were a prospective donor yourself.

People have different personal giving styles. You don't want to offer to hold a tribute dinner in honor of someone who contributes anonymously. And you don't want to downplay a gift from a contributor who relishes public acknowledgement. Some donors prefer the sociability of supporting a cause through a special event, others respond to direct-mail appeals, and still others like to see as much of their money as possible going directly to the service being provided. (If possible, let them see that service with their own eyes!)

Many people forget that foundations are nonprofit organizations with mission statements and their job is to support proposals that further their missions. Your job as a grant seeker is to measure how your goals align with their purposes. For example, many corporate giving programs and company-sponsored foundation programs work to improve the conditions in which their employees live and work. When they discover that their employees are involved in or contribute to a given cause, they may be more inclined to support it.

Government grantmaking programs are created through legislation. If you find a program that seems well suited to your organization's work, going back and reviewing the legislation is worth your time. Doing so helps you fully understand the program's context and intentions. You're able to think like a legislator trout!

Build a Pyramid

Earlier in this chapter, we suggest starting by asking people you know. Imagine your fundraising approach as starting with those people at the peak of a pyramid and working your way down to the broader base. After asking people you know, try to enlist those donors in asking their contacts to support your organization as well. Some are likely to respond (in part because people they know are also contributors). Then ask those new donors to ask their friends. If each contributor leads you to two additional contributors, you steadily build your pyramid.

Make It Easy to Respond

You've written a brilliant appeal letter. You've created a compelling Web site. You've delivered a stirring speech to a room full of prospective donors. You've got them hooked. They want to contribute. But they're glancing around the room with confused looks on their faces. You blew it. You didn't give them an easy way to respond.

Always suggest a specific amount for donors to consider contributing. Connect that amount to what you need and to their potential giving levels (which you can estimate from your research). And always make giving then and there easy for them: Distribute an addressed envelope and reply card with each mailing, put a Contribute Now button on your Web site, or set up a labeled box by the exit where they can leave contributions. Give them pens, stamps, e-mail addresses, pledge cards — any tools to help potential donors respond when you have their attention.

Keep Good Records

After you begin attracting contributors, your donor records become your most valuable fundraising tools. Individuals who give to your organization once are likely to continue giving for three or more years. If you thank them, address them as if they're part of your organization, and generally treat them well, the size of their gifts is likely to increase over time.

Working with foundations, corporations, and government sources is a different story. In their case, you want to keep clear records of your original project goals and outcomes, project budget, and due dates for any required reports. Although these sources may not be willing or able to support your organization year after year, their future support is more likely if you're a conscientious grantee who submits reports on time and keeps clear records.

You can create a simple database on a set of index cards by recording names, addresses, phone numbers, and e-mail addresses, patterns of giving, and personal information (such as whether a donor knows one of your board members or whether he or she is married and has children).

Of course, these days we like to keep databases on computers. You can spend lots of money on commercial database programs known as "fundraising software," but they probably aren't necessary unless you have thousands of donors. One inexpensive option is eBase (www.ebase.org), a free program based on FileMaker Pro. You don't need FileMaker Pro to run the program unless you want to customize it. TechSoup (www.techsoup.org) provides helpful software information.

However you keep it, guard this database carefully. It's one of your organization's most valuable resources.

Part V
Appendixes

The 5th Wave   By Rich Tennant

"I'm sorry we can't help you. Our organization raises money for the homeless, Mr. Branth, the homeless. Not the homely."

In this part . . .

Here we provide some useful tools, including an extensive glossary of nonprofit terms and a selection of print and Web references for further reading. Appendix C is your guide to using the CD that accompanies this book.

Appendix A

Nonprofit Resources

*H*ere you find a cornucopia of reference materials. We didn't have room to list every book, magazine, and Web site that may be of interest to nonprofit folks, but these resources will get you started in the right direction.

Organizations

You'll find the nonprofit organizations (and one government agency) listed here to be helpful for providing guidance and information on everything from the history of nonprofits in America to raising money to support your programs.

Alliance for Nonprofit Management: www.allianceonline.org

American Association of Fundraising Counsel: www.aafrc.org

American Society of Association Executives: www.asaenet.org

The Aspen Institute: Nonprofit Sector Research Fund: www.nonprofit research.org

BoardSource: www.ncnb.org

Center for Civil Society Studies at the Johns Hopkins University Institute for Policy Studies: www.jhu.edu/~ccss

The Council on Foundations: www.cof.org

The Foundation Center: fdncenter.org

Give.org BBB Wise Giving Alliance: www.give.org

Government Printing Office (for regulatory guides): www.gpo.gov

The Grantsmanship Center: www.tgci.com

Independent Sector: www.independentsector.org

Indiana University Center on Philanthropy: www.philanthropy. iupui.edu

Leader to Leader Institute: www.pfdf.org

National Council of Nonprofit Associations: www.ncna.org

Nonprofit Finance Fund: www.nonprofitfinancefund.org

Web Resources

These Web sites have detailed information on a variety of nonprofit topics, including preparing your application for tax exemption for the IRS, finding possible grant sources, and keeping with the latest news about nonprofits.

Keep in mind that Web site addresses change frequently, so if the page isn't where we say it is, use your favorite search engine to track down the new address.

The Catalog of Federal Domestic Assistance (a comprehensive directory about federal funding opportunities): www.cfda.gov

Charity Channel: http://charitychannel.com/forums

CharityVillage: www.charityvillage.com/cv/main.asp

Chronicle of Philanthropy: philanthropy.com

CompuMentor: www.compumentor.org

Congressional Record: www.gpoaccess.gov/crecord/index.html

Department of Commerce, CDBNet (for information about federal contracts): cbdnet.gpo.gov/search1.html

Federal Assistance Monitor (a privately produced guide to federal and foundation programs): www.cdpublications.com/cdpubs

Federal Register (for daily news about federal funding opportunities): www.gpoaccess.gov/fr

The Foundation Directory Online (available for a monthly fee): www.fdncenter.org

Foundation News and Commentary: www.foundationnews.org

Fundraising Forum: www.raise-funds.com

Giving USA Foundation/AAFRC: www.aafrc.org/gusa/

Graduate programs for nonprofit managers: tltc.shu.edu/npo

Grant Advisor (subscription required): www.grantadvisor.com/index.htm

Grassroots Fundraising Journal: www.grassrootsfundraising.org

GuideStar: www.guidestar.org

Help with Form 1023 from Sandy Deja: www.form1023help.com

Internal Revenue Service (information about nonprofits): www.irs.gov/charities/index.html

Internet Prospector: www.internet-prospector.org

National Technical Information Service: www.ntis.gov

Nonprofit FAQ: www.nonprofits.org

Nonprofit Genie, CompassPoint Nonprofit Services: www.genie.org

Nonprofit Management Library: www.managementhelp.org/

The Nonprofit Quarterly: www.nonprofitquarterly.org

The Nonprofit Times: www.nptimes.com

U.S. Census Bureau: www.census.gov

Web surveying: www.zoomerang.com

Books and Print Materials

Here are some books and other publications that you'll find helpful as you learn about the nonprofit sector. You'll also find books to help you through the incorporation process and guides to writing grant proposals.

Accounting For Dummies, 3rd Edition, by John A. Tracy (Wiley)

Corporate Foundation Profiles (The Foundation Center)

FC-Search, CD-ROM (The Foundation Center)

Fiscal Sponsorship: 6 Ways to Do It Right by Gregory L. Colvin (Study Center Press)

The Foundation 1000 (The Foundation Center)

The Foundation Center's Guide to Proposal Writing, 4th Edition, by Jane C. Geever (The Foundation Center)

The Foundation Directory, Directory Part 2, and *Supplement* (The Foundation Center)

The Foundation Grants Index (The Foundation Center)

Foundation Yearbook: Facts and Figures on Private and Community Foundations (The Foundation Center)

Getting Funded: A Complete Guide to Proposal Writing, 4th Edition, by Mary Hall and Susan Howlett (Continuing Education Publications)

The Guide to U.S. Foundations, Their Trustees, Officers, and Donors (The Foundation Center)

How to Form a Nonprofit Corporation, 7th Edition, by Anthony Mancuso (Nolo Press)

Human Resources Kit For Dummies by Max Messmer (Wiley)

Marketing For Dummies, 2nd Edition, by Alexander Hiam (Wiley)

National Directory of Corporate Giving (The Foundation Center)

The New Nonprofit Almanac and Desk Reference: The Essential Facts and Figures for Managers, Researchers, and Volunteers by the Independent Sector, Urban Institute (Jossey-Bass)

Nonprofit Almanac 1996–97, Dimensions of the Independent Sector by Virginia Ann Hodgkinson, et al (Jossey-Bass)

Nonprofit Boards: Roles, Responsibility and Performance by Diane Duca (Wiley)

A Nonprofit Organization Operating Manual: Planning for Survival and Growth by Arnold J. Olenick and Phillip R. Olenick (The Foundation Center)

Principles of Professional Fundraising: Useful Foundation for Successful Practice by Joseph R. Mixer (Jossey-Bass)

Proposal Planning and Writing, 3rd Edition, by Lynn E. Miner and Jeremy T. Miner (Oryx Press)

Securing Your Organization's Future, Revised Edition, by Michael Seltzer (The Foundation Center)

Starting and Managing a Nonprofit Organization: A Legal Guide, 3rd Edition, by Bruce Hopkins (Wiley)

"What You Should Know About Nonprofits," brochure, a joint project of the National Center for Nonprofit Boards — now BoardSource — and Independent Sector

Winning Grants Step by Step, 2nd Edition, by Mim Carlson (Jossey-Bass)

Appendix B

Glossary of Nonprofit Terms

annual report: A voluntary report published by a nonprofit organization, foundation, or corporation describing its activities and providing an overview of its finances. A foundation's annual report generally lists the year's grants.

articles of incorporation: A document filed with an appropriate state office by persons establishing a corporation. Generally, this is the first legal step in forming a nonprofit corporation.

bylaws: Rules governing a nonprofit organization's operation. Bylaws often outline the methods for selecting directors, forming committees, and conducting meetings.

capacity building: A general term used to describe activities to help a nonprofit organization do its job better. Examples include staff and board training, upgrading computer and financial management systems, and consultant assistance for organizational planning.

capital campaign: An organized drive to raise funds to finance an organization's capital needs — buildings, equipment, renovation projects, land acquisitions, or endowments.

capital support: Funds provided to a capital project.

case statement: A brief, compelling statement about an organization's projects, accomplishments, and vision.

challenge grant: A grant that's made on the condition that other funds must be secured before it will be paid — usually on a matching basis and within a defined time period.

charitable contribution: A gift of goods, money, property, or services to a nonprofit organization.

charity: The word encompasses religion, education, assistance to the government, promotion of health and the arts, relief from poverty, and other purposes benefiting the community. Nonprofit organizations formed to further one of these purposes generally are recognized as exempt from federal tax under Section 501(c)(3) of the Internal Revenue Code.

community foundation: A grantmaking organization receiving its funds from multiple public sources, focusing its giving on a defined geographic area, and managed by an appointed, representative board of directors. Technically, it's classified by the Internal Revenue Service as a public charity, not a private foundation.

community fund: An organized community program making annual appeals to the general public for funds that are usually disbursed to charitable organizations rather than retained in an endowment. Also sometimes called a federated giving program.

company-sponsored foundation: A private foundation that derives its grant-making funds primarily from contributions of a profit-making business.

corporate giving program: A grantmaking program established and managed by a profit-making company. Unlike a company-sponsored foundation, gifts of goods and services go directly from the company to grantees.

demonstration grant: A grant made to experiment with an innovative project or program that may serve as a model for others.

designated funds: Restricted funds whose use is defined by those contributing the money. Also called donor designated funds.

distribution committee: A group of individuals responsible for making grant decisions. For community foundations, this committee must be broadly representative of the community to be served by the foundation.

donor advised fund: A fund held by a community foundation or other charitable organization for which the donor, or a committee appointed by the donor, may recommend charitable recipients for grants from the fund.

donor designated funds: Restricted funds in which those contributing the funds specify how the monies will be used.

endowment: Funds intended to be kept permanently and invested to provide income for continued support of an organization.

excise tax: An annual tax of net investment income that private foundations must pay to the IRS.

family foundation: Not a legal term, but commonly used to describe foundations that are managed by family members related to the person or persons from whom the foundation's funds were derived.

federated campaign or federated giving program: Raising funds for an organization that will redistribute them as grants to nonprofit organizations. This fundraising often is led by volunteer groups within clubs and workplaces. United Way and the Combined Federal Campaign are two examples.

fiscal sponsor: A nonprofit 501(c)(3) organization that formally agrees to sponsor a project led by an individual or group from outside the organization that may or may not have nonprofit status. If the outside individual or group receives grants or contributions to conduct an activity, those funds are accepted, approved, and managed on behalf of the project by the fiscal sponsor.

foundation: A nongovernmental, nonprofit organization with funds and a program managed by its own trustees and directors, established to further social, education, religious, or charitable activities by making grants. A private foundation may receive its funds from an individual, family, corporation, or other group consisting of a limited number of members.

gift table: A structured plan for the number and size of contributions needed to meet a fundraising campaign's goals.

grantee: An individual or organization receiving a grant.

grantor: An individual or organization awarding a grant.

independent sector: The portion of the economy that includes all 501(c)(3) and 501(c)(4) tax-exempt organizations as defined by the Internal Revenue Service, all religious institutions, all social responsibility programs of corporations, and all people who give time and money to serve charitable purposes. It's also called the voluntary sector, the charitable sector, the third sector, or the nonprofit sector.

lobbying: Efforts to influence legislation by shaping the opinion of legislators, legislative staff, and government administrators directly involved in drafting legislative policies. The Internal Revenue Code sets limits on lobbying by organizations that are exempt from tax under Section 501(c)(3).

matching gifts program: A grant or contributions program that matches employees' or directors' gifts made to qualifying nonprofit organizations. Each employer or foundation sets specific guidelines.

matching grant: A grant or gift made with the specification that the amount contributed must be matched with revenues from another source on a one-for-one basis or according to another defined formula.

mission statement: A statement of the purpose and key activities of a nonprofit organization.

nonprofit: A term describing the Internal Revenue Service's designation for organizations whose income isn't used for the benefit or private gain of stockholders, directors, or other owners. A nonprofit organization's income is used to support its operations and further its stated mission. Sometimes referred to as an NPO (nonprofit organization).

outcome evaluation: An assessment of whether a project achieved the desired long-term results.

program officer: A staff member of a foundation or corporate giving program who may review grant requests, recommend policy, manage a budget, or process applications for review by a board or committee. Other titles, such as program director or program consultant, also are used.

proposal: A written application, often with supporting documents, submitted to a foundation or corporate giving program in requesting a grant.

public charity: A type of organization classified under Section 501(c)(3) of the Internal Revenue Service. A public charity normally receives a substantial part of its income from the general public or government. The public support of a public charity must be fairly broad, not limited to a few families or individuals.

restricted funds: Assets or income whose use is restricted by a donor.

social entrepreneurism: Creating and evaluating programs in a way that considers social benefits as well as financial results.

tax exempt: A classification granted by the Internal Revenue Service to qualified nonprofit organizations that frees them from the requirement to pay taxes on their income. Private foundations, including endowed company foundations, are tax exempt; however, they must pay a modest excise tax on net investment income. All 501(c)(3) and 501(c)(4) organizations are tax exempt, but only contributions to a 501(c)(3) are tax deductible to the donor.

unrelated business income: Income from an activity that's not within the scope of the organization's mission.

unsolicited proposal: A proposal sent to a foundation without the foundation's invitation or prior knowledge. Some foundations don't accept unsolicited proposals.

venture philanthropy: A style of grantmaking drawing on the business practices of venture capitalists.

Appendix C

About the CD

System Requirements

Make sure that your computer meets the minimum system requirements shown in the following list. If your computer doesn't match up to most of these requirements, you may have problems using the software and files on the CD. You need the following:

- A PC with a Pentium or faster processor; or a Mac OS computer with a 68040 or faster processor

- Microsoft Windows 98 or later; or Mac OS system software 7.6.1 or later

- At least 32MB of total RAM installed on your computer; for best performance, we recommend at least 64MB

- A CD-ROM drive

- A monitor capable of displaying at least 256 colors or grayscale

If you need more information on the basics, check out these books published by Wiley: *PCs For Dummies,* 10th Edition, by Dan Gookin; *Macs For Dummies,* 8th Edition, by David Pogue; *iMac For Dummies,* 4th Edition, by Mark L. Chambers; *Mac OS X Tiger For Dummies,* by Bob LeVitus; *Windows 98 For Dummies,* by Andy Rathbone; *Windows 2000 Professional For Dummies,* by Andy Rathbone and Sharon Crawford; or *Windows XP For Dummies,* 2nd Edition, by Andy Rathbone.

Using the CD

To install the items from the CD to your hard drive, follow these steps.

1. **Insert the CD into your computer's CD-ROM drive.** The license agreement appears.

   Note to Windows users: The interface won't launch if you have autorun disabled. In that case, click Start ➪ Run. In the dialog box that appears, type `D:\start.exe`. (Replace D with the proper letter if your CD-ROM drive uses a different letter. If you don't know the letter, see how your CD-ROM drive is listed under My Computer.) Click OK.

   Note to Mac users: The CD icon will appear on your desktop. Double-click the icon to open the CD and double-click the "Start" icon.

2. **Read through the license agreement, and then click the Accept button if you want to use the CD.** After you click Accept, the license agreement window won't appear again.

   The CD interface appears. The interface allows you to install the programs and run the demos with just a click of a button (or two).

What You'll Find on the CD

The following sections are arranged by category and provide a summary of the software and other goodies you'll find on the CD. If you need help with installing the items provided on the CD, refer to the installation instructions in the preceding section.

Software

You'll find the following software on your CD:

- ✔ **Word Viewer:** Word Viewer is a freeware program that allows you to view but not edit Microsoft Word documents. Certain features of Microsoft Word documents may not work as expected from within Word Viewer.

- ✔ **Adobe Reader:** Adobe Reader is a freeware program that allows you to view but not edit Adobe Portable Document Files (PDFs).

Shareware programs are fully functional trial versions of copyrighted programs. If you like particular programs, register with their authors for a nominal fee and receive licenses, enhanced versions, and technical support. *Freeware programs* are free, copyrighted games, applications, and utilities. Unlike shareware, these programs don't require a fee or provide technical support. *GNU software* is governed by its own license, which is included inside the folder of the GNU product. See the GNU license for more details. Trial, demo, or evaluation versions are usually limited either by time or functionality (such as being unable to save projects). Some trial versions are very sensitive to system date changes. If you alter your computer's date, the programs will "time out" and will no longer be functional.

Chapter files

The following list summarizes all the chapter files on the CD:

CD0101   Classification of Nonprofit Activity Types

CD0102   Chapter 1 Web Resources

CD0201   Sample Fiscal Sponsorship Agreement

CD0202   Chapter 2 Web Resources

CD0301   Sample Mission Statement for the Bay Area Discovery Museum, Adopted in 1995, Included with Permission

CD0302   Sample Mission Statement for the Bay Area Discovery Museum, Revised by Its Board in 2002, Included with Permission

CD0303   Chapter 3 Web Resources

CD0401   Checklist for Forming a Nonprofit Organization

CD0402   Directory of State Offices, with Web connections

CD0403   Writing Bylaws

CD0404   Chapter 4 Web Resources

CD0501   Chapter 5 Web Resources

CD0601   Sample Grid for Planning Board Recruitment

CD0602   Board Officer Position Descriptions

CD0603   Sample Board Contract

CD0604   Sample Board Self-Assessment, Used with Permission from Carter McNamara, Authenticity Consulting

CD0605   Sample Simple Board Agenda

CD0606	Sample Formal Board Agenda
CD0607	Chapter 6 Web Resources
CD0701	Sample Volunteer Job Description, Food to the Table Delivery Volunteer
CD0702	Sample Volunteer Job Description, Take My Hand Adult Mentor
CD0703	Sample Volunteer Intake Form
CD0704	Sample Volunteer Agreement Form
CD0705	Chapter 7 Web Resources
CD0801	Sample Personnel Policies, Adapted with Permission from the San Francisco Study Center
CD0802	Sample Job Description, Executive Director
CD0803	Sample Job Description, Development Director
CD0804	Sample Job Description, Office Administrator
CD0805	Sample Reference Checking Form
CD0806	Sample Hire Letter
CD0807	Chapter 8 Web Resources
CD0901	Sample Planning Retreat Agenda
CD0902	Outline of an Organizational Plan
CD0903	Sample Needs Assessment Survey
CD0904	Chapter 9 Web Resources
CD1001	Sample Organization Budget, Photography Workshops for Teenagers
CD1002	Sample Organization Budget, Mid-sized Sheltered Workshop for Persons with Disabilities
CD1003	Sample Organization Budget, Education/Recreation Program for Homeless Children

CD1004	Total Project Costs for Tutoring Center
CD1005	Tracking Actual Income and Expenses: Sample Organization Simple Budget and Monthly Report of Budget vs. Actual Income and Expenses
CD1006	Tracking Actual Income and Expenses: Sample Organization Budget and Monthly Report of Budget vs. Actual Income and Expenses with Budget Variance Columns
CD1007	Five Year Trend Line, Included with Permission from Susan Stevens and LarsonAllen Public Service Group
CD1008	Monthly Information Every Nonprofit Board Needs to Know, Included with Permission from Susan Stevens and LarsonAllen Public Service Group
CD1009	Cash Flow Worksheet
CD1010	Sample Cash Flow Projection
CD1011	Sample Audited Financial Statement, Community Health Fund Network
CD1012	Chapter 10 Web Resources
CD1101	Sample Audience Survey, Neighborhood Historical Society
CD1102	Sample Participant/Volunteer Survey
CD1103	Sample Press Release, Included with Permission from Carla Befera
CD1104	Sample Press Alert
CD1105	Sample Calendar Release
CD1106	Sample Photo Caption
CD1107	Sample Photo Use Permission Form
CD1108	Sample Public Service Announcement
CD1109	Chapter 11 Web Resources
CD1201	Questions to Ask Yourself About Your Program, Included with Permission from the Nonprofit Finance Fund

CD1503   Sample Benefit Auction Budget

CD1504   Sample Special Event Committee Invitation Letter, Save Our Lakeshore Awards Dinner

CD1505   Sample Special Event Solicitation Letter, Save Our Lakeshore Awards Dinner

CD1506   Sample Special Events Timeline: Tribute Dinner or Luncheon

CD1507   Sample Special Event Timeline: Benefit Concert

CD1508   Sample Benefit Auction Timeline for a Combined Silent/Live Auction

CD1509   Special Event Invitation, International Children's Relief Committee Dinner

CD1510   Chapter 15 Web Resources

CD1601   Foundation Research Checklist

CD1602   Foundation Center Helpful Hints, Included with Permission from The Foundation Center

CD1603   Foundation Prospect Evaluation Sheet

CD1604   Federal Government Program Research Checklist

CD1605   Chapter 16 Web Resources

CD1701   Sample Letter of Inquiry, Save Mount Artemis

CD1702   Sample Foundation Application Form

CD1703   Sample General Operating Support Grant Proposal, Included with Permission from Kevin Walsh

CD1704   Sample Project Grant Proposal, Included with Permission from Jerome Moskowitz and the San Francisco Mime Troupe

CD1705   Final Report to Cultural Equity Grants Program for San Francisco Mime Troupe Project, Included with Permission from Jerome Moskowitz and the San Francisco Mime Troupe

Troubleshooting

We tried our best to compile programs that work on most computers with the minimum system requirements. Alas, your computer may differ, and some programs may not work properly for some reason.

The two likeliest problems are that you don't have enough memory (RAM) for the programs you want to use, or you have other programs running that are affecting installation or the running of a program. If you get an error message such as `Not enough memory` or `Setup cannot continue`, try one or more of the following suggestions and then try using the software again:

- ✔ **Turn off any antivirus software running on your computer.** Installation programs sometimes mimic virus activity and may make your computer incorrectly believe that it's being infected by a virus.

- ✔ **Close all running programs.** The more programs you have running, the less memory is available to other programs. Installation programs typically update files and programs; so if you keep other programs running, installation may not work properly.

- ✔ **Have your local computer store add more RAM to your computer.** This is, admittedly, a drastic and somewhat expensive step. However, adding more memory can really help the speed of your computer and allow more programs to run at the same time.

If you have trouble with the CD-ROM, please call the Wiley Product Technical Support phone number at 800-762-2974. Outside the United States, call 1-317-572-3994. You can also contact Wiley Product Technical Support at `http://support.wiley.com`. Wiley Publishing, Inc., will provide technical support only for installation and other general quality control items. For technical support on the applications themselves, consult the program's vendor or author.

To place additional orders or to request information about other Wiley products, please call 877-762-2974.

Index

• D •

• Q •

• R •

Wiley Publishing, Inc.
End-User License Agreement

READ THIS. You should carefully read these terms and conditions before opening the software packet(s) included with this book "Book". This is a license agreement "Agreement" between you and Wiley Publishing, Inc. "WPI". By opening the accompanying software packet(s), you acknowledge that you have read and accept the following terms and conditions. If you do not agree and do not want to be bound by such terms and conditions, promptly return the Book and the unopened software packet(s) to the place you obtained them for a full refund.

1. **License Grant.** WPI grants to you (either an individual or entity) a nonexclusive license to use one copy of the enclosed software program(s) (collectively, the "Software") solely for your own personal or business purposes on a single computer (whether a standard computer or a workstation component of a multi-user network). The Software is in use on a computer when it is loaded into temporary memory (RAM) or installed into permanent memory (hard disk, CD-ROM, or other storage device). WPI reserves all rights not expressly granted herein.

2. **Ownership.** WPI is the owner of all right, title, and interest, including copyright, in and to the compilation of the Software recorded on the disk(s) or CD-ROM "Software Media". Copyright to the individual programs recorded on the Software Media is owned by the author or other authorized copyright owner of each program. Ownership of the Software and all proprietary rights relating thereto remain with WPI and its licensers.

3. **Restrictions on Use and Transfer.**

   (a) You may only (i) make one copy of the Software for backup or archival purposes, or (ii) transfer the Software to a single hard disk, provided that you keep the original for backup or archival purposes. You may not (i) rent or lease the Software, (ii) copy or reproduce the Software through a LAN or other network system or through any computer subscriber system or bulletin-board system, or (iii) modify, adapt, or create derivative works based on the Software.

   (b) You may not reverse engineer, decompile, or disassemble the Software. You may transfer the Software and user documentation on a permanent basis, provided that the transferee agrees to accept the terms and conditions of this Agreement and you retain no copies. If the Software is an update or has been updated, any transfer must include the most recent update and all prior versions.

4. **Restrictions on Use of Individual Programs.** You must follow the individual requirements and restrictions detailed for each individual program in the About the CD-ROM appendix of this Book. These limitations are also contained in the individual license agreements recorded on the Software Media. These limitations may include a requirement that after using the program for a specified period of time, the user must pay a registration fee or discontinue use. By opening the Software packet(s), you will be agreeing to abide by the licenses and restrictions for these individual programs that are detailed in the About the CD-ROM appendix and on the Software Media. None of the material on this Software Media or listed in this Book may ever be redistributed, in original or modified form, for commercial purposes.

5. **Limited Warranty.**

   (a) WPI warrants that the Software and Software Media are free from defects in materials and workmanship under normal use for a period of sixty (60) days from the date of purchase of this Book. If WPI receives notification within the warranty period of defects in materials or workmanship, WPI will replace the defective Software Media.

   (b) WPI AND THE AUTHOR(S) OF THE BOOK DISCLAIM ALL OTHER WARRANTIES, EXPRESS OR IMPLIED, INCLUDING WITHOUT LIMITATION IMPLIED WARRANTIES OF MERCHANTABILITY AND FITNESS FOR A PARTICULAR PURPOSE, WITH RESPECT TO THE SOFTWARE, THE PROGRAMS, THE SOURCE CODE CONTAINED THEREIN, AND/OR THE TECHNIQUES DESCRIBED IN THIS BOOK. WPI DOES NOT WARRANT THAT THE FUNCTIONS CONTAINED IN THE SOFTWARE WILL MEET YOUR REQUIREMENTS OR THAT THE OPERATION OF THE SOFTWARE WILL BE ERROR FREE.

   (c) This limited warranty gives you specific legal rights, and you may have other rights that vary from jurisdiction to jurisdiction.

6. **Remedies.**

   (a) WPI's entire liability and your exclusive remedy for defects in materials and workmanship shall be limited to replacement of the Software Media, which may be returned to WPI with a copy of your receipt at the following address: Software Media Fulfillment Department, Attn.: Nonprofit Kit For Dummies, 2nd Edition, Wiley Publishing, Inc., 10475 Crosspoint Blvd., Indianapolis, IN 46256, or call 1-800-762-2974. Please allow four to six weeks for delivery. This Limited Warranty is void if failure of the Software Media has resulted from accident, abuse, or misapplication. Any replacement Software Media will be warranted for the remainder of the original warranty period or thirty (30) days, whichever is longer.

   (b) In no event shall WPI or the author be liable for any damages whatsoever (including without limitation damages for loss of business profits, business interruption, loss of business information, or any other pecuniary loss) arising from the use of or inability to use the Book or the Software, even if WPI has been advised of the possibility of such damages.

   (c) Because some jurisdictions do not allow the exclusion or limitation of liability for consequential or incidental damages, the above limitation or exclusion may not apply to you.

7. **U.S. Government Restricted Rights.** Use, duplication, or disclosure of the Software for or on behalf of the United States of America, its agencies and/or instrumentalities "U.S. Government" is subject to restrictions as stated in paragraph (c)(1)(ii) of the Rights in Technical Data and Computer Software clause of DFARS 252.227-7013, or subparagraphs (c) (1) and (2) of the Commercial Computer Software - Restricted Rights clause at FAR 52.227-19, and in similar clauses in the NASA FAR supplement, as applicable.

8. **General.** This Agreement constitutes the entire understanding of the parties and revokes and supersedes all prior agreements, oral or written, between them and may not be modified or amended except in a writing signed by both parties hereto that specifically refers to this Agreement. This Agreement shall take precedence over any other documents that may be in conflict herewith. If any one or more provisions contained in this Agreement are held by any court or tribunal to be invalid, illegal, or otherwise unenforceable, each and every other provision shall remain in full force and effect.

BUSINESS, CAREERS & PERSONAL FINANCE

0-7645-5307-0

0-7645-5331-3 *†

Also available:

- Accounting For Dummies †
  0-7645-5314-3
- Business Plans Kit For Dummies †
  0-7645-5365-8
- Cover Letters For Dummies
  0-7645-5224-4
- Frugal Living For Dummies
  0-7645-5403-4
- Leadership For Dummies
  0-7645-5176-0
- Managing For Dummies
  0-7645-1771-6

- Marketing For Dummies
  0-7645-5600-2
- Personal Finance For Dummies *
  0-7645-2590-5
- Project Management For Dummies
  0-7645-5283-X
- Resumes For Dummies †
  0-7645-5471-9
- Selling For Dummies
  0-7645-5363-1
- Small Business Kit For Dummies *†
  0-7645-5093-4

HOME & BUSINESS COMPUTER BASICS

0-7645-4074-2

0-7645-3758-X

Also available:

- ACT! 6 For Dummies
  0-7645-2645-6
- iLife '04 All-in-One Desk Reference
  For Dummies
  0-7645-7347-0
- iPAQ For Dummies
  0-7645-6769-1
- Mac OS X Panther Timesaving
  Techniques For Dummies
  0-7645-5812-9
- Macs For Dummies
  0-7645-5656-8

- Microsoft Money 2004 For Dummies
  0-7645-4195-1
- Office 2003 All-in-One Desk Reference
  For Dummies
  0-7645-3883-7
- Outlook 2003 For Dummies
  0-7645-3759-8
- PCs For Dummies
  0-7645-4074-2
- TiVo For Dummies
  0-7645-6923-6
- Upgrading and Fixing PCs For Dummies
  0-7645-1665-5
- Windows XP Timesaving Techniques
  For Dummies
  0-7645-3748-2

FOOD, HOME, GARDEN, HOBBIES, MUSIC & PETS

0-7645-5295-3

0-7645-5232-5

Also available:

- Bass Guitar For Dummies
  0-7645-2487-9
- Diabetes Cookbook For Dummies
  0-7645-5230-9
- Gardening For Dummies *
  0-7645-5130-2
- Guitar For Dummies
  0-7645-5106-X
- Holiday Decorating For Dummies
  0-7645-2570-0
- Home Improvement All-in-One
  For Dummies
  0-7645-5680-0

- Knitting For Dummies
  0-7645-5395-X
- Piano For Dummies
  0-7645-5105-1
- Puppies For Dummies
  0-7645-5255-4
- Scrapbooking For Dummies
  0-7645-7208-3
- Senior Dogs For Dummies
  0-7645-5818-8
- Singing For Dummies
  0-7645-2475-5
- 30-Minute Meals For Dummies
  0-7645-2589-1

INTERNET & DIGITAL MEDIA

0-7645-1664-7

0-7645-6924-4

Also available:

- 2005 Online Shopping Directory
  For Dummies
  0-7645-7495-7
- CD & DVD Recording For Dummies
  0-7645-5956-7
- eBay For Dummies
  0-7645-5654-1
- Fighting Spam For Dummies
  0-7645-5965-6
- Genealogy Online For Dummies
  0-7645-5964-8
- Google For Dummies
  0-7645-4420-9

- Home Recording For Musicians
  For Dummies
  0-7645-1634-5
- The Internet For Dummies
  0-7645-4173-0
- iPod & iTunes For Dummies
  0-7645-7772-7
- Preventing Identity Theft For Dummies
  0-7645-7336-5
- Pro Tools All-in-One Desk Reference
  For Dummies
  0-7645-5714-9
- Roxio Easy Media Creator For Dummies
  0-7645-7131-1

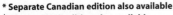

* Separate Canadian edition also available

† Separate U.K. edition also available

Available wherever books are sold. For more information or to order direct: U.S. customers visit www.dummies.com or call 1-877-762-2974.
U.K. customers visit www.wileyeurope.com or call 0800 243407. Canadian customers visit www.wiley.ca or call 1-800-567-4797.

 WILEY

SPORTS, FITNESS, PARENTING, RELIGION & SPIRITUALITY

0-7645-5146-9

0-7645-5418-2

Also available:

- Adoption For Dummies
  0-7645-5488-3
- Basketball For Dummies
  0-7645-5248-1
- The Bible For Dummies
  0-7645-5296-1
- Buddhism For Dummies
  0-7645-5359-3
- Catholicism For Dummies
  0-7645-5391-7
- Hockey For Dummies
  0-7645-5228-7

- Judaism For Dummies
  0-7645-5299-6
- Martial Arts For Dummies
  0-7645-5358-5
- Pilates For Dummies
  0-7645-5397-6
- Religion For Dummies
  0-7645-5264-3
- Teaching Kids to Read For Dummies
  0-7645-4043-2
- Weight Training For Dummies
  0-7645-5168-X
- Yoga For Dummies
  0-7645-5117-5

TRAVEL

0-7645-5438-7

0-7645-5453-0

Also available:

- Alaska For Dummies
  0-7645-1761-9
- Arizona For Dummies
  0-7645-6938-4
- Cancún and the Yucatán For Dummies
  0-7645-2437-2
- Cruise Vacations For Dummies
  0-7645-6941-4
- Europe For Dummies
  0-7645-5456-5
- Ireland For Dummies
  0-7645-5455-7

- Las Vegas For Dummies
  0-7645-5448-4
- London For Dummies
  0-7645-4277-X
- New York City For Dummies
  0-7645-6945-7
- Paris For Dummies
  0-7645-5494-8
- RV Vacations For Dummies
  0-7645-5443-3
- Walt Disney World & Orlando For Dummies
  0-7645-6943-0

GRAPHICS, DESIGN & WEB DEVELOPMENT

0-7645-4345-8

0-7645-5589-8

Also available:

- Adobe Acrobat 6 PDF For Dummies
  0-7645-3760-1
- Building a Web Site For Dummies
  0-7645-7144-3
- Dreamweaver MX 2004 For Dummies
  0-7645-4342-3
- FrontPage 2003 For Dummies
  0-7645-3882-9
- HTML 4 For Dummies
  0-7645-1995-6
- Illustrator CS For Dummies
  0-7645-4084-X

- Macromedia Flash MX 2004 For Dummies
  0-7645-4358-X
- Photoshop 7 All-in-One Desk
  Reference For Dummies
  0-7645-1667-1
- Photoshop CS Timesaving Techniques
  For Dummies
  0-7645-6782-9
- PHP 5 For Dummies
  0-7645-4166-8
- PowerPoint 2003 For Dummies
  0-7645-3908-6
- QuarkXPress 6 For Dummies
  0-7645-2593-X

NETWORKING, SECURITY, PROGRAMMING & DATABASES

0-7645-6852-3

0-7645-5784-X

Also available:

- A+ Certification For Dummies
  0-7645-4187-0
- Access 2003 All-in-One Desk
  Reference For Dummies
  0-7645-3988-4
- Beginning Programming For Dummies
  0-7645-4997-9
- C For Dummies
  0-7645-7068-4
- Firewalls For Dummies
  0-7645-4048-3
- Home Networking For Dummies
  0-7645-42796

- Network Security For Dummies
  0-7645-1679-5
- Networking For Dummies
  0-7645-1677-9
- TCP/IP For Dummies
  0-7645-1760-0
- VBA For Dummies
  0-7645-3989-2
- Wireless All In-One Desk Reference
  For Dummies
  0-7645-7496-5
- Wireless Home Networking For Dummies
  0-7645-3910-8

HEALTH & SELF-HELP

EDUCATION, HISTORY, REFERENCE & TEST PREPARATION

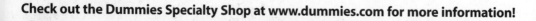